RUN YOUR RACE!

NEW TESTAMENT

WARNINGS

TO CHRISTIANS

DAROLD MEYER

APPRECIATION

Dear Lord, thank you for letting me write this book. I trust that it came out the way You want it. Thank you for the light and life that I received from writing it. I pray that many others will receive the same.

Several of the Lord's saints were quite helpful and encouraging.

John, you proofread and provided many, many, MANY suggestions, corrections, and insights. Such attention to detail. Thank you, brother. I do not know how much embarrassment you saved me!

Ken, thank you for the encouragement and the fellowship. Only the Lord knows how many times I called you, often while we were both driving home from work. Those were precious times in the Lord.

Nate, thank you for your honest insights. You raised an important issue. I and the book are better for it.

Randall, it was a big encouragement to find another brother who realizes the need of the Lord's saints to diligently run their race. I pray that you continue to run yours. Stay true to the Word.

To my sister, my spouse (Song of Solomon), together we will reach the finish line. Forty-five years so far! I love you very much.

* * * * * *

Book Cover Credit: At the time of publication Clayton Aldridge was a Photography and Media Art major at the University of Tennessee Chattanooga. He continues to be an active artist in the Chattanooga area. Clayton did a wonderful job of translating my pencil sketch into exactly what this book is about. I like it. You can see other works by Clayton at www.ccnifty.website

RUN YOUR RACE!
NEW TESTAMENT WARNINGS TO CHRISTIANS

Preface

*Now little children, abide in Him, so that when He appears,
we may have confidence and not shrink away from Him in
shame at His coming.*
(1 John 2:28)

The apostle Paul compared our life in Christ to a race. This life, this race, has a goal, and Paul was quite clear that he was fully engaged in its pursuit. As a pattern of how to pursue Christ, he urged us to follow his example. Implied in that is a warning against not finishing our race.

The Bible has a multitude of warnings, the first being made to Adam, in which God told him of the consequences of eating the fruit of the tree of the knowledge of good and evil (Genesis 2:17). From that point on God has continued to show His mercy to fallen man by giving warnings of impending judgments. Some warnings have been overt, and some not so obvious. Some came through the voices of faithful men, and others through the actions and lives of the same. For example, during the years that Noah spent building the ark, he must have tried to warn his neighbors about the coming flood (2 Peter 2:5), but the ark itself and the building of it were also a clear warning.

We find the rest of God's word to be full of warnings to Israel, to the nations, and to sinners. Warnings are, of course, intended to help the hearer to avoid the judgment that will be coming. All the way to the end of this current age it is God's desire for us to repent and turn our hearts toward Him. Even the calamities revealed in the book of Revelation, while having the declared intention of bringing judgment upon wicked men, have also the hope of causing sinful men to turn to God. Revelation 9:20, 9:21, 16:9, and 16:11 all say, "and they did not repent…"

The church carries out the great commission to spread the gospel. We often include a warning of eternal separation from God as the consequence of rejecting God's salvation through His Son, and without a doubt we can find many scriptures to back that up. By this we warn the unsaved.

My purpose in writing this book is to turn the tables a bit. You see, Matthew 28:19 does not tell us to spread the gospel; Jesus said to "make disciples". The rest of the verse, continuing into verse 20, tells us how to make disciples: *Baptizing them in the name of the Father and the Son and the Holy Spirit, teaching them to observe all that I commanded you.* This **is** the gospel, but does it sound different from what you are used to hearing?

There are many New Testament warnings for us, the born again. We often do not see them, and I will say with some confidence that you probably do not hear them mentioned as being intended for our ears. They are usually assigned to the unsaved or to "false" Christians; or if a text seems to be aimed at us, we might ignore it and hope that it is not so. We might even have confidence that it is not so, because we have the "assurance" that all will be wonderful when we get to heaven.

I would bet that you have heard sermons about parables where someone did well, and we are encouraged to do the same. We want to hear, "Well done good and faithful servant." But have you ever heard a sermon about the flip side: What happens if...? Have you considered what **your** end might be if you were found by the Lord to have not done so well, because you might **not** have been so faithful? Is it guaranteed that we all will hear the favorable words? Apparently not, judging from the parables. What if we do not hear the pleasant words from our Lord?

That's what this work is about. It is not a book about **how** to run your race, but **why** you need to run. By the Lord's grace and (I trust) His leading, I hope to persuade you that we are on dangerous footing if we think that having received the Lord, we can live as though we had not. Maybe we spend an hour or two on Sundays (or Saturdays) with other Christians and try to live right. Does that satisfy the Lord?

I know that my attempts at persuasion can do nothing without the Holy Spirit doing His own convincing. Nevertheless, it is my hope that by putting all of these scriptures together in one place, that they will be impossible to ignore, and by this, the Spirit will have His way.

As you read through, you might get the idea that losing one's salvation is a possible outcome. I do not want you to be distracted by this, so I will say here that I do not believe that the Word says this. But if there are warnings then it follows that there are consequences. I realize, too, that some think that the Word does say that someone can lose their salvation. If you can wait until the concluding chapter, I will lay out what I think the Lord has said to us. But the first step is to show you that there is actually something to talk about and consider.

I will do my best to keep your attention, despite the apparent seriousness of the subject. I do not like to read dry dissertations any more than the next fellow, so I will try to not be dry.

Here are a few ground rules that I decided to employ. 1] Scriptures are quoted from the New American Standard Bible; 2] Direct quotes from the Bible will be in *italics* without quotation marks. I tried several fonts to set apart scripture, but nothing worked as well as good ol' italics. (Even though translators use italics to show words that have been added to aid interpretation, that will be ignored in this book.); 3] Incomplete or partial quotes from the Bible might be enclosed in quotation marks; 4] In order to not have to repeatedly say so, I now declare that **bolding** or any other form of emphasis used in quoting scripture is mine. 5] Any words that are presented as being from original Greek will also be in *italics,* but I do not think there is much danger in confusing these words with scriptural text. The discussion should make it clear enough.

Before we start, consider this warning: *God is not mocked, for whatever a man sows, this he will also reap.* This is not from Proverbs. Neither was it written to the unsaved sinners. The apostle Paul wrote it to the churches in Galatia (Galatians 6:7), thus speaking to **us**.

Contents

Paul's Gospel

Why is the title of this chapter "Paul's Gospel"? Paul himself used the phrase "my gospel" three times: Romans 2:16 and 16:25 and 2 Timothy 2:8.

You might wonder why I start with the letters of Paul rather than the four Gospels. In all honesty, it is because I think I can better make my case this way. Paul himself wrote, *For I would have you know, brethren, that the gospel which was preached by me is not according to man, for I neither received it from man, nor was I taught it, but I received it through a revelation of Jesus Christ* (Galatians 1:11-12). To the church in Ephesus he wrote, *that by revelation there was made known to me the mystery, as I wrote before in brief* (Ephesians 3:3). Paul received the gospel directly from the Lord who revealed Himself, and then he set out to make disciples and build the church.

Since we accept Paul's letters as part of the divine writ of God, there is no danger in examining what he said. We will also look at the writings of the others. After doing so, then we will revisit what the Lord had to say. After all, Paul's gospel did not deviate from our Lord's good news in any way.

This is not to put Paul's words ahead of the words of our Lord, but Jesus used a lot of parables, whereas Paul and the other writers of the New Testament letters spoke plainly and to the point. Since they often addressed certain problems and situations, it was not their intention for their audiences to "seeing, they do not see". With the epistles as background, we will then see if they help us to understand Jesus a little better.

I hope you do not close this book before you give me a chance, but I do want you to understand what is coming, so that you might have a clear mind to accept or reject.

We will look at each book in its order, but in discussing each, there will be a lot of references to other scriptures.

Let's get started!

Romans

This chapter will not be like the remaining chapters of this book. Here I will have a lot more references to other New Testament letters, and so it will read more like a topical study. This is in order to set a foundation for the rest of the book.

Much More

It is appropriate, I think, that the first verse that we cover is Romans 5:10. This will set the tone for the rest of this writing. *For if while we were enemies we were reconciled to God through the death of His Son, much more, having been reconciled, we shall be saved by His life.*

Almost exclusively I would say that Christians acknowledge the day that we received the Lord as the day that we were saved. In a sense this is true and correct, but this verse and most of the New Testament actually show that salvation is **much more** than this. What does it mean to be saved by our Lord's life? How is that different from what was accomplished by His shed blood?

If you are not clear on the difference, it might be helpful to go back to the beginning. In the garden of Eden Adam was made a living soul, and God declared His creation to be very good. But Adam himself was not complete. Yes, he needed a wife, and God provided Eve, but the tree of life in the garden shows us that God wanted to put His life into Adam. Even though Adam had not yet sinned, he still was lacking eternal life. How can we know this? Genesis 3:22-23 shows us that God sent Adam out of the garden so that he would not "take also from the tree of life, and eat, and **live forever.**"

We see then, that after Adam and Eve sinned, the tree of life was no longer available to them, and they were sent out of the garden. Then God put cherubim...where? We usually think of the cherubim at the entrance to the garden, but the Word says, *He stationed the cherubim and the flaming sword which turned every direction to guard the way to the tree of life* (Genesis 3:24). The tree of life is the focus, the center of the garden in Genesis (Genesis 2:9). Now look at the last chapter of the Bible, Revelation 22. The conclusion of God's plan includes verse 14: *Blessed are those who wash their robes, so that they may have the right to the tree of life.* While we pay a lot of attention to washed robes, we do not realize that these are not an end in themselves. The goal is for Christ to be our life, and the only way this happens is by our eating Him as the tree life!

Now, in this age also, God wants to bring man back to the tree of life, which, as I said, is Christ (John 1:4; 5:39-40)! How to do that? Look again at Romans 5:10. It is by reconciliation. Verse 9 adds "justified by His blood". Hallelujah for that! These are two major steps for us sinners, but this brings us only to the position that Adam was in. We have to realize and participate in "much more", which is being saved by His life!

Try to picture a circle with three stop points: eating, washing, being saved by His life. It is a continuous process, and it does not matter whether we go clockwise or counterclockwise. We eat the tree of life, we wash our robes, we are saved by His life. We are saved by His life, we eat the tree, we wash. But understand that this is a life-long process that has a start point that is not on the circle, and that point is the starting line.

Reconciliation and justification got us to the starting line; now there is an entire race ahead of us, and this race involves so many things concerning us and God. Probably for us the biggest is our salvation. Complete salvation is not at the starting line, but at the finish. Romans 12:2 says, *but be transformed by the renewing of your mind.* You can see that there is a process. "Be transformed" means that we are not transformed by standing at the starting line, and "renewing" definitely shows a continuing event. Is it any wonder then that Paul used running and racing as an analogy for the Christian life? (1 Corinthians 9:24, 26; Galatians 5:7, Philippians 2:16, 2 Timothy 4:7.)

This continuing event, our salvation, can be accomplished **only** by His life.....operating in us. We must cooperate with the Holy Spirit as He does His transforming work. You will be able to see this as we go along.

The Olive Tree

Paul's epistle to the Romans goes deeply into the nature and condition of fallen man, and then it brings us into the glorious hope of the Good News. I do not find many warnings in this book that I consider to be directed toward Christians, but in chapter 11 we can find verses 20-22: .... *they were broken off for their unbelief, but you stand by your faith. Do not be conceited, but fear; for if God did not spare the natural branches, He will not spare you, either. Behold then the kindness and severity of God; to those who fell, severity, but to you, God's kindness, if you continue in His kindness; otherwise you also will be cut off.*

You might be very familiar with this section where Paul speaks about our being grafted to the cultivated olive tree, but do you pay attention to the conditions, to the warning? In verse 20 it says, *Do not be conceited, but fear.* Fear what? Paul is very clear: we are to fear being cut off! Again, *If God did not spare the natural branches, He will not spare you, either...*

It used to be that these verses were not in my Bible. I did not think Paul could be really saying what he appeared to say. It was one thing to cut off the Jewish nation for their role in killing their Messiah, but I've been washed in the blood of the Lamb!

We have to be true to the Word, taking it as it is, without inserting our own thoughts about how **we** think things ought to be, or ascribing to God our own feeling of what is just or unjust, right or wrong, righteous or unrighteous. I would also say that we need to be willing to critically look at things that we have been taught. You might not want to believe me, but there really is a lot of leaven in our teachings. If you would search out good Bible teachers in the various media that is available to us, you might find that many agree with that last statement.

But, let us come back to Romans.

If...Then

Look again at verse 22. *Behold then the kindness and severity of God; ....but to you, God's kindness, if...* IF? Nobody told us about "if"! When did you ever hear a sermon about "if"? This is not me trying to twist scripture to make you see something my way. These are plain words, but what do we do with them? If you read my preface, you know what I said about that.

Paul continues: *....if you continue in His kindness; otherwise you also will be cut off.* There is a definite condition and a definite consequence, and there really can be no debate. Does this go contrary to what you have been taught? How are we to correctly understand what Paul means by "cut off"? I will do my best to communicate my understanding of this, but that will come later. For now, I want to stay on the "if" theme. You might be surprised at how prevalent is the word "if" in the New Testament.

Now let's look at Colossians 1:22-23a: *Yet He has now reconciled you in His fleshly body through death, to order to present you before Him holy and blameless and beyond reproach - if indeed you continue in the faith firmly established and steadfast, and not moved away from the hope of the gospel that you have heard.*

Here is a big "if". This one is huge. Do you believe that it is automatic that you will become holy, that we all will stand before Him without blemish, and without reproach? Paul did not say that! Not in any of his epistles!

What is the "if" here? We must continue....continue in the faith, and in that faith we must be established, steadfast. More than that, we have to be not "moved away from the hope of the gospel." What is the hope of the gospel? Traditional thought says "going to heaven." After all, we are promised the sweet bye and bye, are we not? Sorry, that is not the hope that Paul presents.

What is the **real** hope of the gospel? I sincerely believe that you have to grasp the conditioned promises before we can cover that hope, so let us continue.

Partners / Partakers

Hebrews 3:14: *For we have become partakers of Christ, if we hold fast the beginning of our assurance firm until the end.* The translation of this verse gives me a bit of a problem, because some versions read "partners" and some "partakers". Either word can be applied to this discussion.

The verb tenses here are interesting. Paul wrote that "we **have** become" "if we hold" (present tense). Becoming anything (partners or partakers) is a process, and it is not once for all time. As we hold fast, we become true partners of our Lord. If at any moment we cease holding, from that moment we stop being a partner and a partaker. Of course, we do not have to stay in that severed condition. As soon as we return to Him our Savior, the partnership is restored, and we can again partake of the living water and the tree of life. The more we hold fast, the deeper and stronger the partnership becomes, and the more we are strengthened by partaking the divine life.

I believe that the Bible hints that the strength of our partnership with Christ in eternity will match the partnership that we have developed during our life in the flesh. I hope this will become more clear later, but notice the rest of the "if". *"if we hold fast the beginning of our assurance **firm until the end.**"* This theme of "to the end" is echoed in several other places, and we will cover them as we go through the New Testament.

For now, I hope that you are beginning to realize the responsibility that we have to cooperate with the Lord in the work He wants to perform in us. There **are** consequences for not cooperating. Again, I am simply presenting Paul's own words as plainly as I can. It is up to you to agree or disagree, but if you disagree, then you have to find a way to explain the "if" conditions. I skipped over Paul's letters to Timothy. Let's come back to 2

Timothy 2:10-13. I saved this for last because there is a lot here, including four "if" statements.

For this reason I endure all things for the sake of those who are chosen, so that they also may obtain the salvation which is in Christ Jesus and with it eternal glory. It is a trustworthy statement: For if we died with Him, we will also live with Him; if we endure, we will also reign with Him; if we deny Him, He also will deny us; if we are faithless, He remains faithful, for He cannot deny Himself.

I am going to take my time with these verses. Let's take the first "if": *...for if we died with Him, we will also live with Him.* This seems harmless enough. We all anticipate spending eternity with our Lord, and we believe that it is a given. The general thought is that we get saved and go to heaven, right? Then why does Paul attach a condition to it? What does Paul mean by dying with Him? What does it mean to "live with Him"?

These verses echo the Lord's own words, which appear in all four of the gospels. You know the words: *Whoever seeks to keep his life will lose it, and whoever loses his life will preserve it.* (Matthew 10:39, 16:25; Mark 8:35; Luke 9:24, 17:33; John 12:25)

Again, these words appear in all four of the gospels. But more than that, these words appear twice in Matthew and Luke, apparently indicating that Jesus made this statement more than once. In fact, four distinct scenes are portrayed in which Jesus repeats this theme, so there is no telling how many times He said this. In Matthew 10 Jesus is preparing the disciples for the difficulties they will face. In Matthew 16 Peter had just told the Lord to spare Himself from His coming ordeal. This scene in Matthew 16 is repeated in Mark 8 and Luke 9. In Luke 17 Jesus is describing how things will be at the end of the age.

In addition to these, John (12:23) wrote of the Lord's declaration that it was now time for Him, the Son of Man, to be glorified. Then He explained His definition of being glorified (verses 24-25): *Truly, truly, I say to you, unless a grain of wheat falls into the earth and dies, it remains alone; but if it dies, it bears much fruit. He who loves his life loses it, and he who hates his life in this world will keep it to life eternal.*

We must conclude that losing our life must be pretty important. That being the case, we need to understand what it means. There are three Greek words that we translate as "life". They are *bios, psuche, and zoe*. In New Testament usage *bios* refers to the physical, *psuche* to the soul, and *zoe* to the spirit.

When we receive the Lord, the Spirit enters our human spirit, enlivening it (us) with the eternal (*zoe*) life. Our poor (yet marvelous!) body, which is *bios*, remains the earthy flesh until it goes into the ground or until it is transfigured when the Lord returns. But our soul (*psuche*, aka our heart) is the battle ground. It is corrupt, dark, and selfish. Besides all this, it is also under the influence of our flesh, to the extent that there is hardly a dividing line between our soul and the flesh.

Since we have in modern languages only one word for "life" in general conversation, we have to know which of the Greek words was used in the original text. In this case, in talking about losing our life to gain it, the Lord is talking about losing our soul(ish) life, the *psuche*. In all of the scenarios in which Jesus gave this admonition, He is saying that if we hold onto, or even **try** to hold onto, our soulish pleasures, ambitions, pride (all that stuff), we will lose out on the real *zoe* life.

From His foothold in our spirit, the Holy Spirit wants to bring *zoe* life to every part of our soul, every part that makes us "us".

Therefore, the Spirit's objective while we are on this earth is to transform our soul into something that is precious. Philippians 1:6 says, *For I am confident of this very thing, that He who began a good work in you will perfect it until the day of Christ Jesus.* This transforming work in our souls will result in our being "conformed to the image of His Son" (Romans 8:29).

While there might be verses that appear to make this an accomplished fact, all you have to do is look at yourself! Of course, no one expects perfection while we are in this flesh, so we might declare that we **will** be perfect in heaven or when the Lord returns. I advise you not to hang your hat on that. After all, that's what this little book is about.

Now let's look at the second "if" in chapter 2 of 2 Timothy: *if we endure, we will also reign with Him* (verse 12a). Many Christians anticipate ruling and reigning with Christ, but what qualifies us to do so? Are you washed in the blood of the Lamb? That is how we all start, but we are not yet qualified to reign as kings.

Look at the parable of the 10 minas in Luke 19. Starting with verse 12 Jesus tells about a nobleman who gave 10 minas to ten of his slaves before he went away. When the master returned he found out what each slave did with the money that was entrusted to him. Those who were "faithful in a very little thing" were given authority over various cities. But one slave did nothing, and put away his mina into a handkerchief. The result was that everything was taken from him. Jesus inserted that there were many who did not want that master to reign over them, and these were slain when the master returned. This was not the fate of the slave, but he nevertheless went into the next age with nothing.

I hope this helps you to get past the simple concept of spending eternity someplace because you "got saved". The pertinent question is, "What kind of salvation are you experiencing?" Is it folded up in a handkerchief, or have you gained deeper experiences of the Lord? You will take these experiences with you; if you have gained nothing, then you will have nothing to take. The old adage about material possessions is that you "can't take it with you", but our spiritual "possessions" certainly will follow us. Consider in a deeper way Matthew 6:20, which records the Lord saying: *But store up for yourselves treasures in heaven, where neither moth nor rust destroys, and where thieves do not break in and steal.*

But there is still more ground to cover in 2 Timothy 2:12: *if we deny Him, He also will deny us.* This one is hard to swallow. How does this fit in the plan of salvation? How could Jesus deny us? After all, He paid for us with His blood, and we accepted His free gift of salvation!

Paul did not say anything that Jesus himself did not mention....at least twice. As a way of warning, in Matthew 10:33 we can read: *But whoever denies Me before men, I will also deny him before My Father who is in heaven.* It is interesting to note the context. Beginning with verse 16 of Matthew 10 He spoke about the environments of conflict that we will find. This section starts out, *Behold, I send you out as sheep in the midst of wolves.* From verse 26 through verse 31 He encourages us three times to fear neither people nor situations.

Revelation 2 and 3 also portray an environment of hostility toward the saints from outside the church and unscriptural teaching within. To the overcomers in the church in Sardis (Rev 3:5) He says among other things, *I will confess his name before My Father and His angels.* He also commends the church in Pergamum (Revelation 2:13), *...and you hold fast My name.*

So it seems that not denying the Lord is closely related to persecution and false teaching. Notice what Matthew 10:22 says, *You will be hated by all because of My name, but **it is the one who has endured to the end** who will be saved.* You might have come to the Lord 5, 10, or 30 years ago, but do you **really** want to be saved? Endure to the end.

Now we come to the last "if" of this section. I am grateful for the sequence of these "if" statements, because the sequence helps to put this last verse in its context. *If we are faithless, He remains faithful, for He cannot deny Himself.*

What I sometimes heard when I was young (but not so much in my later years) was that it did not really matter if I was faithful or not faithful to the Lord, because He is in me, and He is the one who is faithful, after all. And, since He cannot deny Himself, then everything will be alright concerning me. That seems quite logical, does it not? If this verse stood by itself, it might be hard to argue against that reasoning, but this verse (and all verses) has a context, and the context here says just the opposite.

Simply put, the context says if we died, we will live; and if we endure, we will reign; AND, if we deny Him, He will deny us. How, therefore, can we expect a pass if we are faithless? Is not denying Him related to being faithless? This should be a clear warning to us that if we deny Him, or if we are faithless, then we are pretty much on our own.

Now, you might think that last statement is bothersome, but has the Lord not given us all that we need to live a holy, pursuing, and overcoming life? Most of all, we have the Holy Spirit who indwells us: He is always speaking life to us. We have the Word, which strengthens our spirit and feeds our soul. Plus we have the saints; God's people who nourish us in fellowship.

Therefore, if we are in fact on our own, it is not because the Lord has left us in that state, but it is because we have put ourselves in that situation. But thankfully our loving Lord is always trying to bring us back. Peter's failures and victories are our example and our hope. It is also my experience.

Maybe that is why the Lord is allowing me to write this. I can name dozens who are more qualified, who have been more faithful, who probably love Him and His church more than I, but here we are. This humble brother is writing something that is on his heart, trying to speak to your heart about a matter that can affect your enjoyment in the next age.

The apostle Paul was a particular vessel used by God to establish and strengthen the churches, but he was not a superman. If he were, it would not have been fair for him to encourage us to follow his example in pursuing Christ. But he found the Lord's grace to be his source of strength to run his race. At the end he was able to write to Timothy that he had finished the course.

That is the question before us: Will we finish? Will I finish, or will I stop short? If we give ourselves an excuse now, I am afraid that we will find later that it will not hold up, when we stand before our Lord to give an account. Rather, I think we might be speechless, not even daring to present an argument.

I might have drifted off the main road a little in this section, but my hope is to remove any thought that we can misbehave during our time on earth, and think that it has no bearing in the next age. The Bible does not teach that. In particular the New Testament, in the words of Paul, John, and the rest, and Jesus Himself, does not teach that.

As I wrote at the beginning of this chapter, in order to lay a good foundation for the rest of this book, I branched off into other topics and books of the New Testament. From here on I will mostly stay within the context of each book as it is covered, but I will refer to this chapter quite a few times.

1 Corinthians

While I presented only one selection from Romans, we can look at a few more verses in Paul's first letter to the church in Corinth. Let's look at verses 10 and 13-15 from chapter 3.

Any Man's Work

According to the grace of God which was given to me, like a wise master builder I laid a foundation, and another is building on it. But each man must be careful how he builds on it. ...each man's work will become evident; for the day will show it because it is to be revealed with fire, and the fire itself will test the quality of each man's work. If any man's work which he has built on it remains, he will receive a reward. If any man's work is burned up, he will suffer loss; but he himself will be saved, yet so as through fire.

These verses probably are not ignored by most Christians, but I wonder if the implication is fully appreciated. In the last chapter I asked, "What kind of salvation are you experiencing?" in relation to the unprofitable slave that had everything taken from him. Now, Paul is presenting a similar conclusion to the Corinthians: Will you have something that carries over to the kingdom, or will you suffer loss?

However, there is a difference in these two scenarios. Regarding that slave, there was the issue of fear and lack of motivation. In this chapter the problem is not inactivity, but the kind of activity. Verse 12 reads, *Now if any man builds on the foundation with gold, silver, precious stones, wood, hay, straw.* It is obvious that the good building materials are represented by gold, silver, and precious stones. Gold represents God's nature and person, and silver represents Christ's redemption. The precious stones show us the Spirit's transforming work in us (see 1 Peter 2:5). These are divine, heavenly materials, and they are in contrast to the natural, earthy materials of wood, hay, and straw.

17

What are examples of these earthy materials? I will give an illustration from real life, but please avoid the danger of becoming judgmental of others. As the Lord pointed out, it is easier for us to see the spec in the eye of someone else, and at the same time to be oblivious to the log in our own. So, in assuming that risk I will tell you about a brother that was once in a well known Christian singing group. We went to see that group, and afterward the singers were in the lobby and gift shop area to greet the audience. I was drawn to the one who seemed to have the least showmanship in him. We had some conversation and left, but before I could start the car, I had a strong feeling to give him something to read. I do not even remember what that was or the details of our continued fellowship, but he opened his heart and revealed that some of what goes on behind stage troubled him. While he did not specify, I did not have any feeling that these were sinful things, just the manner of how things operate. He even had some tears. About a year later I saw a brochure for that show, and this brother was not in the photo. I truly hope that the desire of his heart to follow the Lord was the reason.

It is not up to us to say how much of what building materials were in play in that situation. It is easy to pick on those who put themselves in the public eye, but that brother's sentiments say a lot. The Lord will sort out the rest. I think that for the most part, we build partly with the divine materials and partly with the earthy things. At least, I know that is the case with me. Whatever meager building work I have done might be fortunate to survive.

What I find interesting about this portion, *"If any man's work is burned up, he will suffer loss; but he himself will be saved, yet so as through fire",* is that our work is not something that is outside of us. If my work is burned up, it is my salvation that goes through the fire.

Does that sit well with you? Does it go against the kind of salvation that you have been taught? This is the purpose of this book, to make all of us realize that God requires something of us. Yes, we have been washed in the blood of the Lamb (I am assuming that if you are reading this, you probably are a Christian), and we are saved by grace, but that is not the end of our story. Anyway, it ought not to be, according to Paul and according to the Lord, as we will see.

Planting a Building

Most of us are not in a great Christian work, or even in a "minor" work; relatively few are missionaries; most are not even leaders in a local congregation; so what building work do we have part in? What do we do that constitutes "work"? What is the "work" that most of us do that will either burn or survive the fire? I think the clue is in the verses that precede verse 10. Paul wrote about a garden, or field, in verses 6 through 9. He talked about planting and watering. But then curiously he concludes by saying, *you are God's field, God's building,* as though a field and a building are equivalent! He did not say, "you are God's field AND God's building." The word "building" is in apposition (not opposition) to the word "field", meaning that they are the same thing. Only in the realm of the Spirit is that possible!

What this means is that we are growing individually to become a wonderful, beautiful, and solid structure corporately!

So, back to the question...what is the "work" that we do? First you have to realize that if you remain as only an individual plant in the field, there is no chance of you doing any work. Work happens only when you interact with the other plants. It is the work that produces the building. So you can see why Paul transitions from planting and watering in verses 6 through 8 to building in verses 10 through 15. Verse 9 is the keystone. What a divine construction of thought!

But I keep wandering around the question. What is our work, we who are without great works? In one word....SERVICE. This is a significant word. Thinking back to the field, if I remain an individual plant, I am only for myself. I might have deep roots, and I might get my strength from the sun(Son), but unless I get with the other plants, I am of no use to them; I have no way to serve them. Service brings us together. Whether your service is directed **toward**

19

me, or whether your service is **with** me, being together allows the Spirit opportunity to knit our hearts together.

Let's look at chapter four of Ephesians. Verse 11 says that Christ gave gifts to His church in the form of apostles, prophets, evangelists, and pastors and teachers. The reason? Verse 12: *for the equipping of the saints for the work of service.* (It is convenient that the NASB uses the word "service". Other versions use "ministry".) Verse 12 goes on to say that our service is *to the building up of the body of Christ.* You should go to Ephesians 4 and read the verses that follow. They reveal the divine process and progression that is summarized in verse 16. *...according to the proper working of each individual part, causes the growth of the body for the building up of itself in love.*

I hope you see this! It is not the evangelist who builds the church. It is not the preacher who builds the church by giving a sermon every Sunday. Neither is it the Bible teacher. The body of Christ is built by **us** as we serve one another. The gifts to the church, as previously mentioned, have the function of equipping us. Then, being equipped, we serve.

This is what Paul was saying in 1 Corinthians. In verse 3:10 he said, *I laid a foundation, and another is building on it.* He does not acknowledge building anything. Regarding the field, he planted; concerning the building, he laid the foundation. In the field we receive nutrition from the sun and the soil, and God gives the growth (verse 3:7); as the building we cooperate with the Spirit's equipping so that the body builds up itself through our serving.

Reasonable Service

But, what is our service? Please bear with me as I get this out of my system....it is **not** showing up at a Sunday morning "service". I am afraid that in order to placate an offended conscience, Romans 12:1 has been twisted into presenting our bodies at a meeting of the church as a "reasonable service". Our purpose for coming together with the saints (ie, Christians, the church) is to get equipped so that we can go out from the meeting and serve. We need the teaching, we need to hear God's speaking to the church, we need to have our hearts lifted up by singing to the Lord, and we need the encouragement and love that comes from being together. And there are some who are serving. These would be your pastor, ushers, teachers, and others. But for the rest who are parked in a seating apparatus, being there does not qualify as serving.

Serving can take many forms. Some go into the inner city or to other countries to feed the hungry and set up shelters, while many others support those and other causes. Closer to where we live, serving can be having some in your house for dinner. It could be visiting someone who is having a hard time. Serving could be running over to someone's house who suddenly needs help with a plumbing problem. Service can also involve cleaning the bathrooms where the church has its meetings. In other words, our serving can have the aura of being quite spiritual, or it can be very down to earth.

Later verses in chapter four of Ephesians mention some things that you might not consider to be a form of serving, but in my experience they are, and they can be quite precious. Actually, as I list them, they should look very similar to what was mentioned in the previous paragraph.

Verse 28: *He who steals must steal no longer; but rather he must labor, performing with his own hands what is good, so that he will have something to share with one who has need.* Verse 29: *Let no unwholesome word proceed from your mouth, but only such a word as is good for edification according to the need of the moment, so that it will give grace to those who hear.* Verse 32: *Be kind to one another, tender-hearted, forgiving each other*

Now you can know the essential point and the essence of serving. It is our being together in the Lord. Service that is in the Lord (I will even say, in spirit) will have the result of knitting our hearts together, and building with gold, silver, and precious stones.

On the other hand sometimes we forget, and end up talking about all kinds of things, or doing things according to the old creation, and the result is that wood, hay, and straw are added to the building. We need to keep our guard up so that we contribute the divine building materials, and not the other.

Before moving on, we have to look at the last warning in chapter three of 1 Corinthians. Verses 16 and 17: *Do you not know that you are a temple of God and that the Spirit of God dwells in you? If any man destroys the temple of God, God will destroy him, for the temple of God is holy, and that is what you are.*

Because verse 6:19 refers to our body as a temple of the Holy Spirit (*do you not know that your body is a temple of the Holy Spirit who is in you*), for many years I considered verses 3:16-17 in the same way, as referring to me. Eventually the Lord got through my blindness and I realized that in its context (remember context?), "temple" here refers to the local believers.

Of course we do not intend to harm the church, but we can unknowingly do things that are not edifying. The work of building is not an isolationist endeavor, and we need to realize that what we are building is not a vague abstraction. We are building God's holy temple! Only evil men would destroy God's temple, right? To be sure, there were those in Paul's day that were teaching the Gentile believers to keep the law, and Paul had no kind words for them, because that kind of teaching was very destructive to the faith of the saints. It should be no wonder then that God would destroy those with that kind of influence.

However, there is also the warning in verse 18, in which Paul tells us that we should not trust our own wisdom. He says, *If any man among you.* If you have not realized it yet from your own experience and from the Word, your wisdom, man's wisdom, is of the old creation. God's temple is holy, and there is nothing in the old creation that is fit to be used in it or for it. Something might even be good, but if its source is from the old creation, there is nothing holy in it. Wood, hay, and straw typify the old creation, but gold, silver, and precious stones show us the new creation.

The real conflict in this age is new versus old. We tend to see the world situation in terms of right versus wrong, good versus evil. Christians might see the conflict as righteousness versus sin, but consider this. When Adam ate the fruit from the wrong tree, the tree of the knowledge of good and evil, not only did sin enter into man, but oldness entered into all of creation. Today everything is old and every new thing becomes old. But ever since the resurrection of Christ, God has been doing a work of restoration, in us! (See Galatians 6:15 and 2 Corinthians 5:17.) Eventually everything will be restored, as Peter said in Act 3:21, *Whom heaven must receive until the period of restoration of all things about which God spoke by the mouth of His holy prophets from ancient time.*

Do you know why you were saved? Do you know why Christ was beaten with so many, many stripes and then taken to die on the cross? Do you think all of that is so that your sins would be forgiven so that you can go someplace to spend eternity? No! Our sins are forgiven, surely, by our belief in our Savior, but that is the starting point. From that moment on the Spirit's work in us is to transform our oldness to newness (Galatians 6:15). Probably it is even better to say the He is changing **us** from old to new! If you would, read chapters 6 through 8 of Romans with this in mind. Even though you will find the word "sin" used over and over, Paul's point is that having dealt with sin, there is the matter of living in the new creation. For example, the law is of the old creation, but grace belongs to the new. Reflect on Paul's use of the words "new", "newness", and "life". I think you might see that the conflict that Paul describes is, at its core, new creation versus old creation, especially in chapter 8. In fact, I suggest that you read chapter 8 first, at least the first ten verses, then go back to chapter 6 and read through.

Coming back to the materials that are available for building God's temple, you can see now that wood, hay, and straw are of the old creation, and gold, silver, and precious stones represent materials of the **new** creation. Paul is telling us that when we come together, we must be careful to build with materials of the new creation. Old materials will not make it through.

2 Corinthians

Judgment

With what I consider to be an echo back to 1 Corinthians 3:13-15,Paul wrote in his second letter to Corinth (verse 5:10): *For we must all appear before the judgment seat of Christ, so that each one may be recompensed for his deeds in the body, according to what he has done, whether good or bad.*

There is a judgment for unbelievers, and there is a judgment for believers. They are not the same event, and they do not have the same consequences. For the unbelievers there is the great white throne judgment (beginning from Revelation 20:11). This judgment occurs after the millennial reign of our Lord, because Revelation 20:3 describes Satan's temporary release after the thousand years, and verse 5 tells that *the rest of the dead did not come to life until the thousand years were completed.* For this judgment books are opened, and "another book", the book of life, is opened. Everyone is judged according to their deeds, according to what is written in the books. Whoever is not found in the book of life is thrown into the lake of fire.

That judgment, therefore, is for the unbelievers. Those who belong to Christ have a judgment that must occur prior to the millennium, because by this judgment it will be decided who among the Lord's slaves will enter into His joy in His kingdom. I will cover this in much more depth when we look at the gospels, but for now notice that Paul has stated that we will be recompensed, which means to be given wages. "Wages" can mean 1) a soldier's pay, 2) dues paid for work, or 3) the reward of the fruit of one's labor. Recall how Paul stated in his letter to the churches in Galatia that we will reap either corruption or eternal life (Galatians 6:7-8). This judgment is the payoff.

Receive not in Vain

From the end of chapter five into the first couple of verses of chapter six, Paul appears to be preaching the gospel to the Corinthians (5:20 to 6:2). *Therefore, we are ambassadors for Christ, as though God were making an appeal through us; we beg you on behalf of Christ, be reconciled to God. He made Him who knew no sin to be sin on our behalf, so that we might become the righteousness of God in Him. And working together with Him, we also urge you not to receive the grace of God in vain – for He says, "At the acceptable time I listened to you, and on the day of salvation I helped you." Behold, now is "the acceptable time," behold, now is "the day of salvation."*

Paul is reminding the church what the gospel is...and what it is not. The gospel is not a "one time shot". Notice verse 5:21. *He made Him who knew no sin to be sin on our behalf, so that we might* **become** *the righteousness of God in Him.* Paul brings us to a starting line and then shows us the race. Christ was made sin for us (bringing us to the starting line), so that we can **become** righteous in Him. This is a process, a long process.

We all know Romans 5:19 - *For as through the one man's disobedience the many were made sinners, even so through the obedience of the One the many will be made righteous.* John Darby used the word "constituted" in his translation of the Bible. We, who were constituted sinners, are being **reconstituted** righteous! Is this not marvelous? But did it happen at the moment you received the Lord? I can definitely say that I was not instantly constituted righteous! But I will say boldly and in faith that I am **being** constituted righteous!

It is this process that determines whether we have received the grace of God in vain, or not. If, by God's mercy and grace, we get to the starting line, but do not run the race, that is, we do not become the righteousness of God in this context, is that not receiving God's grace in vain? If you disagree with me, remember that it was Paul who said it (2 Corinthians 6:1).

I have run 5k and 10k road races. I get everything ready the night before, and I set two alarms (not to make sure I get up, but to sleep better, knowing that I did not fail to set it!). I get up early enough to arrive at the race 45 to 60 minutes before the start. The time comes, the gun sounds, ...and I stand there. Of course, I do not start there, but how foolish and vain to get to the starting line and not run the race!

How about if I do start running, but get side tracked somewhere and get off the course. Or maybe I think it is too hard and I quit running. I have not done this in a road race, but I have done it in the salvation race. Here Paul is telling the Corinthians that they are in danger of doing the same thing.

But, praise the Lord, we can resume the race! Today is the day of salvation! It is okay to use this verse to persuade sinners to come to Jesus, but keep in mind that Paul wrote this to the church. The first half of verse 6:2 is quoting Isaiah 49:8a, *Thus says the Lord, "In a favorable time I have answered you, and in a day of salvation I have helped you.* Then Paul adds his own summation, *Behold, now is the "acceptable time," behold, now is "the day of salvation".* At some risk, here is my summation of Paul's summation: Listen, Christian, you came to Jesus once as a sinner seeking salvation; now you must keep going! Jesus wants to save us every day from our own unrighteous constitution, so that we can be made, reconstituted, righteous in Him. This is a day of salvation; receive it today and tomorrow and the next day!

Promises, Promises

Now we come to a verse that requires the question, "Why does it matter?" *Therefore having these promises, beloved, let us cleanse ourselves from all defilement of flesh and spirit, perfecting holiness in the fear of God* (2 Corinthians 7:1). If we all go to heaven, having once been saved, what difference does it make whether now, in this life, we cleanse ourselves and perfect holiness? A lot of Christians (maybe most?) know intuitively that we should be holy, but how does holiness in this age prepare us for the next age? Or does it?

What are "these promises" that Paul referred to? We have to go to the previous chapter to see. Verses 6:14 through 6:18 contain various exhortations to separate ourselves to God. The issue is posed in questions like "what partnership...?", "what fellowship...?", "what harmony...?","what...in common...?", and "what agreement...?".

This last "what" reads, *what agreement has the temple of God with idols?* The word "temple" allows Paul to transition to God's **real** temple, which is **us!** *For we are the temple of the living God; just as God said, "I will dwell in them and walk among them; and I will be their God, and they shall be My people"* (verse 16). Just as the physical temple in the Old Testament gave God a venue to be among His chosen people, our **living** God in these days has a living temple that is constituted of all of His redeemed saints. His desire is to dwell in **this** temple, walking and living in **us**. And yet, there is more!

Paul then adds "therefore" in verse 6:17. Do you notice these transitions as you read Paul's letters? In the previous verse (verse 16) he concludes the five "what's" by saying *For we are the temple.....*

Having told us that God wants to dwell in us, walk among us, and be our God, he says "Therefore..." An action is required of us, and that is to *come out from their midst and be separate, ...and do not touch what is unclean.* This puts the ball in our court. Each of us has to approach God in a sincere way to learn by the Holy Spirit what is unclean to us and from whose midst we should remove ourselves. But having done this, the result is (the end of verse 17 plus verse 18), *and I will welcome you. And I will be a father to you, and you shall be sons and daughters to Me.*

In case you lost track, here again are the promises found in chapter 6. *I will dwell in them and walk among them; and I will be their God, and they shall be My people* (verse 16). *I will welcome you. And I will be a father to you, and you shall be sons and daughters to Me* (verse 18).

Now we see the promises that were spoken of in verse 7:1! Do you want the promises that the Spirit has shown us in chapter 6?

Paul's concluding thought in verse 7:1 is this (notice the "therefore"), *Therefore, having these promises, beloved, let us cleanse ourselves from all defilement of flesh and spirit, perfecting holiness in the fear of God.* By this and other scriptures we have covered, we can see that it **does** matter that we cleanse ourselves. So I ask you again, do you want those promises? In our fallen nature we are prone to want "things", but God has promised to give us Himself!

But you might say, "Does not 1 Corinthians 2:9 talk about wonderful things that God has prepared for us?" Here is verse 2:9. *But just as it is written, "Things which the eye has not seen and ear has not heard, and which have not entered the heart of man, all that God has prepared for those who love Him."* What could I possibly have against this verse?! Sorry, but I have to take the "things" out of that verse.

The two words "things which" are actually one word in the Greek, *hos*. *Hos* is used twice in the verse; the second occurrence is where we see the words "all that (*hos*) God has...". *Hos* means who/which/what/that, depending on the context. This word is used many times in the New Testament. Grabbing some verses out of Matthew, you can see the various contexts.

Jacob was the father of Joseph the husband of Mary, by whom (hos) Jesus was born, who is called the Messiah. (1:16)
"Behold, the virgin shall be with child and shall bear a Son, and they shall call His name Immanuel," which (hos) translated means, "God with us." (1:23)
After hearing the king, they went their way; and the star, which (hos) they had seen in the east.... (2:9)
And behold, a voice out of the heavens said, "This is My beloved Son, in whom (hos) I am well pleased." (3:17)
"Whoever (hos) then annuls one of the least of these commandments, ... (5:19)

Without getting lost in too many verses, my point is that *hos* is sometimes translated as "things which" and sometimes as a single word, as in the example verses above. Verses can differ in this respect among the various translations. So, 1 Corinthians 2:9 could just as well be translated as "that which (*hos*) the eye has not seen..." or "what (*hos*) has not entered the heart...," and other versions do present that kind of rendering.

Please forget about **things**, even though our Father surely will have the best of everything in the next age. (I admit that every time I see an extraordinary sunset, I wonder what other wonderful colors we will be able to see.) However, it is more important to realize that what Paul is pointing out is that the real promises are spiritual in nature. He goes on to say in verse 2:10, *For to us God revealed them through the Spirit....* Did you notice the tense of the verb "revealed"? We are not waiting to find out all the wonderful "things" of eternity; God has already shown us, revealed to us, the blessings of the Spirit! These are knowable in this lifetime!

How has He shown us? It is through the Spirit. Verse 2:12a says, *Now we have received, ... the Spirit who is from God.*

What has He shown us? Verse 12 continues, *so that we may know the things* (not *hos*) *freely given to us by God.* Aha! He said "things"! Oh, but these are not ordinary physical things, but spiritual. That is one of the big reasons why the Holy Spirit was sent to us, to reveal to us spiritual things. *Now we have received, ... so that we **may** know.*

Now, let us put that verse to the test. The more time you have spent with the Lord, the more clear your answer should be. Thinking only of your time on this earth before you were saved, did your eyes then see what the Spirit has since shown you? Had your ears heard what the Spirit now speaks to you? Did you have any idea what God had in store for you? Without a doubt we **will** see, hear, and experience in other ways, all the awesomeness of our God, but we get the foretaste now! God has **already** revealed them!

Have I successfully taken the "things" out of 1 Corinthians 2:9? I hope I did. Does that kind of thought now pale? What glory have we already seen? What wonderful things God wants to show us both in His word and in the lives of His saints! What speaking we have received that saves us! What precious experiences we have had as we follow the Lamb!

But, bringing this back to 2 Corinthians, if we are to realize what God has prepared for us we must cleanse ourselves, as 2 Corinthians 7:1 says, *from all defilement,* and we must perfect *holiness in the fear of God.*

Note: For future reference, the word **hos** *here is word number G3739 in Strong's Concordance. It is pronounced like "hoss". There is another* **hos**, *G5613, that has a different meaning and a different pronunciation. The "o" sounds like "host". This second* **hos** *(like host) will come up later, so I hope that this comment will help alleviate confusion then.*

Galatians

It was hard to write about the letters to the church in Corinth. Paul had to deal with some situations that were not pleasant. But we have to appreciate our brothers and sisters who preceded us in the first century church. If they did not have problems, we would be missing a big chunk of the New Testament. Besides, those dear saints are not alone. What would Paul write to us? Would his letters to us have a similar tone? Would he have to deal with some of the same issues? I am sorry to say, but I think so.

In contrast, the next four letters are much more pleasant. It is true that Paul scolds the churches in Galatia, but in explaining things to them, things that they should have already known, we get to read and enjoy some wonderful truths. The Lord is the righteous judge, but whenever I benefit from observing another's fault or downfall (in other words, learning their lesson), my prayer always is that the Lord will go easy on them.

Growing Christ

The first verse we will look at is Galatians 4:19. *My children, with whom I am again in labor until Christ is formed is you...* Paul's tone here is that of a child being formed in its mother's womb. Christ wants to grow in us. He entered into us as the Spirit, joining Himself to our spirit. From there He wants to transform our soul, mainly by renewing our mind (Romans 12:2). In that sense Christ is being formed in us, but the other side of the coin is found in Ephesians 4:15, *we are to grow up in all aspects into Him.* I get the sense that His transforming us from within is His being formed in us, and our being conformed to Him in our actions and living is **our** growing up into **Him**.

Paul touches both aspects, as we will see, but mainly his emphasis toward the Galatians is on the inward. Because our efforts to keep the law (which the Galatians had been enticed to do) can have an appearance of being Christ-like, we have to be brought back to the Spirit, who operates within us to change us from within. What is so crucial that Paul would use an expression like being in labor until Christ was formed in those saints? Actually, he does not say directly. Rather than try to put words into Paul's mouth, I feel like the Lord wants to unveil that through these pages. My prayer is for soft hearts that are open to the Spirit's speaking. Amen, Lord Jesus.

Reap Eternal Life

Here is a verse that is often pulled out of its context. Galatians 6:8 says, *For the one who sows to his own flesh will from the flesh reap corruption, but the one who sows to the Spirit will from the Spirit reap eternal life.*

I have heard messages and encouragements within messages to sow to the Spirit, and this can have many appearances. Spending more time in the Word and less watching TV would be a significant way to sow more to the Spirit. Attending meetings of the church and Bible studies is another good way. But the context of this verse has more to do with fulfilling the **needs** of others than anything else.

Here is the context of chapter 6. Verses 1 and 2 read, *Brethren, even if anyone is caught in any trespass, you who are spiritual, restore such a one in a spirit of gentleness; each one looking to yourself, so that you too will not be tempted. Bear one another's burdens, and thereby fulfill the law of Christ.* Then verse 6: *The one who is taught the word is to share all good things with the one who teaches him.*

Then we have verses 7 and 8: *Do not be deceived, God is not mocked; for whatever a man sows, this he will also reap. For the one who sows to his own flesh will from the flesh reap corruption, but the one who sows to the Spirit will from the Spirit reap eternal life.*

Paul's conclusion is in verses 9 and 10: *Let us not lose heart in doing good, for in due time we will reap if we do not grow weary. So*

then, while we have opportunity, let us do good to all people, and especially to those who are of the household of the faith.
For good measure, here is Hebrews 13:16: *And do not neglect doing good and sharing, for with such sacrifices God is pleased.* It is true that the one "caught in any trespass" has been sowing to his flesh, but I also think that from these verses we can conclude that giving ourselves to others is the truest form of sowing to the Spirit. Usually when I am asked to help with something, my first thought goes to "how much of my time will this take". Right away I care for my own flesh. How much better it is to take the opportunity to die to self and sow to the spirit!

This also ties together some other things. Do you recall my previous discussion on serving? It might look like what you have just read in the preceding paragraph. Do you recall the discussion about losing our soul life? We have just read in the verses above some ways of doing that.

What does it mean to reap eternal life? We saw in chapter four that we are growing Christ; He is being formed in us. This is eternal life, even as John wrote, *This is the promise which He Himself made to us: eternal life* (1 John 2:25); and, *This is eternal life, that they may know You, the only true God, and Jesus Christ whom You have sent* (John 17:3). This is very different from those who pry donations from the saints under the false promise of reaping material benefits. That is not a promise of God's New Testament economy. As stated previously, our Father's desire is to give us Himself!

Walk by the Spirit, Inherit the Kingdom

Now we step backward in Galatians to chapter 5. I chose to cover these verses after chapter 6 because there is a lot more to say.
But I say, walk by the Spirit and you will not carry out the desire of the flesh. For the flesh sets its desire against the Spirit, and the Spirit against the flesh; for these are in opposition to one another, so that you may not do the things that you please. But if you are led by the Spirit, you are not under the Law. Now the deeds

of the flesh are evident, which are: ..... of which I forewarn you, just as I have forewarned you, that those who practice such things will not inherit the kingdom of God (Galatians 5:16-19a, 21b).

Hopefully the title of this section helped you in reading the verses to see that the objective in our walk during this life is to inherit the kingdom of God. The goal is not to be qualified to enter pearly gates or to go somewhere. Inheriting the kingdom of God does not equal going to heaven! This will be brought out more when we get to the Gospels.

In giving you the verses above, I left out the detailed list of no-nos so that the main thought would not be lost. That list runs from the end of verse 19 to the beginning of verse 21. Here now is the list: *immorality, impurity, sensuality, idolatry, sorcery, enmities, strife, jealousy, outbursts of anger, disputes, dissensions, factions, envying, drunkenness, carousing, and things like these.* Does anything strike close to home? Smiley face here!...and three fingers pointing backwards. Our hope, of course, is for deliverance from these things as Christ grows in us, making His home in our hearts.

But Paul's stern warning is that the practice of doing these things will prevent us from inheriting the kingdom. If I ask to whom he is writing, you know the answer, right? He is writing to the churches! He is writing to the saints in those churches. Why would Paul write such a warning if its outcome were not possible?

Please reject the go-to-heaven "gospel". At best you might hear something like, "Christians should live godly lives to honor God and so receive a reward." Did you ever hear that you could miss inheriting the kingdom? If we miss the kingdom, what's left? Does that mean that we could go to hell, even after being saved? In order to put your mind at ease, I will say that I do not think it means that, in fact I am certain of it. I will address that topic at the end of the book. In the meantime, I want to impress upon all who read this that the Lord, because of His loving concern for all of us, has provided these warnings. Satan's subtlety has diminished their impact and even concealed them from many. May we seek our Lord's face as we open our hearts to His speaking.

Ephesians

Ephesians is known as a book with a high altitude vision of the church. This is particularly true in the first half of Paul's letter to that church. At the same time Paul has some down-to-earth advice and admonitions for us in the second half. Among these are three warnings, all of them in chapter five.

Inherit the Kingdom

Ephesians 5:1-2a, 3-5. *Therefore be imitators of God, as beloved children; and walk in love,.... But immorality or any impurity or greed must not even be named among you, as is proper among saints; and there must be no filthiness and silly talk, or coarse jesting, which are not fitting, but rather giving of thanks. For this you know with certainty, that no immoral or impure person or covetous man, who is an idolater, has an inheritance in the kingdom of Christ and God.*

Did we not cover this already? We have, and Paul also had covered this with the Ephesian church previously. Notice that he wrote that they already "know with certainty". Do we? Do we know this with certainty? Forgive my asking the question again: To whom was he writing?

I think it significant that verses 3, 4, and 5 are set in contrast to walking in love, *Therefore be imitators of God, as beloved children; and walk in love, just as Christ also loved you...* (verses 1 and 2a). It is easy to see that immorality, impurity, greed, and filthiness are opposite love, but what is our attitude about silly talk and coarse jesting? If we love someone in truth, would we be so quick with the smart remark or comeback?

It is not that we have to be staid and stiff, lacking in any humor or humanity, but what are we offering to God and to man? Look at verse 2 in its entirety. *And walk in love, just as Christ also loved you and gave Himself up for us, an offering and a sacrifice to God as a fragrant aroma.* How do we smell? Sometimes I realize that I do not smell so good. Christ always smells sweet to our Father, but our death stinks: Our dead words, our dead deeds, and everything else that emanates from us.

In the Old Testament, you can see that when the Israelites came to Jerusalem for their feasts before God, everyone was a partaker of the sacrifices. The priests got their portion, the people who brought the lambs and other animals got their portion, and God got His portion. What part belonged to God? The aroma! Many times that is translated as "sweet savor", but it is the smell of the cooking meat that was God's portion.

That might seem strange to you, but now that it has been explained, realize that the Old Testament points us to Christ. Christ's life was a sweet aroma to God. That is what Paul is calling us to be, a sweet aroma to our Father and also to those around us. Instead of drawing attention to our stinky selves, we should give thanks to our Father for what He has provided to us in Christ, and we should offer ourselves in Christ as a fragrant aroma to God and man. You can probably think of someone who right now fits that bill, a real servant of the Lord, who is selfless in serving. What a sweet aroma!

Think back to the chapter on Romans and the section "Planting a Building". I wrote that our work ought to be service to others, that it does not have to be something big in order to qualify as work. Now consider what a sweet aroma that creates!

Now we have to cover the warning in verse 5: *For this you know with certainty, that no immoral or impure person or covetous man, who is an idolater, has an inheritance in the kingdom of Christ and God.* Rather strong words, do you think? Keep in mind that Paul was not preaching the gospel on the street corner. He was writing to a church, to Christians, to those who have already believed the Gospel! Have you ever heard such a word spoken in a church meeting (Sunday worship service)? How does this square with what you probably hear week after week? Get saved – go to heaven.

Do you think that these things cannot befall a person who has once opened his heart to the Lord? Maybe you have heard such called "false Christians", or "false believers". There have been too many public examples to allow such dismissiveness. No, this was a valid concern in Corinth and apparently in Ephesus, and it remains so today.

With that in mind, what does it mean to inherit (or not) the kingdom? To inherit something means to come into possession of it. But Paul makes it sound as though we could be disqualified from receiving our inheritance.

Does that sound like going to heaven? Do we not pray, following the Lord's example, "Thy kingdom **come**"? The kingdom that we are to inherit is a heavenly kingdom....on earth. Revelation 21 bears this out. Verse 2 describes the new Jerusalem, the holy bride, coming down from heaven to the earth, and verses 24 and 26 says this: *The **nations** will walk by its light, and the kings of the **earth** will bring their glory into it....and they will bring the glory and the honor of the **nations** into it.*

Now that the proper scene has been set, is it easier to imagine how some could inherit the kingdom, while others do not? Of course I am not suggesting that you use your imagination to replace God's Word, but I do contend that man's imagination has already replaced significant portions of the Word and its truth. The Word says that the eternal kingdom will find its place on earth, and the Word, through Paul, says that the man who remains in his flesh will not inherit it. Jesus said the same, and we will cover that when we get to the Gospels.

Sons of Disobedience

Verses 6 and 7 of Ephesians 5 are a continuation of the last section. Speaking of all the impure things listed in verses 3 through 5, Paul continues, *Let no one deceive you with empty words, for because of these things the wrath of God comes upon the sons of disobedience. Therefore do not be partakers with them.*

Therefore *do not be partakers with them.* There is not a lot that needs to be said at the moment, but Paul's clear warning is that we will not be out of reach of God's wrath if we are hanging around the sons of disobedience, engaged in their lawless and sinful activities. Notice how much this sounds like Revelation 18:4. *I heard another voice from heaven, saying, "Come out of her, my people, so that you will not participate in her sins and receive of her plagues."* If you want to disagree, please do not argue with this brother; ask God what He means by these statements.

Careful How You Walk

Now we come to the third portion in Ephesians 5, verses 13-15 and verse 17. *But all things become visible when they are exposed by the light, for everything that becomes visible is light. For this reason it says, "Awake, sleeper, and arise from the dead, and Christ will shine on you." Therefore be careful how you walk, not as unwise men but as wise,.....So then do not be foolish, but understand what the will of the Lord is.* It is coming hot and heavy, don't you think?

There are a couple of warnings here, but how many times are these verses read without taking heed? Verses 7 through 12 continue in the vein that we have been discussing, and then Paul declares that everything will be exposed by the light and calls for us to **wake up**! Wake up so that Christ can shine on us. The shining will come sooner or later, so it is better to be under the shining now, when we can take grace to repent, than later, when the shining will be accompanied by judgment.

For this reason Paul calls on us to not be foolish. The foolishness that he refers to is walking in darkness while we think that all will be well when "we get to heaven", not understanding what God is doing. Rather, Paul says that we **need** to understand God's will. We do not have to be ignorant of God's will, because it is all written in His Book for us to discover.

Do you know God's will? I am not speaking of His will for your life, but I am asking, do you know what He is doing through all of this process of planting a garden in Genesis and putting a man there, becoming Himself a man, enduring the lashes and going to the cross, resurrecting, ascending to the Father, breathing the Holy

Spirit into His disciples, putting His life into millions of believers through these centuries, and returning to set up His kingdom on earth? What God is doing is written in the pages of His Word, and it is not about taking us away somewhere!

Looking back to verse 6, Paul said, *Let no one deceive you with empty words.* What kind of empty words? According to the context, the empty words have to be suggestions to the saints that it is okay if you do not cooperate with the Spirit's attempts to deliver you from captivity and transform you, that it really is okay to stay asleep and hide from the Lord's shining into your heart, because in the end Jesus is going to come back and take us away to glory. Empty words!

Empty words, yet that is what so many have heard for all their lives. Some will argue that God is just, and He will deal with the child that continues to live as though he were still a lost sinner. I have heard that kind of discussion, and while this idea is on the right track, the confidence is lacking in many concerning whether it is true. The one saying this likely is expressing an innate opinion, but it is also likely that he does not know how to back it up with scripture. Those scriptures are what you have been reading in this book, but have you ever heard it presented?

How damaging to God's people have been these empty words? These empty words lead to complacency in some Christians. This has also caused some unsaved to not receive God's mercy, thinking that He is not righteous.

I have read the writings of some other Christians who also believe that the teaching of going to heaven is a false teaching. Some of those think that the idea of going to heaven is what Paul referred to in 2 Thessalonians 2:11 – *For this reason God will send upon them a deluding influence so that they will believe what is false.* The KJV says "send them strong delusion, that they should believe a lie". I do not think that going to heaven is the lie that this verse refers to, but I point it out so that you can see how serious some consider this matter to be.

I showed you a few pages back that "the end of the story" is that Christ returns to set up His kingdom on earth. That is what the last two chapters of Revelation show us. At this point you might have a dozen verses in mind, and you are thinking, "Yeah, but don't these verses talk about heaven, and what about these other verses, and those verses?" If you will stay with me, I feel certain that we will get to those same verses, especially in the gospels.

Philippians

Philippians has some verses that will be difficult for me to discuss. If you read the preface, you know my admission that there are many who are much more qualified than I to write this book. But if the Lord has chosen this brother to discuss these matters, then so be it. He is the head of the body.

Press on...Lay Hold

Philippians 3:12 says, *Not that I have already obtained it or have already become perfect, but I press on so that I may lay hold of that for which also I was laid hold of by Christ Jesus.* This verse lies in the midst of a section that might cause some confusion for you, not really knowing what Paul is talking about. If you hold to the traditional teaching that has been discussed, that Jesus is going to take us to heaven, then it must seem that there is something in these verses that does not quite fit the scenario.

Firstly, here is the apostle Paul, of all people, admitting that he has not yet "obtained it", so he presses on so that he might "lay hold". What is the "it", and what more is there to lay hold of?

The "it" can be found in verse 11, *in order that I may attain to the resurrection from the dead.* This has to be one of the verses that does not square with traditional teaching, because is not the resurrection the one thing we are assured of, the one thing that we are looking forward to? Let me perplex you even more. The beginning of the verse as quoted here is "in order that". This phrase actually means "if somehow", and is similarly translated by KJV (if by any means), New Living Translation (so that one way or another), NIV (and so, somehow), ESV (that by any means possible), RSV (that if possible), and Darby (if any way).

You can see that these expressions, while expressing hope, leave some room for doubt, as if there were a possibility that we might not be resurrected! Fortunately, that is not really the case. The word "resurrection" here actually has a prefix in the Greek,

43

which gives the sense of something extra, or something more. The Greek word is *exanastasis,* the prefix being "ex".

None of the common translations portray this. The only translation of which I am aware that does give the sense of something extra is the Recovery Version (published by Living Stream Ministries), which has a very good footnote. In that version the translation is "out-resurrection". This version is the source of my understanding for this.

Philippians 3:11 is the only place where this word is used. Maybe now you can see how Paul had a special reason for pressing forward. This realization can also give us a new sense to Hebrews 11:35, speaking of the Old Testament saints who endured so much in the name of God: *and others were tortured, not accepting their release, so that they might obtain a better resurrection.* What is this better resurrection? I believe that I see hints of an answer in the Word, that is, in some of the Lord's parables and in Revelation. What I really think, and I hate to say it, is that this better resurrection is what Christians think they are going to experience by the single fact of being a Christian. I think many will be surprised in an unpleasant sort of way, at least during the millennium. If Paul was so earnest to obtain this better resurrection, what makes us so certain of it? I think we ought to follow the example that God provided to us in Paul.

Now, if Philippians 3:11 begins with an expression of some hopefulness, we need to look back at verse 10 to see how that hope can be realized. *That I may know Him and the power of His resurrection, and the fellowship of His sufferings, being conformed to His death.* This seems to be a pretty tall order, but you can see Paul's willingness to suffer anything in order to gain Christ (verse 3:8).

Just as we had to look at verse 10 to better appreciate verse 11, let us look back to verse 9 to see how we get to verse 10. *And may be found in Him, not having a righteousness of my own derived from the Law, but that which is through faith in Christ, the righteousness which comes from God on the basis of faith.* Before we have the deeper experiences of the Lord in verse 10, we need

Christ's righteousness to become ours. How does that happen? How can we know if our righteousness is of the law or of faith?

One way to tell is by the smell test. In the last chapter I wrote about being a sweet fragrance to God. Contrast that with the smell of self-righteousness. Believe me, there have been times when I didn't want to be near me. Awful! Isaiah 64:6 says that our righteousness is nothing more than a filthy garment. I wonder what that smells like!

Sometimes the distinction between righteousness of the law and that of faith is obvious. Even when the difference is clear, we might prefer to hang on to the law. We do not comprehend God's New Testament dispensation, that is, His economy. Here again, it is a difference between oldness and newness.

In verse 6 of the same third chapter Paul was able to say that according to the righteousness "which is in the law", he was blameless. According to the context, I think he was referring to both ceremonial law (circumcision being the example there) and laws for living. But he set aside that kind of righteousness, as we will see. You might think that we are freed from the Old Testament law, but do you realize that we make our own laws? We're really good at it. How should a Christian behave? What kinds of activities are permitted on Sunday?

Look at what Paul said in his letter to the church in Colossae (2:16-17 and 20-23 with highlights). *Therefore no one is to act as your judge in regard to **food or drink or in respect to a festival or a new moon or a Sabbath day** – things which are a mere shadow of what is to come; but the **substance belongs to Christ**. .... If you have died with Christ to the elementary principals of the world, why, as if you were living in the world, do you submit yourself to decrees, such as, "do not handle, do not taste, do not touch!" (which all refer to things destined to perish with use) – **in accordance with the commandments and teaching of men?** These are matters which have, to be sure, the appearance of wisdom in **self-made religion** and self-abasement and severe treatment of the body, but are of no value against fleshly indulgence.*

Regarding the Old Testament law, Colossians 2:16-17 tells us that those things are only shadows, (think images), but the reality of all those things is Christ. Rather than pay attention to those shadows, Paul in verse 2:19 reminds us to hold fast to the Head! Regarding our own laws, verses 20-21 of Colossians 2 list things that give an appearance of religion, but they are nothing more than ideas that have their source in the tree of knowledge of good and evil. How awful it is that these kinds of things have caused confusion and division in the Lord's body over the years and centuries. On a personal level these kinds of things cause us to take our eyes off of Christ, Who wants to be our **life.** He did not die on the cross so that there would be a new kind of religious people on the earth; He had that in Judaism! He rose from the dead and came to us as the Holy Spirit (John 14 and John 20) so that he could live in us. It is up to us to live in the Spirit and pay attention to His leading. This is where "what would Jesus do?" falls short. That thinking causes us to create an instant law for us to follow, rather than take our leading from the Spirit.

Let's come back to Philippians. I stepped you backwards from verse 3:11 to verse 9. Now let us read it forward, beginning at verse 7. I will highlight the connecting words that I pointed out earlier plus others, to help bring out the progression of Paul's experience.

But whatever things were gain to me, those things I have counted as loss for the sake of Christ. **More than that,** *I count all things to be loss in view of the surpassing value of knowing Christ Jesus my Lord,* **for whom** *I have suffered the loss of all things, and count them but rubbish so that I may gain Christ,* **and** *may be found in Him, not having a righteousness of my own derived from the Law, but that which is through faith in Christ, the righteousness which comes from God on the basis of faith,* **that** *I may know Him* **and** *the power of His resurrection* **and** *the fellowship of His sufferings,* **being conformed** *to His death;* **in order that** *I may attain to the [better] resurrection from the dead.*

Do you see any religion in these verses? Definitely not, in my estimation; rather I hope you can see something of the "much more" in Paul's life, being saved in His life.

Enemies of the Cross

Philippians 3:18-19 talk about enemies of the cross of Christ. *For many walk, of whom I often told you, and now tell you even weeping, that they are the enemies of the cross of Christ, whose end is destruction, whose god is their appetite, and whose glory is in their shame, who set their minds on earthly things.* An enemy of the cross in this context is not one who is against the preaching of the gospel to sinners. No, the enemies here do not care for the operation of the cross in their own lives. Paul had just laid out in verses 7 through 10 what it means to him to live a life of the cross. Contrary to his example, these have *their minds on earthly things.*

In the Romans chapter I wrote about losing our soul life to gain the *zoe* life. That is exactly what Paul was writing about here in Philippians. We like to look to the "Old Rugged Cross", but how about the cross that intends to cross out our soul life? This cross hurts a little bit. I am sure that you have felt this cross a least once in a while. Press on toward the goal. The Lord offers grace even while we suffer the loss of some, and maybe all, things.

Colossians

We will cover only one passage in Colossians, but how significant it is!

The Hope of the Gospel

In the earlier chapter on Romans I covered Colossians 1:22-23a in the section titled "If...Then". I ended that section with an unanswered question.

Here are those verses again: *Yet He now has reconciled you in His fleshly body through death, to order to present you before Him holy and blameless and beyond reproach - if indeed you continue in the faith firmly established and steadfast, and not moved away from the hope of the gospel that you have heard.*

I already pointed you to the big "if". I hope you can appreciate it more after having read this far. In that section I asked, "What is the real hope of the gospel?" Let us look into that now.

We can start with the verses just quoted. These verses do not mention one word about going anywhere, but they speak of a complete change of character, inside and out. Holy, because our nature has been transformed; blameless, because our outward expression and actions exhibit nothing of the self; beyond reproach, because our adversary will have nothing to say against us.

And, just as has been discussed previously, these verses show us the starting line, reconciliation. We have been reconciled "in order to". Here again we can see the race: we line up at reconciliation, and then we run until we cross "holy, blameless and beyond reproach". What a finish!

I hope you are starting to question, at least a little bit, the idea that we die and go to heaven just because thirty years ago we got saved. It is true that the book of Revelation has three scenes that show saved ones before the throne in heaven, but their qualifications for being there are clearly stated. Eventually the final three and a half chapters of Revelation show the grand conclusion to be on earth! The Lord descends with His army for the final defeat of Satan and all of those who allied themselves with him (starting at chapter 19, verse 11). In chapter 20 thrones are established (on earth), and Satan leads the last rebellion after a thousand years. The last two chapters are all about the wonderful, beautiful bride, who comes down out of heaven to be with her Husband, who happens to still be on earth! If you remain in heaven, you will miss all of this!

Please see that the hope of the gospel is absolutely NOT about going to another place, it is all about us **becoming** a corporate body that matches our King and Husband in every way! We will be holy, because our Father is holy. The bride, presented as the holy city new Jerusalem, will be holy. Anything that remains unholy will be outside (Revelation 21:27 and 22:11,15).

What are you hoping for now? Has your thinking been changed? I hope so, but if not, maybe something is starting to shake the traditional teaching.

1 Thessalonians

In his first letter to Thessalonica Paul had a little bit to say about our Lord's return. It should be no surprise that I found a couple of other passages related to that.

Establish Your Hearts

Verse 3:13 of First Thessalonians says, *so that He may establish your hearts without blame in holiness before our God and Father at the coming of our Lord Jesus with all His saints.* Again, we can see a process in the preparation of our hearts. Other expressions that can be used for "establish" are "make stable," "make firm," and "set fast." Like we saw in the previous chapter, we must allow the Spirit to do His work in us over a period of time.

What is interesting in this section of scripture is that in verse 12 the foundation of this process is shown: *And may the Lord cause you to increase and abound in love for one another, and for all people, just as we also do for you.* In spite of all the "ways" of arriving at the end, Paul here points to our love toward each other and to all. I find this refreshing! First Corinthians 13 is known as the love chapter, but you can add this as an appendix. Paul said in 1 Corinthians that without love all of our talking is nothing more than a clanging symbol, doing nothing to build up the body of Christ. Now here, Paul echoes the same thought. Do you want to be found blameless before your Lord? Take your eyes off yourself so that you can love others!

Here are verses 12 and 13 together, with added bolding. *And may the Lord cause you to increase and abound in love for one another, and for all people, just as we also do for you,* **so that** He *may establish your hearts without blame in holiness before our God and Father at the coming of our Lord Jesus with all His saints.*

Peter realized this. In his first letter, chapter 4, he says, *Above all, keep fervent in your love for one another, because love covers a multitude of sins. Be hospitable to one another without complaint.*

*As each one has received a special gift, **employ it in serving one another**....* (v 8-10a). Love and service can only be directed toward others. Maybe I am beginning to realize this as well.

But coming back to the point of this section, please note that Christ is not coming back to whisk us away regardless of our condition. We need purified hearts that are ready to receive Him, ready to see Him, at His coming. This word for "coming" is *parousia*, which means not only coming, but also having a presence. This point will be reinforced when we get to John's epistles.

Be Preserved Complete

Here is another verse about our condition at our Lord's return (5:23-24): *Now may the God of peace Himself sanctify you entirely; and may your spirit and soul and body be preserved complete, without blame, at the coming of our Lord Jesus Christ. Faithful is He who calls you, and He also will bring it to pass.*

Once again we can see the process of becoming sanctified. In addition, Paul adds the hope that our tri-part being will be preserved. In case you were not absolutely sure, this is a clear indication that we have a body, a soul, and a spirit, each distinct in function. This is part of what it means to have been created in God's image. Some might think that our soul and our spirit are really the same, but they are not. Remember that Hebrews 4:12 says, *For the word of God is living and active and sharper than any two-edged sword, and piercing as far as the division of soul and spirit,....* We will cover what this means later, but for now, please understand that the Holy Spirit is very desirous of sanctifying us and preserving us, right up to the last moment of our lives or until the end of this age.

We ought to be encouraged by these verses because it is God Himself who will bring this to pass. We cannot sanctify ourselves. We cannot bring light to our darkened hearts. We cannot fix ourselves. But we should be thankful, very thankful, that the One who calls us is the very same who will accomplish everything! As the verse in Hebrews says, the *Logos* is active in our hearts to accomplish our Father's will.

But do not think that we are off the hook, thinking that it is all on God to transform us. Read verses 8 through 22 of this fifth chapter. In these verses can be seen the basis, or foundation, of God's sanctifying and preserving work. The Spirit wants to sanctify us, but we have to allow Him, even cooperate with Him. He wants to move into every corner of our heart, but we must step out of the way. These verses remind us to encourage and build up one another; they tell us how to appreciate those who labor for us; they tell us how to care for each other. In verses 16 to 22 there are encouragements on the personal level, starting with always rejoicing.

After all of these instructions and encouragements, Paul prays that God would sanctify us and preserve us. I think it is very significant that this prayer for sanctification follows those instructions in living before the Lord and in His body.

Paul closes this letter in the same way that John ends Revelation. *The grace of our Lord Jesus Christ be with you.* How precious this is! I have inserted a short chapter on grace before the Gospel chapters. After reading that chapter you might have a deeper appreciation of this last verse.

2 Thessalonians

In one of Paul's shorter letters he again couches a lot of his encouragement in the expected return of our Lord.

Worthy of the Kingdom

In his second letter to Thessalonica, chapter 1, Paul praises the saints for their growing love and for their perseverance and faith in the face of persecutions. In verse 5 he states, *This is a plain indication of God's righteous judgment so that you will be considered worthy of the kingdom of God, for which indeed you are suffering.* The only thought that I wish to convey here is that if some Christians are considered worthy, then others must be considered unworthy. You might think that I am going beyond what the Word says by drawing such a conclusion, but there are a few implications like this, especially in Revelation.

For This He Called You

If you have received the Lord's salvation through His precious blood, for what have you been called? Is it to go to heaven? Paul says in verse 14 of chapter 2, *It was for this He called you through our gospel...* What is "this"? We can see "this" in the second part of verse 14. *It was for this He called you through our gospel, that you may **gain the glory** of our Lord Jesus Christ.* Is glory some **place** where we hope to spend eternity? No! Glory is the expression of God that is gained through a process, and the process is seen in verse 13: *...because God has chosen you from the beginning for salvation **through sanctification** by the Spirit and faith in the truth.*

As this book has been telling you, and as verse 13 again points out, the Christian life is a process, a race that has a goal. The triune God wants to make His home in our hearts. This is not an instantaneous event, proven not only by the Word but by your own experience. We are all in various stages of this transforming process.

Do you want to "go to glory", or do you want to **gain** glory? No doubt some might want to hang on to going someplace, but these verses highlight what is the true message of the good news, that is the true salvation. True salvation is gaining the glory of our Lord....during **this** lifetime.

This is what I hope you will see. This is my challenge. Even though most of what is presented in these pages is the warnings, the result should be that we take the warnings to heart and gain the glory! Be saved! Be saved from the darkness that dwells in your heart. Be saved from the flesh that strives against the Spirit. Be saved in every way, allowing the Lord, the Spirit, Who is the Word, to make home in your heart.

1 & 2 Timothy

I have selected only a pair of verses from 1 Timothy, and these are less of a warning and more of an encouragement.

Store Up to Take Hold

Addressing those saints who do not lack material goods and money, Paul gave this advice. *Instruct them to do good, to be rich in good works, to be generous and ready to share; storing up for themselves the treasure of a good foundation for the future, so that they may take hold of that which is life indeed* (1 Timothy 6:18-19). This is something else that runs through the New Testament, the whole Bible, actually. By helping the poor we store up treasure for ourselves in heaven. That is not hard to understand, but Paul added this curious clause to his statement: *so that they may take hold of that which is life indeed.* "Life" here is that *zoe* word, and some translations do say "eternal life".

What is Paul saying? Can one buy eternal life? I think it is helpful to compare these verses to the account of the young rich ruler who came to the Lord, asking how to inherit eternal life (Mark 10 and Luke 18). Jesus also spoke about treasure. So here and in the two gospels treasure on earth is contrasted with treasure that is stored in heaven.

Again, that should be plain enough, but Paul expands the idea and adds a reason for storing treasure in heaven. First, Paul wrote that this treasure is *a good foundation for the future.* I don't know about you, but I had never considered good works to be a foundation of any kind, but that is what is written. This foundation in turn becomes the basis of experiencing *that which is life indeed.* How does that work? What is this treasure?

In the natural realm we tend to think in terms of things and stuff, but the spiritual realm is about God and things of the Spirit. We think of mansions, but God's Word talks about a spiritual habitation. The use of the word *zoe* is evidence that Paul wrote about something that is a bit beyond our comprehension and knowing. What we can do now is store up treasure by any means. We do not have to be rich in material things to do this, but the Lord and Paul were showing a person with resources one way to store up the true treasure, not trusting in what he has now.

This is also like losing our soul-life now in order to gain it later. There are a few ways to say this same thing. Try to see beyond the natural concepts and understanding. God is awesome and mysterious; the spiritual realm is also, so we are given various illustrations and examples to help our understanding. We do the same when explaining things to children. I do not want to offend you, but that is what we are. The spiritual realm is beyond us, so God gives us word pictures to help our understanding. But, like children, we like the pictures, and the pictures have become part of our belief system. That is exactly why we sing about mansions and pearly gates and a land beyond the sea. Am I too much? Is Jesus really building mansions for us? Read "About Those Mansions" in the Appendix, and see if you can be dissuaded of that notion.

God is the *zoe* life. God in Christ makes the *zoe* life available to us. We receive it instantly as a seed when our human spirit is regenerated by the Holy Spirit, but this life wants to grow in us. It becomes in us a river of water of life in order to flow out to others and also to transform our soul. The *zoe* life is our eternal life now **and** later. It, not some idea of heavenly goods, is the basis of our treasure.

Dear brother, dear sister, you might have heard and learned to desire the Lord rather than what the Lord can give you. That is a good lesson for this life, but it applies also to our eternal future. Do you think a mansion is in your future? Our future **is** Christ!

Chosen to Obtain

What a blessing it is to be called "chosen"! 1 Peter 1:1-2 says that we are chosen according to the foreknowledge of God. What have we been chosen for? The answer might surprise you. Before you read on, consider for a moment what is the reason for God choosing you. For what purpose? To what end? What do you think? Be honest!

Now let's see what the Bible has to say. 2 Timothy 2:10 says this, *For this reason I endure all things for the sake of those who are* **chosen, so that** *they also may obtain the salvation which is in Christ Jesus and with it eternal glory.*

According to these verses we have been chosen for salvation! What lofty purpose did you have in mind? But, how simple! How humble! How wonderful! Salvation! I had to chuckle at myself when I realized this. We do not have to aspire for anything lofty, deep, and profound. But on the other hand, if we have a full understanding of salvation and the full extent of our sinfulness and fallen nature, we would realize how lofty and deep and profound this truly is.

It requires a lot to bring us to salvation. Look at what Paul wrote in 2 Thessalonians (2:13-14). *But we should always give thanks to God for you, brethren beloved by the Lord, because God has chosen you from the beginning for salvation through sanctification by the Spirit and faith in the truth. It was for this He called you through our gospel, that you may gain the glory.* It was for this: Salvation! But salvation comes through sanctification. I cannot say it enough...salvation is not a one step event that was accomplished by once opening your heart to receive Christ. It has to be "obtained".

Salvation is arrived at by sanctification, which is a spiritually metabolic change in one's nature. If Christ is in you, then hopefully you are farther down the path of sanctification than a year ago. But in realizing that you are, it should be glaringly obvious that we need all the time that God grants us on this earth in order to obtain this salvation. Yet it cannot be our accomplishment, can it? There is absolutely no glory in anything that we might do. We have to drop our resistance to the Spirit's work in us, and His work results in true glory.

Did you notice that both of these portions of scripture connect glory with salvation? Look again. 2 Timothy 2:10, ... *so that they also may obtain the salvation which is in Christ Jesus and with it eternal glory.* And 2 Thessalonians 2:13 and 14, *for salvation through sanctification by the Spirit and faith in the truth. It was for this He called you through our gospel, that you may gain the glory.* Once more, glory is not a destination; it is a divine attribute to be gained.

Peter wrote in the same way. In his first letter, verse 1:7, he wrote that *the proof of your faith....may be found to result in praise and glory and honor.* He followed that with verse 9: *obtaining as the outcome of your faith the salvation of your souls.* Glory and Salvation! These are an end result of faith. But the faith that Peter describes is not a passive faith of mere acceptance; rather it is an active faith that is tested and proven. Faith has a purpose, salvation, and salvation has an outcome, glory!

If Then, Again...According to the Rules

I already covered 2 Timothy 2:11-14 in the chapter on Romans, but I will touch on it again in order to make a larger point. *It is a trustworthy statement: For if we died with Him, we will also live with Him; if we endure, we will also reign with Him; if we deny Him, He also will deny us; if we are faithless, He remains faithful, for He cannot deny Himself. Remind them of these things, and solemnly charge them in the presence of God not to wrangle about words, which is useless and leads to the ruin of the hearers.*

I want to point out two verbs that Paul presents in two conditional statements: "died" and "endure". "If we died with Him" and "if we endure" are the conditions. A conditional statement implies a result. In these two cases what results should we see? It is clearly stated that dying with Christ results in living with Him, and enduring will result in reigning with Him.

Those statements are apparent, but I want to take your attention to verses four and five: *No soldier in active service entangles himself in the affairs of everyday life, so that he may please the one who enlisted him as a soldier. Also if anyone competes as an athlete, he does not win the prize unless he competes according to the rules.* It is likely that you have heard messages related to verse four, the soldier, but how about the athlete? What does it mean to "compete according to the rules"? I believe that the rules are laid out in verses 11-13...dying and enduring.

There are many rules in the Bible, as we all know. The first rule (and the first warning) was given to Adam. You could say that Noah was given a certain set of rules that described how to build the ark. After that we do not see any specific rules until God called Abram (but minimal) and until the Exodus, when God first instructed Moses how the nation should conduct the Passover. Later in the wilderness He handed down His ten commandments and the rest of the Levitical law.

When Jesus had His ministry He tightened down the rules, as seen in chapters five, six, and seven of Matthew's gospel and chapter six of Luke's. More than that, He closed all the loopholes, by exposing our thoughts and the intentions behind our actions. He also gave us the golden rule (Matthew 7:12 and Luke 6:31).

So many rules! What should we do? There is an argument in religious circles regarding whether Christians are obligated to keep the Ten Commandments, or whether we are freed from them. I think both arguments miss the main point, and that is that Christ both: 1) made the requirements more strict, as I wrote above; and 2) He invited us (Matthew 11:29-30) to learn from Him and find rest for our souls, because His yoke is easy and His burden is light. This seems to be quite the contradiction. Even though the higher standard leaves the Ten Commandments far in the background, and even though there is a yoke, He makes it bearable. There are burdens, but His are not heavy. How can this contradiction exist?

First, you should understand that Jesus came to unload the burden of outward regulations. In nature there are rules everywhere, but maybe we do not think of them as rules. According to the rules, a tomato plant will always produce tomatoes. A green bean bush will always produce green beans. Even if you plant some tomato seeds in a field of green beans, that plant will produce only tomatoes. You cannot force a tomato plant to grow beans; it's against the rules! Or better said, it is against the law of life of the tomato plant to produce beans.

At the risk of running too far on a tangent, let's look at Romans 8. Paul spent chapters 6 and 7 bemoaning how the law causes us to know sin and our futility in trying to keep the law. He concludes these chapters and transitions to the answer with these four verses in Romans 7:24-25 and 8:1-2: *Wretched man that I am! Who will set me free from the body of this death? Thanks be to God through Jesus Christ our Lord! So then, on the one hand I myself with my mind am serving the **law** of God, but on the other, with my flesh the **law** of sin...... Therefore there is now no condemnation for those who are in Christ Jesus. For the **law** of the Spirit of life in Christ Jesus has set you free from the **law** of sin and of death.*

There is a law at work here, actually two laws, the old law and the new law of life. If you belong to Christ, you have that new law (or set of rules) at work within you. The prior law could only condemn us, but this new law, the law of the Spirit of **life**, is our salvation! The law of the Spirit of **life**, has its own set of rules that cannot be overridden. Just like the tomato plant has a life, with its rules for that life, the Spirit is eternal life, and this eternal, *zoe*, life has a law which governs that life, *...so that the requirement of the Law might be fulfilled in us, who do not walk according to the flesh but according to the Spirit* (Romans 8:4).

But even as the tomato plant will always produce tomatoes, it also needs an environment in which to grow. A dry environment will result in no fruit. The requirement for producing good fruit is a good environment, suitable to the tomato plant.

The Gospels and the epistles, especially Paul's, point out over and over that the divine life that has been deposited within us also needs a good environment. This includes a walk with the Lord, prayer, reading our Bible, fellowship, and more. In this portion of 2 Timothy Paul adds that if we want to "live with Him", we have to die, and if we want to "reign with Him", we must endure.

Our dying and our enduring help to create the environment in our soul for the eternal life to grow. It is **into** our soul, and **in** our soul, that the spiritual growth takes place. Please do not assume that you will reign as a king in the next age (verse 2:12), if you did not provide a good environment in this age for the spiritual seed to grow and mature. What else qualifies you to reign? The shed blood of God's Lamb? Your belief and your baptism? For certain our Lord's stripes and His crucifixion wiped clean our filthy slates (and we are thankful!), but to reign with Christ is a reward and a privilege that comes at a cost.

How about "merely" living with Him (verse 2:11)? Paul points out that this too comes at a cost. You do not have my words in this matter; pay attention to the gospel, as presented by Jesus, and then Paul and others. Please recall the "If...Then" section in the chapter on Romans.

Paul is very serious in this chapter. Do you pick up on that? In 2:14 he says, *Remind them of these things, and solemnly charge them in the presence of God...* Therefore, please do not buy into the idea that our Lord will pat us on the head and say "all is well" even though we might have been unfaithful. If we deny Him, He will deny us (verse 12); if we are unfaithful to Him, do not expect Him to be "faithful" to you (verse 13).

Love His Appearing

Here is a verse that we hear quoted often, at least in part. 2 Timothy 4:7-8: *I have fought the good fight, I have finished the course, I have kept the faith; in the future there is laid up for me the crown of righteousness, which the Lord, the righteous Judge, will award to me on that day; and not only to me, but also to all who have loved His appearing.*

At the end of our days we all would like to say that we have fought the good fight, finished our course, and kept the faith. But do we really know what this means? What if I do not finish my course? Surely I have kept the faith...haven't I? Do I still get a crown?

How could Paul be so confident? Look at what he did. Most of the New Testament was written by him. Compared to him, how can we have any confidence? Are you confident? If you are, where is that confidence placed? If you are not confident, why not? Do you have reason to be a little more confident? What difference does it make, anyway? As long as I get that crown!

Are you confident? Paul was not always so. To the Corinthians he wrote, *but I discipline my body and make it my slave, so that, after I have preached to others, I myself will not be disqualified* (1 Corinthians 9:27). And to the church in Philippi, *Not that I have already obtained it or have already become perfect, but I press on so that I may lay hold...* (3:12).

Now it seems if you are not confident, you have an excuse! If we look at ourselves, we do appear to be helpless (because we are!), but fortunately we have Hebrews 12:1-2! *...and let us run with endurance the race that is set before us, fixing our eyes on Jesus, the author and perfecter of faith...*

Our Jesus is the author of faith, and He will take us to the finish line, but we have to let Him, by setting our eyes on Him, and that means not on ourselves. If you look at yourself, you are automatically in the realm of law. What do you see? You see someone who does not measure up, and cannot measure up. But when you set your eyes on Jesus, you are automatically in the realm of faith. Now, for our confidence we can look at Hebrews 11:1-2! *Now faith is the assurance of things hoped for, the conviction of things not seen. For by it the men of old gained approval.* This is much better! In Jesus we have rest and peace, knowing that He is God, and He can do all things, even perfect **us**!

Now, about that crown. You can hear many songs about getting a crown or crowns, but based on what qualifications? Well, if I am going to rule the nations, surely I must have a crown! You might have some ideas about crowns, but what does the Word say?

As it relates to us, I find six verses that describe various kinds of crowns. Here they are in the order that they appear in the New Testament. See if you can pick out what kinds there are.

Philippians 4:1 – *Therefore, my beloved brethren whom I long to see, my joy and crown, in this way stand firm in the Lord, my beloved.*

1 Thessalonians 2:19-20 – *For who is our hope or joy or crown of exultation? Is it not even you, in the presence of our Lord Jesus at His coming? For you are our glory and joy.*

2 Timothy 4:8 – *in the future there is laid up for me the crown of righteousness, which the Lord, the righteous Judge, will award to me on that day; and not only to me, but also to all who have loved His appearing.*

James 1:12 – *Blessed is a man who perseveres under trial; for once he has been approved, he will receive the crown of life which the Lord has promised to those who love him.*

1 Peter 5:4 – *And when the Chief Shepherd appears, you will receive the unfading crown of glory.*

Revelation 2:10 – *Be faithful until death, and I will give you the crown of life.*

Philippians and 1 Thessalonians point out that the saints over whom Paul labored are his crown. Peter in the same way exhorts the shepherds of the flock of God to take care of those whom God has put under their care. These also, like Paul, might receive a crown of glory.

James says that the Lord has promised a crown of life for those who love Him. Notice that this love is proved, tested, so that the Christian might be approved. In Revelation 2:10 this testing is to the point of death. I think this shows us that all of our situations are different, and one person's testing is not the same as another's. We should be careful, therefore, in making comparisons and judgments regarding what the Lord is doing in the lives of His saints.

Finally, 2 Timothy tells us that the righteous Judge has a crown of righteousness for *all who have loved His appearing.* The question for you, for us, is have we loved His appearing? You might say that you cannot wait for Jesus to return, and you look forward to that day, but in the context of these verses in 2 Timothy 4 can you say that you have loved His appearing by fighting the good fight, by running your course, by keeping the faith?

The New Testament tells us that there will be some (and I mean to say Christians) who will be ashamed at His coming. Did that ever occur to you? If you have been engaged in worldly pursuits, chasing the affairs of this life, do you think you might be ashamed on that day? I will cover more about this later when we get to John's letters.

The point I want to make about these crowns is that they are not headgear. They are not "merit badges" for good works. These crowns are something that will have become an intrinsic part of us. If you receive a crown of life because your love has been tested and found faithful, that is part of what you are. You have laid hold of the life that is really life and did not let go! If you have loved the Lord's appearing in your daily life, then surely you have received His righteousness as your own. Again, this becomes a part of what you are. Finally, if you have ever had the opportunity to develop a youngster in some skill, and he or she performs it well, is that not your glory? How about a grandparent enjoying grandchildren, and maybe even great grandchildren. Is that not a glory? I think Paul means something like that.

Love the Lord's appearing. Paul said the crown of righteousness is for those who have **loved** His appearing. It is an ongoing anticipation, with visible evidence. There will be much more about this when we cover the Gospels.

Titus

In the letter to Titus we will look at the role that grace plays. Since we cannot live the divine life by our own devices and by our own strength, we need something that enables us and empowers us. That something is grace.

We Look...He Purifies

Titus 2:11-14 - *For the grace of God has appeared, bringing salvation to all men, instructing us to deny ungodliness and worldly desires and to live sensibly, righteously and godly in the present age, looking for the blessed hope and the appearing of the glory of our great God and Savior, Christ Jesus, Who gave Himself for us to redeem us from every lawless deed, and to purify for Himself a people for His own possession, zealous for good deeds.*

Grace is a wonderful thing. No matter how many years are behind us, we have not scratched its surface. It is so much more than "unmerited favor". Do not limit yourself or God by that definition. Look at verses 11 and 12 again: *For the grace of God has appeared, bringing salvation to all men, instructing us to deny ungodliness and worldly desires and to live sensibly, righteously and godly in the present age.*

Grace came to us, it has appeared, and in its appearing grace brings salvation. But grace also instructs us to deny the sinful things, and it instructs us how to live before God and man.

Surely grace is unmerited, but it is also indispensable for the race we run. Did God mean to tell Paul that "My unmerited favor is sufficient for you" in 2 Corinthians 12:9? *And He has said to me, "My grace is sufficient for you, for power is perfected in weakness."* God did not say, "Paul, you have my unmerited favor." God said, in effect, "Paul, you have a weakness, and you need something for that weakness. You need power, but I do not give you power; I give you grace."

67

What do you need? Grace comes to you. Do you need to forgive someone? Do you need to ask for forgiveness? Do you have a problem with a particular sin? You do not like the way the other driver ... you fill in the blank! This has equivalence to what I wrote regarding what "things" God has prepared for those who love Him (1 Corinthians 2:9). We think that we need some*thing*, but God gives us grace. We think we need more patience, but what we really need is grace. With grace comes patience.

If you focus on having patience, you never find it, or on being meek, you feel insincere. It becomes a law, and you will be defeated over and over. Or, as I pointed out before, if you happen to succeed, then your flesh has conquered your flesh. You think that you have attained something, but it was your own strength, not the Spirit's operating in you. You have somehow obeyed the law in your own strength, but denied grace in the process.

I invite you to consider Galatians 5:4, *You have been severed from Christ, you who are seeking to be justified by law; you have fallen from grace.* "Fallen from grace" is a well known phrase, and the common understanding of it probably means going to hell, but Paul did not intend that, and the context does not support that. Please read chapters 4 and 5 of Galatians with this perspective of grace.

So Paul wrote to Titus that grace has appeared. This race is not finished by our will power, but by grace. We do not have to try harder. Do you still find that hard to accept? Are you "better" than Paul? Here is just a little of what he said about grace. *But by the **grace** of God I am what I am, and His **grace** toward me did not prove vain; but I labored even more than all of them, yet **not I**, but the **grace** of God with me* (1 Corinthians 15:10). And, *Who has saved us and called us with a holy calling, not according to our works, but according to His own purpose and **grace** which was granted us in Christ Jesus from all eternity* (2 Timothy 1:9).

Grace instructs us, and it does not allow us to be lawless. Being free from law does not equate to lawlessness, as Paul writes in several places. Grace empowers us to overcome, to live rightly before God and men, and to live with an attitude of waiting for our Lord.

I want to make one more point from this portion of Titus 2:14: *Christ Jesus, Who gave Himself for us to redeem us from every lawless deed, and to purify for Himself a people.* We are waiting for the One who gave Himself for us, Christ Jesus. Two reasons are put forth by Paul for what our Lord did: To redeem us **and** to purify us. That little word "and" can be so important. The full gospel is much more than redemption, but it starts there. We are sinners and we do sinful things. Redemption takes care of that, but if we stop there, we miss out on the "much more" from Romans 5:10. (See the chapter on Romans.) Here in verse 14 Paul phrases the "much more…saved by His life" in terms of being purified. Redemption is only the beginning of salvation; purification is our continuing salvation. If we do not follow the Spirit's leading and if we do not cooperate with Him in His purifying work in us, then we neglect (I use this word on purpose) our salvation.

If you have not seen this truth before, I hope it is working its way into you. That is the reason for this book and its title.

Hebrews

In one of the New Testament's longer letters many examples and illustrations are drawn from the Old Testament. We see this quite a few times in letters to the churches, and Jesus, after His resurrection, talked with two disciples who were returning to their homes in Emmaus. Jesus came to them, *then beginning with Moses and with all the prophets, He explained to them the things concerning Himself in all the Scriptures* (Luke 24:27). What a privilege that was!

As we will see, Moses and the prophets also spoke of us, and Hebrews brings this out clearly. The warnings in this letter are therefore for us.

Pay (Much Closer) Attention

The letter to the Hebrews opens with grand declarations and evidences from Old Testament scripture that Jesus is the Son of God, our Creator, and the One who has the right to sit on God's throne.

At the end of the first chapter, the writer shows how far above is this glorious One over the angels, and their purpose is to minister to us who are to inherit salvation (Hebrews 1:14). It is to this point of inheriting salvation that it then says, *For this reason...* (Hebrews 2:1). Here are verses 1:14 and 2:1. *Are they not all ministering spirits, sent out to render service for the sake of those who will inherit salvation? For this reason* (inheriting salvation) *we must pay much closer attention to what we have heard, so that we do not drift away from it.* The writer continues (verses 2:2-3a), *For if the word spoken through angels proved unalterable, and every transgression and disobedience received a just penalty,* **how will we escape** *if we neglect so great a salvation?*

The Hebrew believers are exhorted to not return to the law. There is a danger of drifting back to the law. You might recall that to the Galatians Paul called it falling from grace. There must be a good reason for the advice to *pay much closer attention.* As you continue through this book, I hope that you are beginning to understand the warning.

I repeat what I wrote above, that the warnings are for us who are believers. The writer is not talking to unbelievers about neglecting salvation, but to us, who have come to the Lord but might be neglecting the salvation that we have received!

Now we will skip to chapter 3 and look at some things that we should be paying attention to.

But Christ was faithful as a Son over His house – whose house **we are, if we hold fast** *our confidence and the boast of our hope firm to the end* (Hebrews 3:6). The context of this verse is a comparison between Moses, who was faithful as a servant in his house, and Christ. But in mentioning Christ's house, the writer "throws in" that **we** are the house! But yet, he qualifies that fact with *if we hold fast....* We are Christ's house *if we hold fast our confidence and the boast of our hope.*

Well, that does not seem so hard, does it? I can boast in the Lord that, "I'm washed in the Lamb's blood, and my sins, that once were scarlet, are now white as snow." Why, then, does the writer of Hebrews spend the next 19 verses and more (3:7 through 4:6 at the least) exhorting the saints not to fall short of entering into the Lord's rest, with comparisons to the Israelites' falling short in the wilderness after leaving Egypt?

Hebrews 3:7-11 says, *Therefore, just as the Holy Spirit says, "Today if you hear His voice, do not harden your hearts as when they provoked Me, as in the day of trial in the wilderness, where your fathers tried Me by testing Me, and saw My works for forty years. Therefore I was angry with this generation, and said, 'They always go astray in their heart, and they did not know My ways'; as I swore in My wrath, 'They shall not enter My rest.'"*

After presenting the historical case, Hebrews then gives the present day warning (verses 12-13), *Take care, brethren, that there not be in any one of you an evil, unbelieving heart that falls away from the living God. But encourage one another day after day, as long as it is still called "Today," so that none of you will be hardened by the deceitfulness of sin.*

Then verse 14 repeats the cautionary condition found in verse 6: Recall the section "If...Then" in the chapter on Romans. Hebrews 3:14 is included in that chapter: *For we have become partakers of Christ, if we hold fast the beginning of our assurance firm until the end.* Do you want to partake of Christ in the next age? Hold fast until the end! Again the writer draws on the same Old Testament warning (verses 7-8) in verse 15. *While it is said, "Today if you hear His voice, do not harden your hearts, as when they provoked Me."*

Why has the church not rightly considered these clear warnings? Why has the "be saved and go to heaven" gospel clouded our understanding? Can the warnings be more clear?

But there is more. The author of Hebrews was not done. Verses 3:19 and 4:1 say, *So we see that they were not able to enter because of unbelief.* ***Therefore,*** *let us fear if, while a promise remains of entering His rest, any one of you may seem to have come short of it.*

There was a rest that was waiting for Israel. It was in the land that God had promised to their forefathers (Deuteronomy 12:9-10). There was no rest in Egypt, and there was no rest in the wilderness. But fear and unbelief prevented them from entering into the object of their journey. How does that apply to us? What is this letter talking about? Why use so many sentences to drive home the point? Why do we have all of those other warnings that we have so far covered from Romans through Titus?

In one sentence (and I cannot say this any better than what I heard from another brother and friend) the gospel is about what we are **becoming**, not where we are going. (Thank you, brother Paul S.) If getting to heaven is the goal, wherein we will live in a fine dwelling that Jesus has been preparing for us, then why waste so much parchment on warnings that would seem to not apply to us? But maybe it would be an entirely different story if God's expectation is that we actually **become** the new creation that we think we are, according to 2 Corinthians 5:17 and Galatians 6:15.

We still have not exhausted the exhortations on this matter. Verse 4:2 begins, *For indeed we have had good news preached to us, just as they also....* Have you heard the Good News? Did you hear that you are going to heaven, or did you hear that we are being transformed into the same image as the Lord Himself (2 Corinthians 3:18)? Verse 4:3 supports the latter. It begins, *For we who have believed enter that rest.* Notice that "enter that rest" is in the present tense and that should be a strong indication that it does not mean going to heaven. If we can enter into God's rest **now**, then surely the Good News has to do with what is going on in **this** life, as well as the next!

Since entering into God's rest is for us now, it is absolutely correct to admonish us believers in verse 4:7, *just as has been said before, "Today if you hear His voice, do not harden your hearts."* And again, in verse 4:11 we see, *Therefore let us be diligent to enter that rest, so that no one will fall, through following the same example of disobedience.*

So you see, this rest is available to us today, and we are exhorted to be **diligent** to enter into it, because the danger is in falling away, and in falling, the result will be the unpleasant cutting by God's word in judging those who are His. I just quoted to you verse 4:11; verse 12 continues, *For the word of God is living and active and sharper than any two-edged sword, and piercing as far as the division of soul and spirit, of both joints and marrow, and able to judge the thoughts and intentions of the heart.* We do not want to fall (verse 11), **for** the result will be very unpleasant (verse 12).

But we must endure the unpleasantness, either now, in this life, or later. But if we endure the cutting, dividing, of our soul from our spirit now, the **pleasant result** is rest......**now!** This is the conclusion of the matter that we see in verse 4:16. *Therefore let us draw near with confidence to the throne of grace, so that we may receive mercy and find grace to help in time of need.* This grace (recall the earlier discussions about grace) will result in our rest both now and later.

Better Things for You

For ground that drinks the rain which often falls on it and brings forth vegetation useful to those for whose sake it is also tilled, receives a blessing from God; but if it (the ground) *yields thorns and thistles, it is worthless and close to being cursed, and it ends up being burned. But, beloved, we are convinced of better things concerning you, and things that accompany salvation, though we are speaking this way* (Hebrews 6:7-9).

We are the ground, and from us should come useful vegetation and not thorns. The vegetation is the fruit of the Spirit and also what we see in verse 10. *For God is not unjust so as to forget your work and the love which you have shown toward His name, in having ministered and in still ministering to the saints.* Do we not see in the Gospels that the law is fulfilled in loving God and man?

But we are also quite capable of producing thorns and thistles, and the writer of the letter warns that we can become worthless and close to being cursed, even in the end getting burned! Since this is a book about warnings, I have to point out the warning. "But I am a Christian; I've been saved! That cannot possibly apply to me." Who do you think this letter was written to? The letter is titled "Hebrews", but we know from the letter that these have believed in the Lord Jesus. I remind you also about the being "saved, yet as through fire" in 1 Corinthians 3. There is another, similar, warning written to one of the seven churches in Revelation. We will get to that later.

Now I would like to focus on verse 9, because it also demonstrates that the warning applies to us. *But, beloved, we are convinced of better things concerning **you**, and things that **accompany salvation**, though we are speaking this way.*

I will reverse the phrases in this verse: though we are speaking this way, we are convinced of better things concerning you. Speaking in what way? The speaking in verses 7 and 8. In spite of the warning in verse 8, it is the writer's hope and expectation that the saints would continue in the living way. The warning needs to be heeded, but we have verses 9 and 10! We can have the "better things" that accompany salvation. We can minister to the saints. We can be like verse 12: *So that you will not be sluggish, but imitators of those who through faith and patience inherit the promises.* Dear saints, do you see how many times and in how many ways God has told us that we are not to be passively waiting to go somewhere after we die? Inheriting the promises is not for the sluggish; it is not an assumed outcome. The contrast here between sluggishness and "faith and patience" seems very similar to the difference between Laodicea and Philadelphia in Revelation. Wait for that chapter!

Run with Endurance....Share His Holiness

Chapter ten of Hebrews addresses the urge of some believers to revert to the sacrifices of animals. While there are words and admonitions that can yet pertain to us, I want to bring you down to verses 35-39, which are a summary of the chapter.

Verses 35 and 36 show us the positive side of heeding the writer's encouragement. *Therefore, do not throw away your confidence, which has a great reward. For you have need of endurance, so that when you have done the will of God, you may receive what was promised.* There is a "great reward", but the condition that qualifies us to receive it is endurance. I have already given some attention to this word. It is used quite often in the New Testament, both in noun and verb form, sometimes translated as perseverance and patience. We will see this word many more times.

Verse 37 tells us when we can expect to receive this great reward. *For yet in a very little while, He who is coming will come, and will not delay.* It is then that we will face our Lord at His judgment seat (2 Corinthians 5:10). We want to hear Him say to us, "well done", but this is not guaranteed. Verse 38 continues, *But my righteous one shall live by faith; and if he shrinks back, My soul has no pleasure in him.* Do you have the idea that once "saved" your worries are over? Do you want to appear before the Lord and hear that He has no pleasure in you? Do you think that could not happen?

76

Notice all of the words in verse 39. *But we are not of those who shrink back to destruction, but of those who have faith to the preserving of the soul.* Here "destruction" stands in opposition to "preserving of the soul". Can destruction really be the destiny of one who has received the Lord as his Savior? Judging by the multitude of warnings (and we are not nearly done), the answer must be a definitive "YES!" These verses echo the Lord's own words, which appear in all four of the gospels. You know the words: *Whoever seeks to keep his life will lose it, and whoever loses his life will preserve it.* (Matthew 10:39, 16:25; Mark 8:35; Luke 9:24, 17:33; John 12:25)

Now you might be starting to wonder what "destruction" implies. Could those be correct who say you can lose your salvation? I say "no" to that question, but that is a quick answer to a question that is not that simple. Please, let us continue to look at everything, and then come back to it at the end of the book.

Accept Our Father's Discipline

In Hebrews 12:1, a verse probably familiar to you, the writer returns to the idea of a race, *Therefore, since we have so great a cloud of witnesses surrounding us, let us also lay aside every encumbrance and the sin which so easily entangles us, and let us run with endurance the race that is set before us.*

In the rest of chapter 12 it is explained what we can expect if we lack endurance or if we become entangled with cares of life or sin. But even if we do not become entangled and even if we do run the race, we can expect our Father's discipline. That is because He loves us as the sons we are. We ought not deceive ourselves, because no one has ever run a perfect race except Jesus. So we have discipline discussed from verse 5 through 11, and the key verse, I think, is verse 9, *Furthermore, we had earthly fathers to discipline us, and we respected them; shall we not much rather be subject to the Father of spirits, and live?* Verse 10b explains, ... *but He disciplines us for our good, so that we may share His holiness.*

Did you get saved so that you could go to heaven? How about the gospel that is actually presented in the New Testament, the gospel of being sons on the road to holiness? What is the best outcome that have you heard? Get a crown? Maybe get some reward for a vague reason that you cannot recall? This gospel in Hebrews (preached to believers, by the way) says that God wants to share His holiness with us! In order to do that, we cannot go through life and remain as we are.

Verse 11 has more to say. *... yet to those who have been trained by it, afterwards it yields the peaceful fruit of righteousness.* Again, we can see that real salvation is a process. Training does not happen overnight, and some of us require more time than others. This is a good reason to thank the Lord for another day above ground – we have another day in which our loving Father can train us up, if we submit to the training.

Now understand, maybe in a different light, verses 12 and 13. *Therefore strengthen the hands that are weak and the knees that are feeble, and make straight paths for your feet, so that the limb which is lame may not be put out of joint, but rather be healed.* A young child needs to grow in many aspects. As he or she grows, more can be learned and accomplished. But if you have a child that is weak and sickly, you will surely love him, but he might be limited in how much he can benefit from training. Maybe the parents of such a child might spoil him, being unwilling to discipline him properly. Therefore, in order to advance properly in life, there must be healing and strengthening. Maybe the weakness is not physical, but mental or emotional. I have more appreciation for those who care for the mental and emotional health of others than I used to have.

Even though there is no limit to God's love for us, there might be limitations on the race that we are able to run. Even so, there is no need to condemn others or yourself. Verse 14 of this chapter 12 says, *Pursue peace with all men, and the sanctification...* I think we all can do this, but only in the grace of the Lord, not by our own strength... and we need to. In accordance with the purpose of this book, it must be pointed out that the second part of verse 14 is, *and the sanctification without which no one will see the Lord.*

Here we go again. Why are the Hebrew Christians being warned that they will not see the Lord if they miss out on sanctification? Have you always thought that this passage concerns only unbelievers? I hope you can see that such a thought does not fit the context.

The book of Hebrews has some wonderful verses, but also a lot of warnings. When you next read this book, I encourage you to read it soberly. As verse 12:25 says, *See to it that you do not refuse Him who is speaking. For if those did not escape when they refused him who warned them on earth, much less will we escape who turn away from Him who warns from heaven.*

We need to heed the warning, but neither do we have to fear. The same letter also reminds us that we have a sympathetic high Priest (Hebrews 4:15), and we can come **with confidence** to the throne of grace. Here we find mercy and grace. Our Father's heart is saddened when we turn away, but He always draws us back to Himself. Receive His grace to run.

James

James wrote a very practical letter. He set his tires in the snow and showed us what the tracks look like. Some like to point out the differences between his letter and Paul's letters. I also used to do that, but eventually I realized that both were saying many of the same things, but from different angles. I have attached an article I wrote at the end of this book to explain what I mean. See "Faith and Righteousness ... Paul and James."

Be Perfect

Apparently James was not big on lengthy introductions (unlike Paul). In just one verse he identifies himself and his audience, and then he jumps in with both feet.

Right away he talks about trials and testing and what should be our reaction to them. He shows a progression (like Paul, but enough comparisons) in the desired effect upon our being. Be joyful (verse 1:2) because testing results in endurance (verse 3), and endurance, if we allow it, will have a "perfect result". That result (verse 4) is being made perfect and complete, lacking in nothing.

The word for "perfect" has the sense of the end result, being full grown and mature. And the word for "complete" implies being unblemished and faultless. It seems that the meanings are assigned to the wrong word, that "perfect" should mean unblemished and faultless, and "complete" should mean full grown and mature. But we should understand what the writer intended in the day that he wrote. That is not easy, but with online Bible web sites, it is easier these days. In addition to those sites, I looked up "perfect" in a dictionary. One definition reads "obsolete: Mature". Even though that definition is now obsolete, it still is a pleasant confirmation.

We might think ourselves as being so sinful and wicked at heart. Surely, while we are in this flesh, we should trust neither our "righteousness" nor our motives, but at the same time, we can put aside false humility. It is the Spirit's job to transform us into

Christ's likeness, and that has to look like something, even in this life time. After all Jesus said, *Therefore you are to be perfect* (same word), *as your heavenly Father is perfect* (Matthew 5:48). We can never be sinless while we are in this flesh in this age, but nevertheless we can become perfect! In the life of a Christian this is not a contradiction. It might be easier if I say "become perfected". That might be easier for us to acknowledge, but nevertheless, Jesus said that we **are** to be perfect, so it must be possible. We need the faith that makes it possible.

But after all of that, I do not want to lose the point to be made here. If we do not grow in Christ and become mature Christians, then surely we must have hindered the Spirit's operation in us. Everything we go through has an intended purpose. James calls it being made perfect and complete. This is the real meaning of Romans 8:28, *And we know that God causes all things to work together for good to those who love God, to those who are called according to His purpose.* This is not about happy endings like in story books. History and our own eyes tell us that those kinds of endings did not happen for many people of God. The best ending for all of us is to be made perfect and complete, and once again, James, like Paul, shows us that this is a process that takes time. It is not a given, nor an automatic result of opening the heart one time to Jesus.

The Crown of Life

I have already discussed the various crowns in the chapter on 2 Timothy. In that chapter I wrote the following regarding James 1:12:

James says that the Lord has promised a crown of life for those who love Him. Notice that this love is proved, tested, so that the Christian might be approved.

Here is the verse. *Blessed is a man who perseveres under trial; for once he has been approved, he will receive the crown of life which the Lord has promised to those who love Him.* Do you want the crown of life? Did you realize that you have to be approved? You cannot hide behind the Lord's blood and hope that it will come to you. Our Savior's blood is VERY effective against our sin, but if you want the crown of life, then you have to pass the test.

But here is something else that I realized. I have to tell you, at the exact moment that I was typing out the verse above, James 1:12, I realized that there is no indication that the reward of this crown has to wait until after we die or until the Lord's return. Have you met anyone who is already wearing the crown of life? After thinking about this, I realized that I do know some who are wearing it. They have been through the suffering and the trials, and it seems that the Lord has already given them their crown.

Many say that the twenty-four elders in Revelation 4:10, who cast their crowns before the throne, are us. I have not thought about it in that way for many years, even before I looked more closely at the crowns. The crowns, as I mentioned, are not headgear that you can take off. These crowns are a manifestation of the glory that produced in us by the work of the Holy Spirit. By re-examining the crown of life, I am all the more convinced of this, and I hope that you are beginning to see the need to go past any shallow understanding of the Word and God's plan, and go deeper into Him who saved us for His glory.

Be Saved

Speaking of being saved, I see salvation as a three part process. When we first come to the Lord and believe in Him and His atoning death on the cross, we are saved from sin, and we are saved from death, which is the consequence of sin (Romans 6:23 and James 1:15).

Secondly, by being baptized, we are saved from the world. It is our declaration that we are dead to the world, and we live a new life in Christ!

You can see both of these aspects in the Exodus from Egypt, firstly in Passover and then in the crossing of the Red Sea, which put Egypt (the world) in the rear view mirror.

A third aspect of being saved is to be saved from our old nature, the old creation, and to be made new. This also is seen in two aspects in Exodus and in Joshua. In the wilderness Moses continually had to deal with the complaining and rebelling Israelites. Their immaturity and selfishness were continual problems. When they finally entered the good land, the issue became that of cooperating with God to fight the battles in order to conquer their enemies and gain the land. This typifies the battle for our soul today. We must cooperate with the Holy Spirit, who is joined to our spirit, as He does His transforming work in us. We should understand James in this way in verse 1:21, *Therefore, putting aside all filthiness and all that remains of wickedness, in humility receive the word implanted, which is able to save your souls.*

In practical terms, because "that's the kind of guy he is," James is saying the same thing as Jesus when the Lord said that we need to lose our life in order to gain it. Here is what I wrote about that subject in the "If...Then" section of the chapter on Romans.

Since we have in modern languages only one word for "life" in general conversation, we have to know which of the Greek words was used in the original text. In this case, in talking about losing our life to gain it, the Lord is talking about losing our soul(ish) life, the *psuche*. In all of the scenarios in which Jesus gave this admonition, He was saying that if we hold onto, or even **try** to hold onto, our soulish pleasures, ambitions, pride, (all that stuff), we will lose out on the real *zoe* life.

From His foothold in our spirit, the Holy Spirit wants to bring *zoe* life to every part of our soul, every part that makes us "us".

Therefore, the Spirit's objective while we are on this earth is to transform our soul into something that is precious. Philippians

1:6 says, *For I am confident of this very thing, that He who began a good work in you will perfect it until the day of Christ Jesus.* This transforming work in our souls will result in our being "conformed to the image of His Son" (Romans 8:29).

The salvation of our souls, as James phrased it, is the same thing as gaining life, the *zoe* life! James said that we need to put aside filthiness and wickedness (because it yet remains in us), of which he used lust and anger as examples. In putting aside that stuff, we open ourselves to receive the Word, which is able to save our souls. Jesus said that we need to lose our soul life in order to save it (Matthew 16:24-26 and Mark 8:34-36). As I wrote in that chapter, Jesus said this more than once, so we need to understand and heed His words!

Judge Not

The following subject will be covered in more detail later, when we get to the gospels, but James echoes a recurring New Testament theme in verse 9 of chapter 5. *Do not complain, brethren, against one another, so that you yourselves may not be judged; behold, the Judge is standing right at the door.*

But James is talking about complaining, not judging. Is it not true that complaining is a form of judging? Its roots are in judging. Before we complain, we do in fact make a judgment, and certainly not a positive judgment, else there would not be anything to complain about! We might even preface a comment with "I'm not complaining, but...". So even if we allow that we are not making a complaint, have we not already judged? How deceitful is the heart!

What is the warning here? James points out that we will be judged according to our complaining. But are we not covered by the Lord's blood? Have we not always heard that God looks at us through the lens of Christ? How then can we be judged? Well, we can be (see the beginning of the chapter on 2 Corinthians, Judgment), and James ominously points out that *the Judge is standing right at the door.* James is inferring, just like Jesus said, if we judge, we will be judged. But the Lord also said that if we do not judge, then neither will we be judged. Oh, there is hope! Who can bear to stand up to judgment? I cannot; none of us can. The remedy, dear saint, is to not judge. "But it is too late!" you might say. "How judgmental I have been! In so many ways, toward so many people." Thankfully, in spite of what I wrote in the paragraph above, we do have the blood that was shed for us. *If we confess our sins, He is faithful and righteous to forgive us our sins and to cleanse us from all unrighteousness* (1 John 1:9). Hallelujah! The Lord might also require a confession and an apology to the offended person, and that heals the rift in His body and knits our hearts together.

But do not forget the second half of that verse: *and to cleanse us from all unrighteousness.* We can be forgiven, but we also need to be cleansed. This reminds me of Romans 3:23, *for all have sinned and fall short of the glory of God.* We usually just run this verse together, but I see our condition in two aspects here. Not only do we sin, but we also fall short of God's glory. You can say that we fall short because we sin, and that is true. But if you know yourself well enough in the blazing light of God, you know that even without sinning, you fall wa-a-ay short of His glory! In other words, even if we were to not commit another sin, we still fall short.

This is why the Spirit is in a continual fight against the fallen nature that remains with us, a fight that He cannot win in this age without our cooperation. He will win eventually, but He can win in this age if we allow Him to make His home in our hearts, and we can be cleansed from our unrighteous, judging nature. This is so promising!

Turn a Sinner from Death

We now come to James' last thought in verses 5:19-20. *My brethren, if any among you strays from the truth and one turns him back, let him know that he who turns a sinner from the error of his way will save his soul from death and will cover a multitude of sins.*

Are you familiar with these two verses? Did you catch the phrase *save his soul from death*? What do you think about this? What **have** you thought before reading it just now? First, let us establish that James was writing to Christians; that is a given. Also verse 19 begins by addressing the readers as brethren, and he says "if any among **you**." I hope that you can clearly see that James is stating that a Christian is saved from death when he is turned back from straying from the truth.

This is the first time in this book that we have faced directly that a Christian can face spiritual death. But this is not the first time in the epistles that you could have read it. Paul warned us in Galatians 6:8: *For the one who sows to his own flesh will from the flesh reap corruption, but the one who sows to the Spirit will from the Spirit reap eternal life.* This has implications for both this life and the next.

The next-life scenario is literally laid out in 1 and 2 Corinthians. In 1 Corinthians 5:5 Paul, speaking about the man who was living with his father's wife, says, *I have decided to deliver such a one to Satan for the destruction of the flesh, so that his **spirit may be saved** in the day of the Lord Jesus.* Later then, in 2 Corinthians chapter 2, Paul tells the church to comfort and love the repentant brother.

Please compare what James wrote, *he who turns a sinner from the error of his way will save his soul from death,* to Paul's statement, *so that his spirit may be saved in the day of the Lord Jesus.* What sober words from both of them!

From this point there will be more challenging scriptures like this. Please be patient and let the Lord open His word to you. Let the Spirit guide us into all understanding. Please make that your prayer.

1 & 2 Peter

Peter is famous for writing concerning Paul, *as also in all his letters, speaking in them of these things, in which are some things hard to understand* (2 Peter 3:16a). He said "some things" are hard to understand, but what is **not** included in the hard to understand things is the principal subject of this book. Backing up to verses 3:14 and 15, we can read what should be perfectly clear, but is not, to many. *Therefore, beloved, since you look for these things, be diligent to be found by Him in peace, spotless and blameless, and regard the patience of our Lord as salvation; just as also our beloved brother Paul, according to the wisdom given him, wrote to you, as also in all his letters, speaking in them of these things.*

The speaking by the Spirit through both Paul and Peter is consistent in this matter: *be diligent to be found by Him in peace, spotless and blameless.*

The Outcome of Your Faith

Coming to the first chapter of 1 Peter, I have to return to something I have mentioned a few times in this book. I beg your patience.

Did you answer an altar call one day in your past? If not, maybe you prayed by yourself on a mountain and felt the life changing presence of God. Maybe a couple of Christian friends helped you come to the Lord. There are the profound stories of someone at the edge of death making a deal with God. We found salvation in various ways, and we give glory to God.

But, here is the "but". That was your beginning, a glorious beginning, but it is also the start of a life-giving, life-saving, journey. Peter briefly traces this journey in the first chapter. Verse 3 begins, *Blessed be the God and Father of our Lord Jesus Christ, who according to His great mercy has caused us to be born again...* Hallelujah, there is the first step!

After this Peter tells us that for our journey: [1] we will have God's protection (v. 5); [2] we will be distressed by various trials (v. 6); and [3] our faith will be tested by fire (v. 7).

Wow! Number 1 sounds good, but those last two do not seem very pleasant! But look at the results. *So that the **proof** of your faith, being **more** precious than gold which is perishable, even though **tested** by fire, may be found to **result** in **praise** and **glory** and **honor** at the revelation of Jesus Christ* (v. 7). *And though you have not seen Him, you **love** Him, and though you do not see Him now, but **believe** in Him, you greatly **rejoice with joy** inexpressible and full of glory* (v. 8). How about that?! If we, like the Lord and so many of His saints, can keep the present and future joy in view, then perhaps we might allow the Spirit to perform His work in us!

I write these things as one who has not been tested by fire, as I view that term. Many saints have been sorely tested through history. You might have had thoughts like this. We can be faithful only where God has put us and in the circumstances in which we find ourselves. By comparison to the suffering of many, my suffering is not suffering at all, but mostly inconvenience. Like many, I and my family have gone through periods of joblessness, under employment, and other struggles of life and living. It is up to our Father to place us where we are according to His purpose, so be faithful where you are. We cannot compare ourselves to others, but if need be, use the witness of the Lord's faithful ones to be encouraged and strengthened. We are all running this race in the midst of a cloud of witnesses, so take the Lord's discipline as it comes, and find the joy of the Holy Spirit in it.

Back in verse 3 we see that we were born again "to a living hope", and in verse 9 we see that going through the trials and tests of verses 4-7 results in *obtaining as the **outcome** of your faith the salvation of your souls.* Does this mean that when we stand before the Lord, He will declare us "saved" or "not saved", based on this outcome? In some fashion that is apparently the case, but not in the way that you are probably thinking, not as in going to heaven or to hell. I will discuss this more when we get to John's letters, but in 1 John 2:28 we read, *Now, little children, abide in Him, so that when*

*He appears, we may have confidence and not shrink away from Him **in shame** at His coming.* If we have been washed in His blood, how could it possible for us to have shame at His coming? I hope that you are understanding by this time that it is possible, if we have not taken advantage of the salvation that is available to us. But you might say, "I took advantage of salvation 10 years ago!" My answer, according to what I read in the Word, is that you took that first step 10 years ago. The continuous salvation (which is our race) is available to us through our trials and circumstances and the little things that come to us every day.

When something comes up, our first reaction shows us who and what we are. We might count to ten, but that does not change what was revealed about our inward condition in that initial moment. However, if we would confess our fault, the precious blood covers our sin, and a little more transformation, i.e. salvation, can occur in our hearts. I have my own logs to deal with, so I am not going to point out anyone's splinters. But this becomes our daily salvation: dealing with logs, saying "amen" to our Father's discipline, turning to our spirit (which is one with the Holy Spirit) instead of going along with our emotions. In so many ways, so many times every day, salvation is available to us: salvation from our impure motives, salvation from ungodly thinking, salvation from selfishness, salvation from a stubborn will, and salvation from so many other things within us that are against God.

If we would abide in Christ, instead of in ourselves, we will receive the salvation that His sacrifice has made available, and we can know the salvation that Peter described and the confidence that John desires for us.

An Abundant Entrance

In his second letter Peter again exhorts his readers to be diligent in demonstrating their faithfulness. In the first chapter verses 10 and 11 give us a concluding thought of verses 5-9. *Therefore, brethren, be all the more diligent to make certain about His calling and choosing you; for as long as you practice these things, you will never stumble; for in this way the entrance into the eternal kingdom of our Lord and Savior Jesus Christ will be abundantly supplied to you.* Did Christ call you? Did He choose you? If you can answer "yes", then Peter tells you to be diligent to make them (the calling and the choosing) certain! "But I have 'blessed assurance'! Why do I have to make sure of His calling?"

Peter's answer is in verse 11. *For in this way the entrance into the eternal kingdom of our Lord and Savior Jesus Christ will be abundantly supplied to you.* Are you now getting bothered by all of this? Does this sound like the die-and-go-to-heaven gospel? What does it mean to have an abundant entrance into the kingdom? These kinds of words are prevalent in the New Testament, but have you seen them? Have your heard a sermon about them? I pray that the compilation of these scriptures will help you to see what God is really doing, and how we have such an important part to play.

Now, having seen the conclusion of Peter's discussion, let us see how Peter brought us here. Verse 10 says, *as long as you practice these things, you will never stumble,* so let us see what "these things" are.

Like Paul often did, Peter runs through a sequential list of characteristics that we should exhibit, starting in verse 5, and we should apply "all diligence". *Now for this very reason also, applying all diligence, in your faith supply moral excellence, and in your moral excellence, knowledge, and in your knowledge, self-control, and in your self-control, perseverance, and in your perseverance, godliness, and in your godliness, brotherly kindness, and in your brotherly kindness, love.*

Then the conclusion in verses 10 and 11 is that by practicing "these things", we will have an **abundant** entrance into the **kingdom**! What does **this** mean? What is an **abundant** entrance? According to the Word, some of us will find out. But also some of us will find out the opposite. Think back to 1 Corinthians 3. *But each man must be careful how he builds on it. ...each man's work will become evident; for the day will show it because it is to be revealed with fire, and the fire itself will test the quality of each*

92

man's work. If any man's work which he has built on it remains, he will receive a reward. If any man's work is burned up, he will suffer loss; but he himself will be saved, yet so as through fire (verses 10b, 13-15). This last part must surely be an entrance that is **not** abundant. No one would want to be saved "yet as through fire", but some will. The Bible is quite consistent in its themes. I hope that this one is becoming clear.

Peter directed the words "diligent" or "diligence" three times to his readers in his second letter. We have looked at the first two. The last occurrence can be found in verse 3:14. *Therefore, beloved, since you look for these things, be **diligent** to be found by Him in peace, spotless and blameless.* Peter puts together three ideas in a unique way. He equates being at peace with being spotless and blameless. I can see in myself the point that he must be making. If I am to be blamed for something, something I did or something that I did not do but should have, then I have no peace. If I am unhappy with myself, I do not have peace. If I see something about you that bothers me (you know, one of those splinters), then I have no peace.

What can we do, since we are in this fallen condition? How can I be peaceful about the condition of my devious heart? The best answer I have is this from Philippians 1:6, *For I am confident of this very thing, that He who began a good work in you will perfect it until the day of Christ Jesus.* What an answer! The same Spirit that enlivened me is very eager to complete the work that He started. I cannot fix myself; no amount of fretting and feeling sorry for my condition will ever accomplish anything. I do not have to keep score. I can be at peace, knowing that our Lord is more **willing** and more **able** than I am to make me spotless and blameless. He wants to do the same in you. My picking at your splinters (or mine) does not do any good for you (nor for me). However, we have the Spirit! The Spirit in me is also the Spirit in you. He is working in all of us, His church, for a glorious result!

Concerning the church Paul wrote to the Ephesians that Christ wants to *sanctify her, having cleansed her by the washing of water with the word (rhema), that He might present to Himself the church in all her glory, having no spot or wrinkle or any such thing; but*

that she would be holy and blameless (v. 5:26-27). This **will**
happen! I think we see its fulfillment in Revelation 21:2, *And I saw
the holy city, new Jerusalem, coming down out of heaven from God,
made ready as a bride adorned for her husband.* But realize that
this wonderful event happens after a whole lot of other stuff,
including the millennium.

This is the age for our transformation and sanctification by the
Spirit's speaking life into our soul. But if we are not diligent, and if
it does not happen now, then when can it happen? I will let you
think on that.

1 John

John is known as the apostle whom Jesus loved, and John's letters are the most tender-hearted. Even so, he spoke the truth with clarity. He told us that we lie *if we say we have fellowship with Him and yet walk in the darkness* (1 John 1:6). That is crystal clear, do you think?

Two Problems, Two Solutions

John also wrote that we deceive ourselves *if we say that we have no sin* (1 John 1:8), but the good news is in verse 9: *If we confess our sins, He is faithful and righteous to forgive us our sins and to cleanse us from all unrighteousness.* This is good news, but could we have a more complete understanding? I think this is how most read the verse: If we confess our sins, He is faithful and righteous to forgive-us-our-sins-and-to-cleanse-us-from-all -unrighteousness. I previously discussed Romans 3:23 in this manner. To that church Paul wrote, *for all have sinned **and** fall short of the glory of God.* That also should not be understood as have-sinned-and- fall-short.

We have two problems. One is that we sin; the other is that we sin because we **are** sinners. I am sure that you have heard this before. We have sinned **and** we fall short. Our sins need to be forgiven **and** we need to be cleansed because our constitution is unrighteous! Isaiah wrote, quoting God, *Though your sins are as scarlet, they will be as white as snow* (verse 1:18). But Ezekiel wrote *Moreover, I will give you a new heart and put a new spirit within you; and I will remove the heart of stone from your flesh and give you a heart of flesh* (verse 36:26). You can see distinctly two problems. Isaiah wrote about our sins, and Ezekiel wrote about our hearts. This helps us to see that John covered both prophets in his one sentence. *If we confess our sins, He is faithful and righteous to forgive us our sins* (Isaiah) *and to cleanse us from all unrighteousness* (Ezekiel).

We know that our Lord has taken care of both problems, but the second is resolved differently from the first. His shed blood removes our sins if we confess them. From where we stand that is all we have to do. He suffered such a cruel death and shed so much blood, especially at the business end of those heinous whips, so that we can do nothing but receive what He has made available. He drank His cup so that we could *lift up the cup of salvation and call upon the name of the Lord* (Psalm 116:13). Lord, help us to appreciate even more what you endured so that you could redeem us to Yourself.

But how does our heart get changed? Jeremiah wrote, *The heart is more deceitful than all else and is desperately sick* (verse 17:9). I hope that you can see your own heart for what it is. Jeremiah saw me clearly. The more that we follow the Lord, the more we should see this. But what to do? We cannot help ourselves in this matter any more than we can earn forgiveness for our sins.

The change that is required in our hearts is accomplished by the Spirit operating in us, to cleanse us from our defilement. A verse that shows this well is 2 Corinthians 3:18. *But we all with unveiled face, beholding as in a mirror the glory of the Lord, are being **transformed** into the same image from glory to glory, just as from the Lord, the Spirit.* This is how we get a new heart! This "beholding" is one way that our heart gets renewed.

Another is found in Ephesians 5:25-27. This passage starts with the verse about husbands loving their wives, which serves as an illustration of the Lord's desire: *Just as Christ also loved the church and gave Himself up for her, so that He might sanctify her, having cleansed her by the washing of water with the word, that He might present to Himself the church in all her glory, having no spot or wrinkle or any such thing; but that she would be holy and blameless.* Here you can see the ultimate goal of our Lord's suffering on the cross. He gave Himself up, not so we can go someplace after we die, but so that the church can become holy and blameless! This is more than forgiveness; this requires new hearts in all of us, hearts that have no spots and no wrinkles! So you see, "and" is very important. *He is faithful and righteous to forgive us our sins **and** to cleanse us from all unrighteousness.* Sins are what we do; unrighteousness is what constitutes us. We need a change, but we cannot do it ourselves. The law was (and is) not sufficient for our need. This is why the Old Testament prophets pointed to a future time, as the verses from Ezekiel indicate. See also Jeremiah 24:7 and 31:33-34 and Ezekiel 11:19. This is validated in chapter 8 of Hebrews, in which scripture is drawn from the Old Testament to make this very point.

Finally, consider this from Paul's letter to the churches in Galatia. *For if a law had been given which was able to impart life, then righteousness would indeed have been based on law* (Galatians 3:21b). Our Father's desire is to impart life, **His** life, into us, specifically into our hearts. The law cannot do this, but the eternal life, the *zoe* life, operates in us, writes in us, cleanses us from all unrighteousness, and transforms us!

Thank the Lord that He gave up all and gave all to remedy our outward problem **and** our inward problem.

<u>Do the Will of God, Have Confidence</u>

Now we will look at two verses in chapter 2 of 1 John. At first glance they might not appear to be related, but on a deeper level they are. Verse 17 reads, *The world is passing away, and also its lusts; but the one who does the will of God lives forever.* Verse 28, *Now, little children, abide in Him, so that when He appears, we may have confidence and not shrink away from Him in shame at His coming.*

I'll bet that you are counting on living forever, since you have been washed in the blood of the Lamb. But, having been washed, are you doing the will of God? If *the one who does the will of God* will live forever, then what should we extrapolate about the one who does **not** do the will of God?

Now you might think that I have gone too far with verse 17, but what do you do with verse 28? If you are a Christian, no doubt you are waiting for the Lord's return, but John is telling us that we might not be so glad to see Him! When the Lord appears, will you have confidence or will you have shame? Did you ever think about that? Truth be told, Jesus warned us of this, but we will get to that when we cover the gospels.

In the previous chapter we saw that Peter wrote the same thing. *Therefore, beloved, since you look for these things, be diligent to be found by Him in peace, spotless and blameless* (2 Peter 3:14). Two brothers, who spent a bit of time with the Lord, wrote the same thing. I think we should give more weight to what they said than to the gospel that promises heaven in the sweet bye and bye.

If you are starting to become convinced of the seriousness of living to please the Father, what should you do? What should we all do? Verse 17 says that we should do the will of God, but what does that mean? Let's try to simplify.

We covered in chapter 1 of First John about confessing our sins and allowing the Word to cleanse our hearts. John follows that by saying, *My little children, I am writing these things to you so that you may **not** sin* (verse 2:1a). But John knows, as well as we, that we are going to sin, so he reminds us that *we have an Advocate with the Father, Jesus Christ the righteous* (verse 2:1b).

With that understood, sinning or not sinning isn't the main point. The main point is found in verse 3, *By this we know that we have come to know Him, if we keep His commandments.* If the only gospel that you have heard is about having your sins forgiven, then you have **not** heard the whole gospel! Just as I pointed out in the previous section, we need our sins to be forgiven, **and** we need to be cleansed from all unrighteousness. Being cleansed in the heart goes hand in hand with knowing Him, and knowing Him means keeping His commandments!

"Wait! Slow down!" you say. "Didn't you just quote Galatians 3:21, about the law not imparting life? And now you say to keep his commandments? How can both be true? The Bible is so confusing, so full of contradictions!"

There are many occasions in the gospels where the word "commandment" is used without the Ten Commandments being in view. Consider John 12:49, *"For I did not speak on My own initiative, but the Father Himself who sent Me has given Me a commandment as to what to say and what to speak."* There are many examples, as I said, so I think we have to understand verse 3 in this way.

Now it is "simple" again. Think of it as receiving a direct order from your superior in the military. The Spirit is always speaking to us, and sometimes the speaking is an instruction, or order. But we do not like taking orders, do we! However, in John 14:21 we see the Lord saying, *He who has My commandments and keeps them is the one who loves Me.* I do not see a lot of wiggle room here. As John might say it, "If we say that we love the Lord, yet ignore His speaking, we are just fooling ourselves." Oh, wait... John did say that. *The one who says, "I have come to know Him," and does not keep His commandments, is a liar, and the truth is not in him* (verse 2:4). Did I not say that John spoke the truth with clarity?

Now, allow me to finish John 14:21. *He who has My commandments and keeps them is the one who loves Me; and he who loves Me will be loved by My Father, and I will love him and will disclose Myself to him.* This verse starts with *he who has My commandments and keeps them*, and it ends with *I...will disclose Myself to him.* Do you see the parallel to 1 John 2:3? *By this we know that we have come to know Him, if we keep His commandments.* This is very similar to what Paul wrote to the Corinthians. Do you remember 2 Corinthians 6:16-18? Verse 17 says this, *Therefore, come out from their midst and be separate, says the Lord. And do not touch what is unclean; and I will welcome you.*

Let all of that sink in. I think there is nothing that I can add to that.

Jude

Jude wrote a very short letter. His intention was to write about *our common salvation* (verse 3), but instead he felt the necessity *to write to you appealing that you contend earnestly for the faith* (also verse 3). It seems that his burden was similar to mine, or mine is similar to his.

As Some of Them Did

There are many warnings in Jude's letter. Let us look at verse 5, *Now I desire to remind you, though you know all things once for all, that the Lord, after saving a people out of the land of Egypt, subsequently destroyed those who did not believe.* I will ask a question similar to what I asked in the last chapter: Did Jude go too far? Is he really warning Christians that they could be destroyed? If this really is a possible outcome for us, how does that square with everything we have been taught?

As I have tried to do throughout this book, I prefer to let the Word speak for itself. I hope you have noticed that I have not done a lot of interpreting. I have done a lot of "talking", but mostly I have been laying the Word before you and writing about what has been in front of us all these years. I am trying to present what the apostles and others have written (given to us as the breath of God) in a way that forces you to go to the Lord about what **they** said.

Now let us come back to verse 5. Do you realize that Paul wrote the same thing? Speaking about those who escaped Egypt, he wrote, *Nevertheless, with most of them God was not well-pleased; for they were laid low in the wilderness. Now these things happened as examples for us, so that we would not crave evil things as they also craved* (1 Corinthians 10:5-6). Paul continued. *Do not be idolaters, as some of them were* (verse 7). *Nor let us act immorally, as some of them did* (verse 8). *Nor let us try the Lord, as some of them did* (verse 9). *Nor grumble, as some of them did* (verse 10). He concluded, making the same point as above, *Now these happened to* *them as an **example**, and they were written for **our instruction**, upon whom* (us) *the ends of the ages have come. Therefore let him who thinks he stands take heed that he does not fall* (verses 11-12). We covered similar verses in the chapter on Hebrews. *Do not harden your hearts as when they provoked Me, as in the day of trial in the wilderness* (Hebrews 3:8). How many times can we read these things and not see the warning? I know the answer personally: many times. It does not help us either that traditional teachings have ignored this matter.

But there is hope! Verse 10:13 of 1 Corinthians says, *No temptation has overtaken you but such as is common to man; and God is faithful, who will not allow you to be tempted beyond what you are able, but with the temptation will provide the way of escape also; so that you will be able to endure it.* We have heard this verse many times, I am sure, but now look at it in its context (see the verses two paragraphs up). God does not want us to fall. He is there for us! He is faithful!

Look at Jude's final word on the matter! After so many dire and depressing warnings, he cannot say enough to encourage us. Pardon me while I quote all six verses (20-25). I cannot leave out any. *But you, beloved, building yourselves up on your most holy faith, praying in the Holy Spirit, keep yourselves in the love of God, waiting anxiously for the mercy of our Lord Jesus Christ to eternal life. And have mercy on some, who are doubting; save others, snatching them out of the fire; and on some have mercy with fear, hating even the garment polluted by the flesh. Now to Him who is **able to keep you** from stumbling, and to make you stand in the presence of His glory blameless with great joy, to the only God our Savior, through Jesus Christ our Lord, be glory, majesty, dominion and authority, before all time and now and forever. Amen.*
AMEN! Hallelujah! While writing that I have to say that I got excited! What a conclusion! Thank you, Lord. Jude used to be merely the last book before Revelation, but I had never read those six verses like **that** before!

I know you might not have felt the same as you were reading, so go back and look at that again. We who are "prone to wander" have a God, a Savior, who is able to keep us. Oh, I know that for sure, and I praise Him and thank Him.

Not Done Yet

Well now. This seems like it should be the end of the book, but we have a lot more to cover. I said that we would look at the Gospels after looking at the epistles. That is next. What about Revelation? It seems good to me to save it for last. It is the conclusion of the Bible, and the conclusion of God's journey with man in this age. I think it will have the final word about these warnings to us.

Next we will see what Jesus had to say, but before we do that I think it is important to review a matter that is crucial to our understanding. How does grace fit into all of this?

What About Grace?

It might be that you have some confusion after reading this far. (Or, you might think that I am confused.) The law was of the Old Testament, and it was ineffective, and it did not impart life, so why do I (rather, not I, but the writers of the New Testament) seem to be insisting that we have to "do good"? Are we not saved by grace, and grace alone? Is this a contradiction on the highest order?

I have talked about grace here and there in the previous chapters, but even so, I understand that it can be difficult to get past life-long held concepts. In this chapter I will review some of what was previously discussed and add other supporting scripture and thoughts.

The long-held concept (rather, definition) that gets in our way is that grace is unmerited favor. Grace **is** unmerited, for sure, but this definition by itself limits our understanding and appreciation. There is so much more!

It is not hard to see this traditional definition of grace while reading Romans. Here are some of the verses.

5:15b - *...much more did the grace of God and the gift by the grace of the one Man, Jesus Christ, abound to the many*
5:20 – *The Law came in so that the transgression would increase; but where sin increased, grace abounded all the more*
6:1 – *What shall we say then? Are we to continue in sin so that grace may increase?*

As we continue in Romans, however, it can be noted that this definition of unmerited favor begins to come up short. Consider these verses.

12:3a – *For through the grace given to me I say to everyone among you not to think more highly of himself that he ought to think.*
12:6 – *Since we have gifts that differ according to the grace given to us...*
15:15-16a – *But I have written very boldly to you on some points so*

*as to remind you again, because of the grace that was given me
from God to be a minister of Christ Jesus to the Gentiles*

Notice that in the verses quoted from chapters 5 and 6 Paul is presenting a basic Gospel, but later he speaks of his own experience and also of everyone's place and function in the body of Christ. These experiences all require grace, but "unmerited favor" is not an adequate explanation for what is needed.

In verse 12:3 Paul says that he is able to speak through the grace that was given to him. It is because of grace that he is able to speak. Verse 12:6 says that grace is given to us so that we can function in the body of Christ, and the verses in chapter 15 tell us that Paul was given grace to be a minister, which is his function in the Body, corresponding to verse 12:6. I hope you see now that something much deeper than the common definition is at work.

Let us look at other examples from Paul's letters. In 1 Corinthians 3 Paul wrote that grace is needed to build God's habitation. *According to the grace of God which was given to me, like a wise master builder I laid a foundation* (verse 10). In the preceding verse he wrote, *For we are God's fellow workers* (verse 9). Grace has to be the realm and the means by which we work (even for us small-potato brothers and sisters), and this is shown in the context of verses 10 and 12-13. *According to the grace which God has given to me, like a wise master builder I laid a foundation, and another is building on it. But each man must be careful how he builds on it.* Verses 12-13: *Now if any man builds on the foundation with gold, silver, precious stones, wood, hay, straw, each man's work will become evident; for the day will show it because it is to be revealed by fire, and the fire itself will test the quality of each man's work.*

Usually a message on these verses will center on the three precious materials versus the three earthy materials. How can we know for sure what materials we are using? It must not be completely evident to us, because Paul said that our work will be proved by fire. But do we really have to wait until we stand before Christ to know if our work will survive?

Evidently Paul had some confidence about this. He said that he laid a foundation *according to the grace of God which was given to me.* He also later wrote (verse 15:10), *But by the grace of God I am what I am, and His grace toward me did not prove vain; but I labored even more than all of them, yet not I, but the grace of God with me.* Paul could say that he worked more than all of the other apostles, but he could also say, *not I, but the grace of God with me.* Paul was not idle. He labored, but it was not his labor alone. Grace was his companion.

Again I ask, how can we know for sure what materials we are using? You can guess the answer now: Grace! But still, that answer is not clear enough. How can I know that I am doing something in grace, according to grace, and with grace?

For me it is like this. If I feel frustrated, I am outside of grace. If I am too demanding of myself or others, I am not in grace. The negative feelings are a big clue. On the other hand, if I have peace with myself and others, if I have assurance in what the Lord is doing though me and in me, then I am in grace. Self confidence is not grace, but confidence in the Lord is.

Sometimes we might start in grace, but after some time the tension arrives. Frustration builds. This is not necessarily a sign that we are doing the wrong thing, but maybe we need to pause, and give grace its proper place. There have been a couple times when I was doing something to help someone, but after some time of helping, I no longer felt the grace to continue. Sometimes it feels difficult to pull out of the situation, but continuing would have been an exercise in unblessed obligation. I found that even withdrawing requires grace to do it the right way.

I hope it is clear that grace is our way. It is so much more than unmerited favor. Did Paul need unmerited favor when he asked the Lord three times to remove a thorn from his flesh? You know the Lord's answer. *My grace is sufficient for you* (2 Corinthians 12:9). You also know that was not the complete answer. The Lord continued, *for power is perfected in weakness.* We think we need something that meets our situation, like Paul prayed for the removal of his problem, but the Lord says that we need grace. Our problems make us feel weak, but grace prevails! There is something much deeper here that we all need to experience. May the Lord lead us into this.

For ministering to the body of Christ we need grace. Romans 12:6 says, *We have gifts that differ according to the grace given to us.* 1 Corinthians 12 also talks about spiritual gifts, but without mentioning grace. Instead, Paul speaks of the Spirit as the source and means of the operation of gifts to minister to the Lord's body.

Can you see where I am going? We think we need some-**thing** for functioning in the Lord's body, and we need some-**thing** for our problems, but what we really need in all cases is grace. So now that we understand the need for grace, do we still understand grace to be another "something"? By looking at Romans 12 and 1 Corinthians 12 together, we can see that grace is not some-**thing** that the Lord provides, but grace is the Spirit Himself come to us!

I am writing this book in the realm of grace and by the means of grace. I am able to write because the Holy Spirit is with me. I would not dare to write this otherwise!

I hope this brief discussion helps you to understand better what we have. We need grace to run this race, and this grace is nothing other than the Lord Himself come to us as the Spirit to impart His life to us.

The Gospels

Introduction

Having covered the New Testament letters, I hope that you can admit that I am making a good case that there are many warnings to us who call ourselves Christians. Remember, the authors of these letters were not writing to unbelievers; they were writing to the churches, to those who have believed in the Lord.

Now let us look at what Jesus had to say. Mostly He spoke obliquely or in parables, and not very often in a direct manner except to His disciples.

Many of the things that Jesus said are recorded in more than one gospel, so rather than go through Matthew and then Mark, etc., I will mainly go through Matthew's gospel, because Matthew presented more parables than the others. But, while examining Matthew's gospel I will refer to the other gospels. Where the other gospels mention something that Matthew leaves out, I will either insert them where the context allows, or I will present them in other chapters.

Matthew – Part 1
(Matthew 6 and 7)

Debts

But of course, the first scripture we cover will not be a parable. This might be unexpected, but let us start at the Lord's prayer. There is this little phrase (Matthew 6:12) wherein we ask our Father to forgive our debts. We certainly want and need our debts (a metaphor for sins) to be forgiven, but there is a condition attached. As many times as you have said this prayer, did you ever realize that you are actually attaching a condition to God's forgiveness?

Luke 11:4 records it like this, *And forgive us our sins, for we ourselves also forgive everyone who is indebted to us.* Here it sounds like the Lord has ground to forgive us, **because** we forgive others! How can that be? A response might be, "Jesus paid the price for all of our sins! And I have accepted His free gift by faith, the cleansing by His precious blood. How can there now be a condition to God's forgiveness?"

But there is more! Look at Mark 11:25. *Whenever you stand praying, forgive, if you have anything against anyone, so that your Father who is in heaven will also forgive you your transgressions.* Here again we see cause and effect. Our Father will forgive **my** sins if I forgive **anyone's** (everyone's) offenses toward me. I forgive "so that" I will be forgiven.

Now we come to a parable, to me a very powerful one. It is in Matthew 18:23-35. Because of its length, I will not write all of the verses here, but please take a minute to read it.

This parable about the unforgiving slave should be familiar to you. This slave owes a debt, 10,000 talents, to the king. He cannot pay, but out of compassion the king forgives the debt. This slave, however, was not as merciful to another who owed a debt to him of 100 denarii. For comparison, a denarii was a day's wage, and a talent was more than 80 pounds, more than 15 **years** of wages according to a footnote. And this guy owed the king 10,000 **times**

15 years of wages! This slave had his fellow slave thrown into prison because of that smaller debt of 100 denarii. Verse 18:34 tells us the king's reaction. *And his lord, moved with anger, handed him over to the torturers until he should repay all that was owed him.*

This is serious! The Lord's concluding statement on the matter is, to me, His most somber warning in all of the gospels. *My heavenly Father will also do the same to you, if each of you does not forgive his brother from your heart.* My soul trembles a little every time I read this. Saved by grace? Well, sure, but, do I have any grudges? Saved by grace? Yes, but have I forgiven everyone that has offended me? What does it mean to be handed over to the torturers? If that sounds extreme, you can go with some versions that say "jailers", but others say "tormentors" and "inquisitors" and "jailers to be tortured".

You get the point; so, what does that have to do with us? Why would Jesus draw such a conclusion and direct it to His disciples, and to us by extension?

The word that comes to my mind is responsibility. We will see that theme in many of the parables, and you probably have some in mind. God did not put His life into us, bring us into His fellowship, and invest so much into our salvation, for us to receive it all with an unthankful heart. We are to be the same toward others as our Father is to us.

So as to not end this section on a negative tone, I want to finish with a discussion on the last three words of Matthew 18:35, "from your heart". Sometimes we pay lip service to forgiveness, and this leaves the other party and us feeling unfulfilled. Please read in the Appendix an article titled "Making Pearls". Do not feel condemned if every situation cannot turn out as well as what I describe there, but it might help us to see what forgiveness looks like when it has its best result.

The Way You Judge

Now we come to a topic that hits close to home for nearly all of us (as if the last one did not). I will say "nearly" just to allow for a margin of error on my part, but if I say "very, **very** nearly," do you think I would be mistaken? *Do not judge so that you will not be judged. For in the way that you judge, you will be judged; and by your standard of measure, it will be measured to you* (Matthew 7:1-2).

I mentioned in the previous section that the parable spoken of there makes my soul shudder. Do these two verses have any similar effect? Is this not a real problem with our sick hearts, our broken nature?

Here is how Mark reports another occasion when the Lord spoke similar words. *And He was saying to them, "Take care what you listen to. By your standard of measure it will be measured to you; and more will be given you besides* (Mark 4:24)." Did you catch the part about *and more will be given you besides?* I think that I do not want more of my judgments piled on top of me! By my standard of measure I will be measured...and then some!

Luke gives us the Lord's positive slant on this. *Be merciful, just as your Father is merciful. Do not judge, and you will not be judged; and do not condemn, and you will not be condemned; pardon, and you will be pardoned* (Luke 6:36-37).

Who has not expressed an opinion about someone? It does not matter whether the opinion is accurate or not. Do not forget, Adam ate of the tree of the **knowledge** of good and evil. Since we think we know what is right and wrong, and since we tend to act like God (Genesis 3:22), we have opinions about everything! But we have no right to judge others; judgment belongs only to the Son (John 5:27). To discourage us from usurping what is His (but I think not the only reason), Jesus gave this warning that **we** will be judged in the same way that we pass judgment, even using the same measuring stick that we use on others. How many of us would crumble before Him?

The alternative is to be kind and generous in our attitudes, which is not easy much of the time, but this is pleasing to God and to man.

Let us look at Ephesians 4:29-32. These verses contain the admonition to not grieve the Holy Spirit. I will tell you now, that I had not paid attention to its context until right now, while writing this chapter. Verses 25 through 32 contain a list of instructions from Paul, seemingly unconnected, including verse 30, which says, *Do not grieve the Holy Spirit of God, by whom you were sealed for the day of redemption.* But look at the three verses that surround verse 30. *Let no unwholesome word proceed from your mouth, but only such a word as is good for edification according to the need of the moment, so that it will give grace to those who hear* (v 29). *Let all bitterness and wrath and anger and clamor and slander be put away from you, along with all malice* (v 31). *Be kind to one another, tender-hearted, forgiving each other, just as God in Christ also has forgiven you* (v 32).

It is quite significant, I think, that Paul mentions grieving the Holy Spirit right in the midst of telling how we should speak and act toward one another. Surely the Spirit is grieved when I sin, but how much more when I mistreat those around me!

Is it any wonder, then, that the Lord warned of speaking ill of a brother in Matthew 5:22? *But I say to you that everyone who is angry with his brother shall be guilty before the court; and whoever says to his brother, "You good-for-nothing," shall be guilty before the supreme court* (Sanhedrin) ; *and whoever says, "You fool," shall be guilty enough to go into the fiery hell.* Where the NASB reads "shall be guilty," many versions use the phrase "shall be in danger off," but you get the point here: Jesus will not tolerate bad behavior toward His own, including such behavior by us!

The Narrow Way

Now we come to a couple of verses that I expect to be turned upside down and inside out for you. I feel quite challenged and inadequate to relate to you all the thoughts and feelings that I have related to these verses. May the Lord be merciful to help me relay what He meant and also to help you to receive.

Surely by the title of this section you know what the verses are. I will spend quite a bit of ink to cover as much as possible.

Enter through the narrow gate; for the gate is wide and the way is broad that leads to destruction, and there are many who enter through it. For the gate is small and the way is narrow that leads to life, and there are few who find it (Matthew 7:13-14).

Do I have to lay out here what is the traditional teaching related to these verses? Here it is in a nut shell as I understand that teaching...Jesus is the gate and the pathway to heaven and, as Acts 4:12 says, There is no other name. The names of Buddha and Mohammed cannot save us, so Jesus is the narrow gate and the narrow way.

But in telling us that there does exist a wide gate and a wide path that lead to destruction, I believe that Jesus was saying that many will try to follow Him and think that they are, based on a gospel that requires nothing from us except "faith".

I think Jesus revealed the narrow gate in verse 24. *Therefore everyone who hears these words of Mine and acts on them, may be compared to a wise man who built his house on the rock...* You know the rest. The wide gate is seen in verse 26. *Everyone who hears these words of Mine and does not act on them, will be like a foolish man who built his house on the sand.* You know the rest of this passage also.

The wise one is the one who acts on (many translations say "does") the Lord's words. This matches Matthew 28:19-20. *Go therefore and make disciples of all the nations, baptizing them in the name of the Father and the Son and the Holy Spirit, teaching them to **observe** all that I commanded you.* Do Matthew 7:24 and 28:20 say the same thing? I think so. 7:24 tells us to act on (do) the Lord's words, and 28:20 tells us to observe all that the Lord has commanded. This must be the gospel as God intended it.

Jesus would know what the Gospel is, don't you think? Three times in Matthew it is written that Jesus preached the "gospel of the **kingdom**" (verse 4:23, 9:35). In addition, Mark 1:14, Luke 4:18, and 20:1 mention that Jesus preached the gospel. What do you suppose **He** told the people? Do you really think that He told the people that they would be going to heaven after death? Maybe you think He couched that idea in words like "finding life". I am doing my best, with His help, to show that this was not our Lord's intention at all.

In saying that the narrow way leads to life, Jesus is **not**, absolutely **NOT**, talking about going to heaven. I hope I did not lose you by saying that. Jesus was talking about **life**! Again, this is the *zoe* life. If you need a review of *zoe* life, please reread the If...Then section in the chapter on Romans. The go-to-heaven lens that covers the eyes of many prevents them from seeing a distinction between life and going to heaven, even though Jesus clearly said "life". The New Testament, even the entire Bible, is a book of *zoe* life! This life is revealed to us, it is dispensed into us, and it will grow and mature in us, and it satisfies our Father, from Whom it came. Please decide today to understand this *zoe* life. I have a Bible in which I wrote the letter "z" where the Greek word *zoe* was used. It helps me to understand what kind of life is discussed.

Life, specifically *zoe* life, is the goal of our Christian walk. These verses in Matthew 7 parallel John 14:6: *Jesus said to him, "I am the way, and the truth, and the life; no one comes to the Father but through Me."* In John 14 and here in Matthew 7 we have "the way" and we have "life". These are inseparable. If you want life, Jesus is the way. If you are in the correct way, then you will find life. In John 17:3 Jesus said in His prayer to His Father, *This is eternal life, that they may know You, the only true God, and Jesus Christ whom You have sent.* Jesus is life (*zoe*), and life is knowing our Father and Christ.

Satan, the subtle enemy, was quite successful in changing the gospel from *zoe* to going someplace when we die. Because of this, the real meaning of verses such as Matthew 7:13-14 and John 14:1-6 has been veiled. Please read about John 14 in the Appendix, "About Those Mansions".

Let us come back to Matthew 7. If "leads to life" does not equal "go to heaven", then it follows that we have to reconsider these two verses, and find out what Jesus was really saying.

Jesus talked about gates and paths. It is difficult for me to distinguish the gate from the path in the following sense. The gate matches the path. If you have a road that leads to your house, the gate has to be as wide as the road. If the road is wide enough for a car, then the gate must accommodate a car. If you have a walk that leads from the street to your door, then the gate is only as wide as a person or two. You would not have a narrow gate on a road, and neither would you have a wide gate for a walk. Therefore Jesus says to enter the narrow gate, because the path on the other side of the gate will also be narrow.

The important factor then is the path, not the gate. Nevertheless, we have to go through the correct gate in order to be on the path that leads to life. We might want to get on the correct path, but we have to recognize the proper gate. What is the gate? I have wondered about this for years, but it seems to me that the wide gate and the narrow gate are shown to us in verses 7:15-20. (Remember: context, context, context!)

The wide gate is represented by false prophets, wolves, thorns, thistles, and bad trees. We have to recognize these types so that we do not receive their "gospel". Eventually we see in verse 7:23 that these are those *who practice lawlessness,* even while they claim to be working in the Lord's name.

From observation and according to Paul's letters, I think there are mainly three kinds of wide gate: 1) an insistence that you follow the law, 2) an insistence that there is no law (meaning I can do whatever I want), and 3) that which I will call "the prosperity-and-feel-good- about-yourself gospel."

Examples of the first kind of wide gate, referring to law givers, are those who require certain adherence to outward demonstrations of religion. In Paul's day it was mainly the Jewish religion that got in the way. These days it is Christian religion. We think that by being religious or by doing things in a certain way that we are brought closer to God. God already had a religion that He designed, and He instructed His chosen people in performing and maintaining it. Do you really think that He sent His Son to the cross just so that we, fallen and corrupt, could make up another religion?

You might think that religion is a narrow way, but really it is not. It might appease our conscience and make us feel good, but it hinders us from a living relationship with Christ. If you want to be religious, how religious do you want to be? Which Christian denomination do you follow? There are so many to chose from! Or, make up your own version of Christian religion. It really is a broad way after all.

Besides all of that, the teachers of religion must have forgotten, or do not realize, that the requirements of the kingdom *zoe* life are higher and stricter than what even they have in mind. Is this not one of the points that Jesus tried to make in His sermon on the mount when He referenced adultery and murder within the heart?

On the other hand, those who suggest that we are free of law are also forgetting, or do not realize, the same thing, that the kingdom life is high, and that it demands certain things. The kingdom *zoe* life has its own spiritual law. I learned this many years ago from Witness Lee. If an apple tree did not follow the law of the apple tree life, how could it ever produce apples? Being free from "the law" does not mean lawlessness.

There is such a thing as the law of the Spirit of life. This law surpasses the former law, and it also does not leave us lawless. Paul was so eloquent in the letter to the church in Rome about this subject. We see in verse 8:2, 3a and 4, *For the law of the Spirit of life in Christ Jesus has set you free from the law of sin and of death. For what the Law could not do, weak as it was through the flesh, ...(verse 4) so that the requirement of the Law might be fulfilled in us, who do not walk according to the flesh but according to the Spirit.*

The law still has a requirement, and it must be fulfilled, even as Jesus said that He did not come to abolish the law, but to fulfill it (Matthew 5:17). But He drove the Pharisees crazy, because His fulfilling of the law was by the Spirit, not by the flesh. In the same way Paul in Romans 8:4 said that the law will be fulfilled **in** us. How is this so different from following the old law? I refer you again to the Sermon on the Mount. The old law said not to murder; the law that is fulfilled by the Spirit, exposes hate in our heart, and writes love in its place. The old law said not to commit adultery; the law that is fulfilled by the Spirit exposes lust in our heart and writes purity in our heart. This is how the law is fulfilled **in** us. As the Spirit of life writes God's law on our heart (Jeremiah 31:33), this begins to have an outward manifestation, so that even though we remain clay vessels, God begins to have an expression through us. What a marvelous thing this is!

Now let us look at the same subject from a slightly different angle. Consider these two verses from Romans 6, verses 15 and 22. *What then? Shall we sin because we are not under law but under grace? May it never be!* (verse 15). *But now having been freed from sin and enslaved to God, you derive your benefit, resulting in sanctification, and the outcome, eternal life* (verse 22).

The implication behind verse 15 is that being under grace does not allow for lawlessness; being free from the law does not equal being free to sin. More than that, verse 22 shows us that there is a result that is derived from being under grace, a two-fold result, actually. The first result is that grace leads us to sanctification, and the second is that sanctification brings to us **eternal life!**

Did you think that we get eternal life for free? I bet you have a verse to prove that we do. In fact the verse might be Romans 6:23 in the same chapter that we are discussing. *For the wages of sin is death, but the free gift of God is eternal life in Christ Jesus our Lord.* Nothing can be more clear, right? Eternal life is a free gift, but, can we possibly see this verse in a new light? I have just showed you that eternal life is an outcome of sanctification, and sanctification in turn, is a result of living under grace! So let us put verses 22 and 23 together. *But now having been freed from sin and enslaved to God, you derive your benefit, resulting in sanctification, and the outcome, eternal life. For the wages of sin is death, but the free gift of God is eternal life in Christ Jesus our Lord.* (If you still are not clear about what is grace, please read again the previous chapter.) If you still think that eternal life is free, I will be the first to say that you are correct! Am I contradicting myself? Once again, putting things into their context (verses 15-23) we can see that while eternal life **is** free, it does not come without a condition. That condition is that we live a life enslaved to God! Is that too strong for you? Okay then, we can say it this way. The condition is that we live under grace. If you can see it properly, there is no difference between living under grace and living as a slave to God. He provides the grace to do what He asks of us. I can testify to my own small experiences, but you can hear the testimonies and read the books of those who have deeply experienced God in this way.

It is okay to preach the gospel and tell people that eternal life is a free gift from God, but as we become mature Christians, we need to move beyond basic understanding so that we can receive all that God wants to teach us and give us. Therefore, please understand that verse 23 of Romans 6 is a summary of all the discussion that preceded it, even starting all the way back to verse 1 of the chapter.

Eternal life is a free gift; the Bible says so, but it is also an outcome. The more that the Spirit is able to sanctify me, the more eternal life is wrought into my soul. You already have eternal life since the day that you received the Lord, but you received this life as a seed. That was your beginning. Now this eternal life needs to be cultivated and allowed to grow and spread into your heart. This growth is our sanctification, *and the outcome, eternal life.*

If I was not able to make this completely clear, please ask the Lord to help your seeing and your understanding. He is the One who said, *Ask, and it shall be given to you; seek, and you will find; knock, and it will be opened to you* (Matthew 7:7).

After spending almost two pages on the first two teachings, now we have to come back and cover the third "gospel", the prosperity gospel. I hope that you can see through this one, but the allure must be great, judging from all the people that flock to it. A whole other book could be written by someone more qualified, but I want to touch one point: motivation. Here is a portion from Paul's letter to the church in Philippi. *You yourselves also know, Philippians, that at the first preaching of the gospel, after I left Macedonia, no church shared with me in the matter of giving and receiving but you alone; for even in Thessalonica you sent a gift more than once for my needs. Not that I seek the gift itself, but I seek for the profit which increases to your* account (not bank account). *But I have received everything in full and have an abundance; I am amply supplied, having received from Epaphroditus what you have sent, a fragrant aroma, an acceptable sacrifice, well-pleasing to God* (Philippians 4:15-18).

I quoted quite a bit here from Paul's letter, but I want you to get a sense of the love in the motivation, both in the giving and in the receiving. Drawing from Old Testament offerings, Paul called the gift from the saints a fragrant aroma. Is this a good description of our giving? Maybe you have heard of "the smell test". Well, we can see here an early application. How does our giving smell? Is it attractive, well-pleasing, to God? Whether God decides to materially reward one's giving, or if He chooses not to, should not be our motivation. Our one desire should be to have a pleasing aroma, even **be** a pleasing aroma, to our God.

Have you ever smelled yourself? I know that sounds funny, but did you ever smell your own righteousness? I have (mine of course...not yours)! It truly does stink! The truth is, we should not be aware of our own aroma when it is pleasing to God. It is for Him to enjoy.

Concerning the matter of adding to their account, it is clear that Paul is not suggesting in any way that God will reward them with financial security. Paul's words perfectly echo the Lord's when He said to store up treasures in heaven (Matthew 6:20). That is all I am going to say on that.

After all that you have just read about the wide gate, we need to recognize the narrow gate for its positive aspects, not only as an absence of the prior mentioned negatives. A point of review is that the gate matches the way. The object is to go through the correct gate so that you will be on the correct way. The narrow way leads to *zoe* life, so it should be our desire to find its gate.

Matthew 7:20, after the Lord talked about good and bad trees, concludes by saying, *So then, you will know them by their fruits.* Is the gate before you demonstrating fruits of the Spirit? Galatians 5:22-23a has a good list. *But the fruit* (notice the singular noun) *of the Sprit is love, joy, peace, patience, kindness, goodness, faithfulness, gentleness, self-control.* Some of these can be imitated for a time, so you have to be aware, be patient, and use what discernment you have at your stage of spiritual growth. The gate that opens to the way of life, will direct you to Christ in all of these things, not as a way of changing behavior or turning over a new leaf.

Not included in the list in Galatians 5 is another fruit of the Spirit. Notice these verses...

Hebrews 12:11 --- *All discipline for the moment seems not to be joyful, but sorrowful; yet to those who have been trained by it, afterwards it yields the peaceful fruit of righteousness.*

Philippians 1:9-11 --- *And this I pray, that your love may abound still more and more in real knowledge and all discernment, so that you may approve the things that are excellent, in order to be sincere and blameless until the day of Christ; having been filled with the fruit of righteousness which comes through Jesus Christ, to the glory and praise of God.*

Ephesians 5:8-10 --- *For you were formerly darkness, but now you are Light in the Lord; walk as children of Light (for the fruit of the Light consists in all goodness and righteousness and truth), trying to learn what is pleasing to the Lord.*

I like the way Ephesians 5:10 ends the phrase, *trying to learn what is pleasing to the Lord.* Some translations use the word "proving". The proper gate will lead to the way that pleases the Lord; it will not use scripture to justify an opinion or way of life. The proper gate will show us our Father's loving discipline and the cross, which we must eventually bear.

I pray that the difference between the two gates is clear. I cannot help but think that the gates actually represent people. Nearly all of us probably came to the Lord through contact with another person. Right away or eventually we find ourselves under someone's ministry. I was very fortunate that at a young age, about two years after coming to the Lord, I found a group of Christ-seeking Christians in Akron, Ohio. What a wonderful gate that was for me. I learned about my human spirit and God's eternal purpose. I learned how to "eat" the Word, which is eating Jesus according to John 6. The person behind the ministry in this case was Witness Lee. I received a good foundation that has stayed with me through my ups and downs.

The point about remaining on the way is important, because I found out that we can switch paths. Finding the narrow gate and starting out on the narrow path does not guarantee, or even imply, that we will remain on it. It is too easy to wonder off. We might suddenly find ourselves following a different gospel. Maybe we become religious and come to depend on something that looks like Christ, but is just a shell. Or we could take for granted our liberty in Christ, and become lawless.

Even the apostles could find themselves off the narrow way. In Galatians 2 we read that Peter associated himself with the Gentile believers until "certain men from James" showed up (Galatians 2:11-14). Dare I say that even Paul went off the narrow way when he went to Jerusalem in Acts 21? He was persuaded to participate in a traditional Jewish purification ritual with some Jewish believers. A riot ensued, and Paul was prevented from completing the event. This led to his arrest and later transport to Rome.

The Lord is merciful to bring us back to the narrow way if we seek Him again. He is so very willing put our feet back on the narrow way, to seek Him alone and the good of His church.

Here is a question for you. How narrow is the narrow way? Another question: How few is "few"? Luke 13:23-24 says this, *And someone said to Him, "Lord, are there just a few who are being saved?" And He said to them, "Strive to enter through the narrow door; for many, I tell you, will seek to enter and will not be able."* You might be inclined to think in terms of Jesus being the only way to enter heaven, as discussed above. But, again, keep in mind that Jesus was always talking about the kingdom.

Here are the next few verses in Luke 13. *Once the head of the house gets up and shuts the door, and you begin to stand outside and knock on the door, saying, "Lord, open up to us!" then He will answer and say to you, "I do not know where you are from." Then you will begin to say, "We ate and drank in Your presence, and You taught in our streets"; and He will say, "I tell you, I do not know where you are from; depart from Me, all you evildoers." In that place there will be weeping and gnashing of teeth when you see Abraham and Isaac and Jacob and all the prophets in the kingdom of God, but you yourselves being thrown out* (verses 25-28).

Notice that in Matthew 7 Jesus mentioned a narrow gate, and here in Luke 13 He talked about a narrow door. They are distinct words in the Greek. The picture that I get is one of the narrow gate opening to the narrow path, which leads to the narrow door. The goal is that door, hence the need to strive for it.

Based on these verses we can understand that when Jesus said that many will seek to enter (verse 24), He is talking about seeking to enter the kingdom. This refers to His kingdom that He will establish on this earth when He returns. Just in case I need to make it clear, He is **not** talking about going to heaven. Those who enter by the narrow door (we have to strive for it), will be able to participate in the enjoyment of His glorious kingdom!

It is not automatic. Inviting the Lord into my heart some time ago does not qualify me for the kingdom. Recall that Paul wrote to the church in Corinth, *But I discipline my body and make it my slave, so that, after I have preached to others, **I myself will not be disqualified*** (1 Corinthians 9:27). It is this disqualification that concerned him, being left on the outside of the kingdom age.

You read previously about losing our soul life in order to gain the *zoe* life. The entrance into the kingdom is a large part of what is to be gained. On the other hand, seeking now to preserve our soul life will result in loss later. The loss will be our being left out of participation in the kingdom. This is quite serious, because this will be a thousand years of being left out of the joy of the Lord!

Will we trade what few years remain in our lives for a thousand? We do that in so many little choices we make every day. How many times do we chose what we prefer, what we like, what suits us? Lord have mercy on us...on me.

I Never Know You

In Matthew 7 and in Luke 13 we have these verses where the Lord claims to have never known someone (Matthew 7:23) or to not know from where someone has come (Luke 13:25,27). The verses in Matthew follow the Lord's discussion of gates and paths, false prophets, and good and bad trees. After all of my discussion above, can you see how this scenario can take place? But the question is, who are these that say, "Lord, Lord"? Many say that these are "false Christians" or some other term that suggests that they had never been born again.

Here is Matthew 7:21-23. *Not everyone who says to Me, "Lord, Lord," will enter the kingdom of heaven, but he who does the will of My Father who is in Heaven will enter. Many will say to me on that day, "Lord, Lord, did we not prophesy in Your name, and in Your name cast out demons, and in Your name perform many miracles?" And then I will declare to them, "I never knew you; depart from Me, you who practice lawlessness.*

There are two obvious points to discuss here: 1) Who could stand before the Christ and say "Lord, Lord," and 2) what did Jesus mean in saying that He does not know someone? Regarding the first point I will admit that my argument is not as strong as for the second point, and you might not agree with my argument, but I think that the two points together make a stronger argument than either by itself, like two strands of twine.

1 Corinthians 12:3b says, *and no one can say, "Jesus is Lord,"* *except by the Holy Spirit.* While Romans 14:11 and Philippians 2:10-11 say that "every knee will bow" to Jesus and every tongue will confess that He is Lord, this plea of "Lord, Lord" is not like that.

These in Matthew 7 are defending themselves by declaring all that they had done in Jesus' name. Again, remember the context of this chapter. By various illustrations and examples, Jesus is showing us how, and how not, to live before Him. No one can stand before the righteous King and lie, and Jesus did not deny that they had done these wonderful things. Instead He says that He never knew them.

So, who is it that might stand before the Lord saying "Lord, Lord"? I firmly believe that these are born again believers, but believers who did not do the will of their Father. I remind you that I was in that camp, though not doing anything like these claimed to have done. I was "farther" away than that.

This brings us to the second strand of twine, that Jesus said He never knew them. In the Greek there are mainly two words for "knowing". One refers to a knowing of facts and ideas; the other refers to an experiential knowing.

Oida is the word for knowing facts and ideas. A good example in scripture is Ephesians 6:21: *But that you may know about my circumstances, how I am doing....*

The other word for knowing is *ginosko*. This kind of knowing is based more on experience and even intimacy. Two good examples of the use of this word are in Galatians 4:9 and 1 Corinthians 13:12.

Galatians 4:9a – *But now that you have come to know God, or rather to be known by God...*

1 Corinthians 13:12 – *For now we see in a mirror dimly, but then face to face; now I know in part, but then I will know fully just as I also have been fully known.*

A wonderful example of both words used together is John 21:17. See if you can determine which word is *oida* and which is *ginosko*. I'll bet you can! *He said to him the third time, "Simon, son of John, do you love Me?" Peter was grieved because He said to him the third time, "Do you love Me?" And he said to Him, "Lord, You know all things; You know that I love You." Jesus said to him, "Tend My sheep."*

Lord, You know all things; You know that I love You. You are correct if you thought that the first "know" is *oida* and the second is *ginosko*. How can you know that someone loves you, except by intimate knowledge? That is *ginosko*. You can "*oida*" all things, but you can love someone only by "*ginosko*-ing" that person.

Think about the sunrise. A scientific person can tell you all sorts of things about the rising sun: rotation, refraction, etc. That person *oida*s the sunrise. But if you have been camping, you know the cool air, the wakening birds, the building color. You *ginosko* the sunrise! This is knowing by experience; this is true knowing. So then, when Jesus in Matthew 7:23 said that He never knew them, the word is *ginosko*! Like Peter, we might understand that the Lord knows (*oida*) all things, and therefore we might understand how it could be that He might not *ginosko* someone.

Please read John 17. This is the chapter with the **real** Lord's prayer. The word "know" is used many times in this chapter, and in every case it is *ginosko*. The first time is in verse 3, *This is eternal life, that they may know You, the only true God, and Jesus Christ whom You have sent.* Eternal life is to *ginosko* God!

This is a key point in this book. Religious people who do not allow God to know them do not fulfill His purpose. He does not want a bunch of actors, the original meaning of "hypocrite". His desire is for us to allow Him into every aspect of our lives.

Are you getting to know God? Do you show up once a week on Sunday and think that this is your "reasonable service" (Romans 12:1, KJV)? Or are you getting to know God in a real way? Look again at Galatians 4:9a. *But now that you have come to know God, or rather to be known by God...* Even though it might be hard for the natural mind to grasp, you can see the thought here, that while we are getting to *ginosko* God, He is getting to *ginosko* us! He might *oida* all about you, but He wants to *ginosko* you!

This idea is also in 1 Corinthians 13:12b, when Paul said, *just as I also have been fully known.* Fully known by whom? By God, of course!

Coming back to Matthew 7, here is someone (even a brother) who, by whatever means, came to the Lord for his salvation. Eventually he did things according to his own will and his own ideas, and he did not allow the Lord to direct his way. Do you think this is not possible? Never mind those with ministries like that described in verse 22, ...what about us? Do we go through the motions in our Christian walk? Do we do things according to our concept?

It might concern you at this point how it is that I can call these lawless ones my brothers, meaning that they would be Christians, and yet the Lord told them to depart! In verse 21 He said, *Not everyone who says to Me, "Lord, Lord," will enter the kingdom of heaven...* I think that the strongest parallel to these verses in Matthew 7 can be found in 1 Corinthians 3:13-15. *Each man's work will become evident; for the day will show it because it is to be revealed with fire, and the fire itself will test the quality of each man's work. If any man's work which he has built on it remains, he will receive a reward. If any man's work is burned up, he will suffer loss; but he himself **will be saved**, yet so as through fire.* Fire is God's judgment. It is also the means by which He purifies us, but this purification implies judgment against all that is impure. We all will appear before the judgment seat of Christ as Paul wrote in 2 Corinthians 5:10: *For we must all appear before the judgment seat of Christ, so that each one may be recompensed for his deeds in the body, according to what he has done, whether good or bad.*

In Paul's first letter to Corinth he wrote of judgment by fire and in his second letter he wrote about being recompensed according to our deeds. There is definitely the possibility of negative consequences at the judgment seat of Christ, but in no way does Paul suggest that we lose our salvation if this judgment does not go well for us. Neither does he suggest that we had not been saved. I see no reason, therefore, to assume that these in Matthew 7 were not saved. Keep this in mind while reading the next chapter.

Matthew – Part 2
(Matthew 10)

Endure to the End

In chapter 10 of Matthew we see the Lord sending His disciples out to the cities and towns of Israel. Besides giving them instructions, Jesus also gave them a warning about hostile environments that they might encounter. The warning was not just for that present moment, but also for the future, the church age. Please read for yourself verses 6 through 21. In verse 22 we have Jesus saying, *You will be hated by all because of My name, but it is the one who has endured to the end who will be saved.* Mark 13 has a parallel passage, and the familiar discourse in Matthew 24 contains the same statement, *but the one who endures to the end, he will be saved* (verse 24:13). We have covered Hebrews 3:6, *but Christ was faithful as a Son over His house – whose house we are, if we hold fast our confidence and the boast of our hope firm until the end.* Revelation 2:26 also has a similar statement, *He who overcomes, and he who keeps My deeds until the end, to him I will give authority over the nations.*

I wrote in the preface that by putting together so many scriptures in one place, my hope is that they would be too hard to ignore. Here I have shown you five passages that tell us how important it is to hold fast until the end: Matthew 10:22, Mark 13:13, Matthew 24:13, Hebrews 3:6, and Revelation 2:26. These are in our Bibles, so what do we do? Jesus spoke it at least twice, Paul said it explicitly once and wrote on the same thing by implication many times, and John quoted Jesus saying it plainly one more time to the churches.

Coming back to the theme of a race, does it do any good to run a race but stop short of the finish line? We have to endure to the end! The 100 meter sprint is not won at 99 meters. A 5 kilometer race, which is about 3.1 miles, is not finished after 3 miles. The loudest cheers are for the winner, but do you know who usually receives the second loudest cheers? The one who finishes last! This one completed the course. He or she was not the fastest, not the most skilled, but this faithful one endured to the end and completed the course. From the first to the last, this is us. I know that Paul said only one receives the prize in a race, but he was giving an example about **how** to run the race (1 Corinthians 9:24). The reality is, however, that all who finish the course that the Lord has laid out are counted as faithful and worthy, as these five verses (and more) tell us.

But, we must finish. The trouble is, we do not know how long is the race. Some, like Paul, run until they can see their finish line. It might be a life span, or it could be until the end of a terminal disease. The race can also be cut short by a fatal accident or other tragedy.

Whatever is our course, and however long is our race, it is ours to run. Hebrews 12:1 encourages us to *run with endurance the race that is set before us.*

No one can run it for us, BUT, we can run together! Check out these verses!

Romans 15:30 - *Now I urge you, brethren, ...to strive together with me in your prayers...*
2 Corinthians 7:3b - *...you are in our hearts to die together and to live together*
Ephesians 2:5b - *...(God) made us alive together with Christ...*
Ephesians 2:21 – *in whom the whole building, being fitted together, is growing into a holy temple in the Lord*
Ephesians 2:22 – *in whom you also are being built together into a dwelling of God in the Spirit*
Ephesians 4:16 – *from whom the whole body, being fitted and held together...*
Philippians 1:27b - *...that you are standing firm in one spirit, with one mind striving together...*

Colossians 2:2a – *... that their hearts may be encouraged, having been knit together in love*
Colossians 2:13b – *...He made you alive together with Him...*
Colossians 2:19b - *...the entire body, being supplied and held together...*
Hebrews 10:25a – *not forsaking our own assembling together...*

God did not intend for us to run alone. In fact, His purpose is not accomplished unless our spirits and hearts are knit together. Look at the verses again, and see the phrases "fitted together", "built together", and "held together". The result of all this together-ness is a holy temple and a dwelling of God!

Some of us are loners by nature, but we have to allow the Spirit to knit our hearts with other hearts. As Paul wrote to the church in Corinth, we need each other. *The eye cannot say to the hand, "I have no need of you,"* (1 Corinthians 12:21). We need the fellowship; we need the encouragement; we need the spiritual building up. When I run by myself, rather than with someone, the temptation to stop is stronger when I am tired. When I run with others, however, it is also much easier to press on. Even more so, when I run a race with a friend, it is especially easier for **both** of us to endure, because we are running for each other. Neither wants to be the one who says, "I need to stop for a while."

Confess Me Before Men

This next section is related to the previous. The previous section is an encouragement to endure to the end; this section is about the one thing that hinders us the most: fear. Matthew used the word "fear" four times in this tenth chapter, and in a parallel passage Luke in chapter 12 used "fear" four times and "be afraid" twice.

Finally, the Lord says in verses 31-33, *So do not fear; you are more valuable than many sparrows. **Therefore** everyone who confesses Me before men, I will also confess him before My Father* *who is in heaven. But whoever denies Me before men, I will also deny him before My Father who is in heaven.* See also Luke 12:8-9. I have learned to pay attention to the ifs, buts, and therefores in scripture. What does our value over sparrows have to do with our confessing Christ before men, and His confessing us before His Father? We have to look at the whole context; I think you will get it.

In Matthew 10:19-20 the Lord had previously said, *But when they hand you over, do not worry about how or what you are to say; for it will be given you in that hour what you are to say. For it is not you who speak, but it is the Spirit of your Father who speaks in you.* Do you see the value? God, our Father, knows everything that goes on with every little sparrow, and He also knows how many hairs are on our heads. To borrow a phrase that is often heard these days, He's got this! How much more valuable can one be than to be a speaking vessel for God! Even the "how" will be given. Do not fear; the confession before men will be given to us, and our Lord will confess us before His Father.

But, after that encouragement there is the warning. Verse 33 says, *But whoever denies Me before men, I will also deny him before My Father who is in heaven.* He had to go and say it.

After this the Lord gives examples of the difficulties to be faced. We will be betrayed, put to death, and hated (verses 21 to 22). Jesus will become an example of what to expect (verses 24-25), but in verse 28a He encourages us with, *Do not fear those who kill the body but are unable to kill the soul.* Our value lies in our soul, but our fear is laid bare in the first part, killing the body.

It might be helpful to look at the apostle Paul at this point. In Philippians 1:18-20 we find this familiar passage. *What then? Only that in every way, whether in pretense or in truth, Christ is proclaimed; and in this I rejoice. Yes, and I will rejoice, for I know that this will turn out for my deliverance through your prayers and the provision of the Spirit of Jesus Christ, according to my earnest expectation and hope, that I will not be put to shame in anything, but that with all boldness, Christ will even now, as always, be exalted in my body, whether by life or by death.*

Here is a real life application of Matthew 10. Paul did not fear those who could kill the body, because they could not touch his soul. When he declared *this will turn out for my deliverance,* he was not talking about freedom from his captors. Many translations use "deliverance", and many use "salvation." If we think "salvation" I think this helps to show Paul's attitude, because he wrote *this will turn out for my deliverance... whether by life or by death.*

In many places of the world today Christians face such an outcome. Beheadings and torture are carried out in the name of another god. May we find such boldness and steadfastness if days like these come upon us.

I wrote previously that the matter of confessing the Lord before men has a lot to do with persecution. This will be seen again when we get to Revelation. "Dear Lord, may we not fear. We look to You for grace and courage when the perilous times come. May we uphold Your Name, just as so many have, who have endured before us."

Not Worthy of Me

We all know that we are not worthy of salvation. We cannot save ourselves and we cannot earn salvation. It is only through our Lord's shed blood that our salvation was purchased. How is it then that we have consecutive verses where Jesus describes those who are not worthy? Here is Matthew 10:37. *He who loves father or mother more than Me is not worthy of Me; and he who loves son or daughter more than Me is not worthy of Me.* And verses 38-39. *And he who does not take his cross and follow after Me is not worthy of Me. He who has found his life will lose it, and he who has lost his life for My sake will find it.*

By now the explanation will make sense, I hope. Before we come to the Lord we have nothing and we can do nothing. At the beginning of our walk with the Lord we are new born babes. We can surely tell people about Jesus, but the divine life within us needs to be nourished so that it can grow. Eventually we should begin to mature in *zoe* life, and it will start to require more of us. There is a price that we have to pay to become more like Him, and that price is our soul-life, our *psyche* life. We love so many things, but we should love nothing more than, or above, the Lord.

It might make us uncomfortable to hear or read the words "is unworthy of Me," but I cannot apologize for the Lord's speaking. I did not say them; He said them. These cannot be intended to the unsaved because, of course, they cannot be expected to love the Lord. He is clearly speaking to us who claim to be His. There can be no expectation of the unsaved person to love Christ more than family, and there can be no such expectation for the unsaved to take up their cross.

I love the song *Just As I Am*. I came to the Lord under the singing of that hymn. On that day He showered me with His love and grace. Today I still come to Him just as I am, and today His love and grace are still with me, but He also says, "Just as you are is not suitable for the kingdom." Today I come just as I am to the throne of grace so that He can help me to love Him above all and to lose my soul-life. The promise is that if we lose our soul-life in this age, we will have it in the next for our complete enjoyment of the kingdom life.

In Philippians 3 we can see what this meant to Paul. I promised back in that chapter that we would look at it again here in Matthew. Notice what it means for him to take his cross and what it means to lose his soul-life. Here are verses 8 and 10. ***More** than that, I count **all** things to be loss in view of the surpassing value of knowing Christ Jesus my Lord, for whom I have suffered the loss of all things, and count them but rubbish so that I may gain Christ. ...that I may know Him and the power of His resurrection and the fellowship of His sufferings, being conformed to His death.* (Note: "knowing" and "know" here are both *ginosko*, the intimate knowledge that comes by experience.) When in verse 17 he wrote, *Brethren, join in following my example,* verses 8 and 10 are the example he is talking about. He continued, *and observe those who walk according to the pattern you have in us.* Just in case we think that this is too high, or too difficult, we are left with no excuses. We can follow the example of others. More than that, we can **be** examples.

Paul then contrasts his life and pattern to those who do not take the way of the cross, as seen in verses 18-19. *For many walk, of whom I often told you, and now tell you even weeping, that they are enemies of the cross of Christ, whose end is destruction, whose god is their appetite, and whose glory is in their shame, who set their minds on earthly things.* As I mentioned briefly in the chapter on Philippians, Paul is not talking about someone who is necessarily against gospel preaching or against speaking about the Lord's death on the cross. The cross here is not the cross on which Jesus hung, but the cross that should be effective in us in order to kill our impurities and so transform us.

Paul's description of these might hit home. He talks about their god being their appetite. Some translations use the word "belly" or "stomach". They brag about shameful things or exult in their shame, and their minds are set on earthly things. The indwelling Spirit wants to cross out these things…in us. This is not to say that we become like monks in a monastery, but that our thinking, desires, and ways of doing things, become more like Christ. This should not become a code of behavior, but a real change inside of us.

Coming back to the verses in Matthew, we can see that the Lord has to have our best love, He demands that we take our own cross and follow Him in order to be worthy, and we have to lose our soul-life in order to gain it. These are the demands of the kingdom. It is absolutely **not** a simple matter of being saved and going to heaven.

Whoever Receives You

At the end of chapter 10 the Lord comes back to the mission. In verse 14 He talked about those who would not receive the disciples, and we covered all of that in the first two subtitles of this chapter. Now He talks about those who did receive the disciples. *He who receives you receives Me, and he who receives Me receives Him who sent Me. He who receives a prophet in the name of a prophet shall receive a prophet's reward; and he who receives a righteous man in the name of a righteous man shall receive a righteous man's reward. And whoever in the name of a disciple gives to one of these little ones even a cup of cold water to drink, truly I say to you, he shall not lose his reward* (verses 40-42). I want you to notice here that Jesus is talking about reward, not for the disciples, but for those who help them in some way. I am planting a seed for now. We will come back to this thought later.

Matthew – Part 3
(Matthew 13)

Parables

After Jesus presented the parable of the sower in chapter 13, the disciples asked why He spoke in parables. The Lord answered, *To you it has been granted to know the mysteries of the kingdom of heaven, but to them it has not been granted* (13:11). That seems clear enough; that settles it then. The Lord said that they, the disciples, get to know, but the others do not. But, as with most things that I am presenting in this book, it is not that simple.

In the next verse we read Jesus saying, *For whoever has, to him more shall be given, and he will have an abundance; but whoever does not have, even what he has shall be taken away from him* (13:12). I used to wonder whether this verse was cause or whether it was effect. By that I mean, do the conditions described in verse 12 precede the Lord's statement in verse 11, or is verse 12 a result of verse 11? Now I think I am clear. The disciples did not have much, but they had Jesus. It is true that Jesus scolded them a bit for being slow to learn, but they were doing their best. They wanted to be with Him. They wanted to be a part of what He was doing. They had open hearts. Therefore, they get to know the mysteries.

The "them" in verse 11 had their religion, which was the law and man-made traditions. All of this was a filter through which they received the Lord's speaking. So, hearing, they did not hear. They heard the words, but they did not hear the message. What they did not have were open hearts to hear God. For this reason Jesus said that they do not have, and even what they had, their religion, would be taken away. Eventually it was taken from them with the destruction of Jerusalem and the temple in 70 AD.

How is it with us? Are we without filters? If you are starting to agree with what you have read in this book, or if you might only be thinking on it before the Lord, why did you never see it before? These verses have been there. It is because of filters!

We always have to be on guard for new filters. Every time we see something in the Word, that new thing has the potential to become a filter, including the subject of this book. Whenever we come to the Word, we have to pray for the Spirit to have an open way to speak into us. We need Him to help us drop our filters, our concepts, our backgrounds, our traditions, our denominations, our new learning, everything!

A personal testimony: If you were to look at any of my Bibles, you will not see any writing in them except added marginal references and an indication of the Greek for words like "life" and "love". It is not because I am religious about not writing in my Bible; it is so that an underlined or highlighted passage does not prevent me from seeing what the Spirit wants to speak today. I am not making a rule for anyone else, but I want to present an example of being serious about wanting to be as open as absolutely possible, to be empty of anything that can hinder my hearing the Lord.

I asked why you might have never seen these scriptures in this way before. Many will not like this, but I contend that the biggest reason has to do with the thickest filter, and that is the be-saved-and-go-to-heaven gospel. Why do you think that many interpret Matthew 7:14 in that way? *For the gate is small and the way is narrow that leads to life, and there are few who find it.* "Leads to life" does **not** equal "go to heaven!" We have already looked at that in covering Matthew 7. This shallow "gospel" is why teachers have to contort their reasoning in order to explain the parable of the sheep and goats in Matthew 25. This is what leads to not understanding John 14, where Jesus said that no one comes to the Father except through Him. If we have to wait to go to heaven in order to come to the Father, then we have little hope in this life. (I cover John 14 in great depth in the Appendix.) This brings us to the next chapter.

Matthew – Part 4
(Matthew 16)

Leaven in the Teaching

In chapter 16 we see that Jesus and the disciples crossed the Sea of Galilee, and they had forgotten to bring bread. Jesus used this, what we now call a teaching moment, to say, *Watch out and beware of the leaven of the Pharisees and Sadducees* (verse 6). After some discussing and explaining, Jesus told them plainly that He was not talking about bread, and the disciples figured out that He was talking about teachings.

Leaven often refers to sin, but there are New Testament instances of leaven being used exemplify inaccurate teaching, as well as sin. Mark 8 and Luke 12 have accounts of Jesus teaching His disciples about leaven. Paul used leaven in 1 Corinthians 5:6-8 to portray the effects of not dealing with sin. In Galatians 5:8 Paul refers to unscriptural teaching that hindered the saints in the churches of that region.

Leaven is not good. Yet the parable in Matthew 13:33 is often taken as a positive declaration of the kingdom of heaven, i.e. the Gospel, spreading around the world. Here is the one-verse parable. *He spoke another parable to them, "The kingdom of heaven is like leaven, which a woman took and hid in three pecks of flour until it was all leavened."* It might be that since this was a parable of the kingdom, then it must be assumed that this is a positive story, but I remind you that the parable of the wheat and tares in the same chapter is **not** entirely positive.

In the parables of Matthew 13 Jesus illustrated what will be the state of affairs on earth during this age, the age of the gospel. Not all is good. You can see many troubles in the church in the various letters of the New Testament and in chapters 2 and 3 of Revelation, and some of that is caused by erroneous teachings.

We should not be surprised then to find both good and bad in the parables of the kingdom. And if this parable is showing us the bad, how are we to understand leaven? If it is in the teachings, what are some examples?

The first, and I think prime example, was covered in the last chapter. Has not the whole become leavened with the teaching of spending eternity in heaven? The church's understanding of many scriptures is tainted by this, as explained previously. Besides that, there are things like mansions, Saint Peter at the pearly gates, the golden shore. I will not belabor the point. Please read in the Appendix "About Those Mansions."

There is other leaven in the church, and I mentioned briefly the prosperity gospel when discussing Matthew 7. The best thing we all can do is read the Bible for ourselves. Do not be afraid to question anything and everything you have been taught. It's okay, God can handle it. It is the Spirit's pleasant job to lead us into understanding. He will enlighten the scriptures, as He leads your understanding. By being open in this way, those things that are true will become more sure in your understanding, and you will not be shaken.

Matthew – Part 5
(Matthew 18)

Enter Life

We come now to chapter 18, in which are a couple of parables that have to be perplexing to many. If we are saved by grace, and not by works...if we cannot earn our salvation...if we are eternally secure...then what place do these parables have in the Gospel? Here is the first, although I do not actually consider it a parable. Verses 8-9: *If your hand or your foot causes you to stumble, cut it off and throw it from you; it is better for you to enter life crippled or lame, than to have two hands or two feet and be cast into the eternal fire. If your eye causes you to stumble, pluck it out and throw it from you. It is better for you to enter life with one eye, than to have two eyes and be cast into the fiery hell.* (A parallel description is given in Mark 9:42-48. See also Matthew 5:22,29-30.)

Jesus gave two illustrations that seem to have some determining factor in our eternal destiny. One result is entering into life, and the other is being cast into the eternal fire and fiery hell. But if we are saved by grace, then how can my cutting off a hand (presumably to keep me from sinning) make me any more qualified to spend eternity with the Lord, and less deserving to spend eternity in hell?

I am reminded again of the hymn *Just As I am.* There is no requirement for a sinner to do **anything** to qualify himself to come to the Lord. There is no requirement because there is no possibility. We **have** to conclude that these verses are not intended for the lost as a prerequisite to opening their heart to receive salvation.

As I attempt to offer my explanation for this quandary, please keep in mind the reason for the book and all that you have read so far. There is a consistency in all of this, so I hope that I can help you to realize that Jesus has not said anything different here from what has been said by Him in many ways, and later by Paul. So here are two reminders. The first reminder is that Jesus said a few times that we have to lose our soul-life now in order to gain it later. The second reminder is that Paul wrote to the Corinthians about being saved "yet so as through fire" (1 Corinthians 3:15).

At the risk of being repetitious, these kinds of warnings are scattered all through the New Testament. By bringing them together in one book, my hope is that Christians will begin to see the truth and love in the warnings and begin to take them seriously.

Speaking of fire, I will cheat a little and look ahead to Revelation 2. Verses 8 through 11 comprise the letter written to the church in Smyrna. Verse 11 concludes the letter. Here is the second part of that verse. *He who overcomes will not be hurt by the second death.* The second death is defined for us in Revelation 20:14 and 21:8 as the lake of fire.

Keep in mind that the letters in chapters 2 and 3 of Revelation were written to churches! In these churches the sovereign Lord is looking for those who will be overcomers. As I am trying to show, no one is automatically an overcomer. I have heard preachers and teachers try to say so (actually, they do say so), but the Word reveals something else.

So, we read in the letter to Smyrna that the overcomer will not be "hurt" by the lake of fire, the second death. Is this something different from being "cast into" the lake of fire? It must be. I have presented three scriptures that talk of fire in relation to God's people. Again, these are Matthew 18:8-9, I Corinthians 3:15, and Revelation 2:11. Can you admit that there must be something to this?

Maybe the next parable will help.

Forgive from Your Heart

Matthew 18:23-35 is one of the longer parables. It was already covered in the chapter Matthew – Part 1. I will not present all of the verses here, but please read them before continuing.

Jesus had just talked to the disciples (and us) about forgiving our brothers (verse 22) seventy times seven times. That comes to 490 times, so if you want to keep score, well good luck with that. But we have to know that our God has forgiven us in Christ seventy times seven times seventy times seven...times! When God stops forgiving us, then we might have cause to not forgive someone else. Jesus begins the parable by saying "for this reason". The reason is that we might be tempted to think we have forgiven someone enough times or maybe that the offence toward us was too great. In the parable a slave is owed 100 denarii by another slave. The 100 denarii is 100 day's wages. That might seem like a lot, and it is. If you work 6 days per week, as back then, 100 days is about one-third of your annual wages! But what is that compared to 10,000 talents that the slave owed to the king? If we try to compare how much we forgive to how much we have been forgiven, we can never catch up.

As you know, the one slave had the other thrown into prison for the debt. This was after the king had forgiven the slave's 10,000 talent debt. When the king heard of it, he withdrew his mercy. The parable ends like this: *And his lord, moved with anger, handed him over to the torturers until he should repay all that was owed him. My heavenly Father will also do **the same to you**, if each of you does not forgive his brother from your heart.*

I will give you two more verses. Matthew 6:14-15 read, *For if you forgive others for their transgressions, your heavenly Father will also forgive you. But if you do not forgive others, then your Father **will not** forgive your transgressions.*

Hmmm, Matthew 6. There is something familiar about that chapter. Did you realize that Jesus spoke this right after He gave us the example on how to pray? Here is a snapshot. *Our Father who is in heaven* (verse 9), *forgive us our debts, as we also have forgiven our debtors* (verse 12). *For if you forgive others for their transgressions, your heavenly Father will also forgive you. But if you do not forgive others, then your Father **will not** forgive your transgressions* (verses 14-15).

Here we find the second Greek word *hos*. This is the *hos* that is pronounced with a long "o", like "host". This *hos* means "like", so when we say *forgive us our debts, as we also have forgiven our debtors* we are actually saying *forgive us our debts,* **like** *we also have forgiven our debtors.* We are really saying, "It is okay with me, God, for you to grant me the same forgiveness that I extend to others!" We are agreeing with that parable in chapter 18! That is something to keep in mind the next time you recite that prayer. Sobering, is it not?

Returning to the parable, we see in verse 33 that the king said to that slave, *Should you not also have had mercy on your fellow slave,* **in the same way** *that I had mercy on you?* Would you like to guess the Greek word behind the phrase "in the same way"? It is *hos*!

Some have an understanding about this, but the conversation seems to stop short of drawing a conclusion. It seems to me that the reason for stopping short is.... well, you either go to heaven or you go to hell, right? Is this not a quandary?

Do you remember how the parable in chapter 18 ends? *And his lord, moved with anger, handed him over to the torturers* **until he should pay** *all that was owed him. My heavenly Father will also do the same* **to you,** *if each of you does not forgive his brother from your heart* (verses 34-35). What will the Father do to us? We will be required to repay! How would we repay? I do not know, but this does have a conclusion; there is an "until." I do believe that this involves missing at least part of the millennial kingdom. The parables in the coming chapters strongly suggest this.

Matthew – Part 6
(Matthew 22)

Dressed in Wedding Garments

The first fourteen verses of Matthew 22 are a synopsis of God's history with His people. We come into the story in verse 9: *Go therefore to the main highways, and as many as you find there, invite to the wedding feast.* Throughout history this is what God has been aiming at. Whatever might be our agenda, and no matter what was our motivation for receiving salvation, God's desire has always been the wedding!

In verse 10 we see that many are gathered to the wedding feast, but there was one there who was not wearing wedding garments (verse 11). This parable does not tell us how the others came about their wedding garments, but somehow, this one missed out. He answered the invitation like all of the others, but apparently he thought that all he had to do was show up and enjoy the feast. Dear saints, are we like this? Do we think that having been once saved, all we have to do is wait for "that day?"

In Revelation 3:4-5 we can see garments mentioned in the letter to the church in Sardis. There the Lord speaks of those who will wear white garments *for they are worthy.* Then in verse 3:18 those who are in the church in Laodicea are urged to **buy** white garments from the Lord. What is the difference between receiving the free gift and buying a wedding garment? Consider again the section "The Narrow Way" back in my first chapter on Matthew. Here is the key paragraph from that section:

> If you still think that eternal life is free, I will be the first to say that you are correct! Am I contradicting myself? Once again, putting things into their context (verses 15-23) we can see that while eternal life **is** free, it does not come without a condition. That condition is that we live a life enslaved to God! Is that too strong for you? Okay then; we can say it this

way. The condition is that we live under grace. If you can see it properly, there is no difference between living under grace and living as a slave to God. He provides the grace to do what He asks of us. I can testify to my own small experiences, but you can hear the testimonies and read the books of those who have deeply experienced God in this way.

Recall, too, the discussion about losing our soul-life in order to gain *zoe* life. These passages in different ways say the same thing!

Matthew – Part 7
(Matthew 24 and 25)

Sensible or Evil

Now we arrive at some very significant parables in chapters 24 and 25 that cause a lot of discussion about who is who. I am glad that we can start with this parable in chapter 24. After coming this far, I hope that you can agree that it is quite clear.

You might be familiar with chapter 24. Jesus mentioned the destruction of the temple in verse 2, and the disciples later asked Him when this stuff was going to happen. Jesus described a lot of things and then we have this parable in verses 45 to 51.

Who then is the faithful and sensible slave whom his master put in charge of his household to give them their food at the proper time? Blessed is that slave whom his master finds so doing when he comes. Truly I say to you that he will put him in charge of all his possessions. But if that evil slave says in his heart, 'My master is not coming for a long time,' and begins to beat his fellow slaves and eat and drink with drunkards; the master of that slave will come on a day when he does not expect him and at an hour which he does not know, and will cut him in pieces and assign him a place with the hypocrites; in that place there will be weeping and gnashing of teeth.

Who is this slave? It is crucial to properly identify him. The clues to his identity are these:

* He is a slave to his Master.
* He is in charge of his Master's household to feed them.
* He expects his Master to return

An unsaved person cannot possibly fit any of these criteria. The unsaved are slaves to the world and to sin, but certainly not to God. Likewise the other two items cannot apply to a person who has not come to the Lord.

Therefore, this slave must be, has to be, a Christian. He is expecting the return of his Master, but his Master isn't due for a while. Instead of being faithful to his responsibility, he thinks he can abuse his fellow slaves and carouse with the world. Eventually the Master surprises the unfaithful slave by returning unexpectedly. There are two possible outcomes in this parable. One is quite good and the other is very unpleasant. The only thing that made the difference in this slave's outcome was his faithfulness or his lack of faithfulness. The issue was not whether he was saved or not saved, but whether he was obedient to carry out his assigned task, which was to feed those entrusted to him.

Now, in saying this, I can understand that the ending of the parable might bother you greatly: *cut him in pieces and assign him a place with the hypocrites; in that place there will be weeping and gnashing of teeth.* Luke 12 has the same parable in verses 42-46, with the same ending, but Luke records some additional words in verses 47 and 48a. *And that slave who knew his master's will and did not get ready or act in accord with his will, will receive many lashes, but the one who did not know it, and committed deeds worthy of a flogging, will receive but few.*

Can you see that the Lord is speaking to us? Do you know your Master's will? If you are not sure of that answer, I can understand; but eventually we need to know the Lord's leading in our lives. An unbeliever certainly cannot know such a thing. When I was young I used to hear sometimes about one who is "backslidden." Do you think this parable might apply? Do you know someone that is a Christian, yet not following Christ, but at the moment is pursuing his own path? I tell you, you are reading a book that is written by such a person. By the Lord's mercy, He allowed me to turn back to Him.

Recall the parable about the forgiven slave, who was thrown into prison and delivered to the torturers because he would not forgive. Jesus concluded that parable by saying (Matthew 18:35) *My heavenly Father will also do the same to you, if each of you does not forgive his brother from your heart.* Does this shake you? I really am not happy about writing this. I want to think that this could not possibly be true. Would the Lord not be reneging on His promise to cleanse us from our sins and to save us? What about "by His stripes we are healed"?

Peter in his first letter referred to that phrase, written by Isaiah (Isaiah 53:5). 1 Peter 2:24 says, *and He Himself bore our sins in His body on the cross, so that we might die to sin and live to righteousness; for by His wounds you were healed.* Yes, Jesus did bear our sins on the cross, and thank the Lord for that! But, as I have been saying, that is not an end to itself. His bearing our sins was for a greater purpose. We are healed by His wounds for a glorious eternal reason that fulfills God's purpose. In this age those two things, His wounds and the cross, give us new life, *so that we might die to sin and live to righteousness.* But what if we do not? Providing for God's people, as in the parable, is living to righteousness; being drunk with the entertainment of the world is not.

Jesus spoke these harsh words to warn us. I have to write (also to myself) what is in the Word. Even if no one has pointed out these things to you, these words have been there all along.

Wise or Foolish

The next parable is at the beginning of Matthew 25, verses 1-13. It is the parable of the ten virgins, another where the less fortunate
five are usually relegated to the status of the unsaved. Please read the parable in your Bible before continuing.

I hope you can more easily recognize that all ten could be representative of the Lord's people. There are two keys points.

Number one, they all have oil, which in scripture typifies the Spirit. That the oil is in their lamps shows that God's Spirit is in their spirit. This is evidenced by Proverbs 20:27, which says, *The spirit of man is the lamp of the Lord, searching all the innermost parts of his being,* and by Romans 8:16 which says, *The Spirit Himself testifies with our spirit that we are children of God.*

Number two, all ten are waiting for the bridegroom. Only God's people could be waiting for their bridegroom. The world certainly is not. This is very much like the identifying clues in the previous parable.

Now, the difference between the two groups of five is singular, five were wise, and five were foolish. If you tell me that the wise are saved and the foolish are unsaved, then I ask you, do you consider yourself to be wise because you opened your heart to the Lord one day?

Having the oil shows that all ten have the Lord. The foolish are foolish because they do not have oil in their **vessels**. Verse three says, *For when the foolish took their lamps, they took no oil with them.* They had oil in their lamps, but that was all they had. They had nothing more in their vessels. This shows us that while they had been regenerated by the Lord in their spirits, the subsequent transformation had not occurred in their souls.

About the wise virgins verse 4 says, *But the prudent took oil in flasks along with their lamps.* Here the NASB uses "flasks". Many, if not most, translations use "vessels". The definition of the Greek word is: a vessel, receptacle, pail, reservoir. The significance is that one of the ways that God sees man is as a vessel to contain Him. 2 Corinthians 4:7a, for example, says, *But we have this treasure in earthen vessels...* Therefore, even though "flask" might be a logical word to use, I like the word "vessel" here, because the parable is not about lamps; it is about us.

Man has a spirit (1 Thessalonians 5:23, Proverbs 20:27), and at the time of our regeneration God, as the Spirit, entered into our spirit. This is not the end, but the beginning of His experience with us and our experience with Him. He wants to move into every corner of our hearts, making His home in our hearts (Ephesians 3:17a). This is what is shown by having oil in the vessels. This is having an abundant portion of the Spirit. This is what made five of the virgins wise. We cannot and dare not claim wisdom in coming to the Lord, **but** let us be wise in allowing the Lord to make His home in us.

As one who was once aligned with the foolish (and pray that I never again will), my wish is that you will be wise, or become wise, so that the door will not be shut for you. Yes, this door to the wedding feast (verse 10) is a door for those who are the Lord's. Verse 10 talks about the foolish going away to buy the needed oil. *And while they were going away to make the purchase, the bridegroom came, and those who were ready went in with him to the wedding feast; and the door was shut.* "But if the oil represents the Spirit, how do you buy that?" To the church in Laodicea the Spirit instructed John to write (verse 3:18), *I advise you to buy from Me gold refined by fire so that you may become rich, and white garments so that you may clothe yourself, and that the shame of your nakedness will not be revealed; and eye salve to anoint your eyes so that you may see.* The saints in that church were told to buy gold, white garments, and eye salve. Oil is not mentioned here, but the principal is the same. These things are not free!

What is the price of these precious items? Maybe you already know. Hopefully, if I have written clearly and if you have received it, you will know that the price is your soul-life. Lose your soul-life to gain the *zoe* life! That should sound familiar!

Is God's word not consistent? It also has continuity. Do not look at scripture here and scripture there, and try to interpret the various passages without the larger context. That is how the church, even while understanding that Christ will reign on earth for a millennium, still teaches that He will break the eastern sky and take us away to a home far away. I find absolutely no continuity in that.

I keep wandering away......let's get back to Matthew. The five wise virgins had bought the oil for their vessels prior to the Groom's arrival. The foolish had not. Yet it had to be bought. I emphasize that it **had to be bought**. But because of being late in making the purchase, the foolish ones missed the wedding feast. The unsaved have no thought of a wedding feast. They have no chance of entering into that enjoyment. All ten of the virgins did have a chance, but some were late in making their purchase. They had not permitted the Spirit to spread into their hearts (fill their vessels).

We all like Romans 8:28. In the chapter on James I mentioned it. *And we know that God causes all things to work together for good to those who love God...* I did not mention what is that "good". God does not promise happy endings for our problems and situations. The good is in the two verses that follow, ending with glorification. *For those whom He foreknew, He also predestinated to become conformed to the image of His Son, so that He would be the firstborn among many brethren; and these whom He predestinated, He also called; and these whom He called, He also justified; and these whom He justified, He also glorified.*

Wow, that sounds wonderful! But...it starts with, *For those whom He foreknew, He also predestinated to become conformed to the image of His Son.* Some are not comfortable talking about predestination, while some do not have a problem. Some do not believe it, and some do. But, even if you believe it, what has been your understanding of it? God's word is very clear here that we have been predestined to be conformed! That means the outcome is certain. We **will** be conformed to the image of God's Son!

That also means that it must happen sooner or later. If we do not submit to the operation of the Spirit in us while we walk this earth, when will it happen? Do you think that at the resurrection we will be automatically conformed to Christ? Do you remember this verse, 1 John 2:28? *Now, little children, abide in Him, so that when He appears, we may have confidence and not shrink away from Him in shame at His coming.*

If we shrink away from Christ at His return, then it must be obvious that we have not abided in Him so that we might be conformed to His image. It will mean that we had not bought the oil, the gold, the white garments, and the eye salve. It will mean that we had preserved our soul-life instead of exchanging it for the *zoe,* eternal, life. And, it will mean that Christ was not able to make his home in our heart.

Do you understand my burden for this book? Surely we want to save the lost, but on the other hand, how many Christians will miss the wedding feast because they have not heard the **whole** gospel? How many do not understand how crucial it is to abide in Christ now, while we are living in the age of grace?

The parables show us that there will not be grace and mercy when this age ends. Do we not appreciate the seriousness of Paul's words to the church in Rome? *But you, why do you judge your brother? Or you again, why do you regard your brother with contempt? For we will all stand before the judgment seat of God. For it is written, "As I live, says the Lord, every knee shall bow to Me, and every tongue shall give praise to God." So then each one of us will give an account of himself to God* (Romans 14:10-12). We usually apply the bowing of the knee to the rebellious sinners, but here Paul mentions it in connection to **our** standing before God!

The question for us, then, is whether we are bowing our knees before the righteous King now, in this life. Consider 2 Corinthians 5:9-10. *Therefore we also have as our ambition, whether at home or absent, to be pleasing to Him. For we must all appear before the judgment seat of Christ, so that each one may be recompensed for his deeds in the body, according to what he has done, whether good or bad.*

The judgment seat is not the Great White Throne judgment that we see in Revelation 20. The Greek word for judgment seat is *bema*, while the word for throne is *thronos*. This judgment seat of Christ is for the believers. It is this judgment that this book addresses, and which is behind all of the warnings to Christians given by Christ and the New Testament writers.

In the previous parable the Lord said that the slave could be either sensible or evil. In this one the difference is between being wise and being foolish. Paul echoes the Lord perfectly in Ephesians 5:15-18. *Therefore be careful how you walk, not as unwise men but as wise, making the most of your time, because the days are evil. So then do not be foolish, but understand what the will of the Lord is. And do not get drunk with wine, for that is dissipation, but be filled with the Spirit.*

Be wise, or be foolish. Fill your vessel by making the most of your time. Be **filled** with the Spirit. If Paul is exhorting the saints in Ephesus in this manner, are we not safe in suggesting that the Lord is likewise in these parables giving a loving warning? The wise virgins did fill their vessels, showing that they did exactly what Paul advocated: Being careful in their walk, making the most of their time, being filled with the Spirit. The unwise virgins did not, and so their vessels were empty. As the Lord's parable suggested, Paul showed us that we can be wise or unwise in our walk in the time that we have in this life.

Luke presents a different parable on the same theme. *Be dressed in readiness, and keep your lamps lit. Be like men who are waiting for their master when he returns from the wedding feast, so that they may immediately open the door to him when he comes and knocks. Blessed are those slaves whom the master will find on the alert when he comes* (Luke 12:35-37a). He concludes in verse 40, *You too, be ready; for the Son of Man is coming at an hour that you do not expect.*

After this Peter asks (verse 41), *Lord, are you addressing this parable to us, or to everyone else as well?* The Lord, as was His way, did not answer directly, but with another parable, and this parable is the one that we covered in the previous section about the faithful and sensible slave who is supposed to provide food to the others. Does that answer the question sufficiently?

Here is another parable.

Good and Faithful Versus Wicked and Evil

We say that we want to hear the Lord tell us, "Well done, good and faithful servant." But that desire also carries with it the possibility that we might not hear those words. But have you ever heard anyone say so? That is what the next parable is about (Matthew 25:14-30), and no doubt you are familiar with it.

Like the last parable, it is comprised of many verses, so I ask that you read the parable before continuing.

Again I have the task of convincing you that all three of the slaves in this parable are the Lord's redeemed, that not one of them is unsaved. In all respects there is no difference among them. Verse 14 says that he *called his own slaves and entrusted his possessions to them.* Is there any possibility that an unsaved person could be the Lord's own slave, or that He would entrust **anything** to that person? I hope you can answer, "of course, not." The next verse says that slaves were given talents according to their ability. There is nothing to suggest a condition of being saved or unsaved. All three start out comparatively equal, differing only in their ability to handle the Lord's resources. Based on their abilities, He gave them varying amounts of His possessions, money according to verse 18.

While the master was away, the slaves had possession of and responsibility for the money. Two made additional money, but one buried his in the ground. When the master returned, he complimented the two who had made money and they were rewarded. To both he said, *Well done, good and faithful slave. You were faithful with a few things, I will put you in charge with many things; enter into the joy of your master.*

For the third slave he did not have any kind words, and it is his punishment that confuses many about who he is...just like the five virgins. But remember that in the beginning of both parables all had the same standing before the Lord. And like the slave that was charged with feeding the household and his fellow slaves (24:45-51), they had the opportunity to be faithful or unfaithful.

The slave in chapter 24 was caught unawares when his master returned unexpectedly. The five foolish virgins did not have oil in their vessels. The lazy slave did nothing with what the Lord had given him. They ended up in similar circumstances. The chapter 24 slave went to a place of weeping and gnashing of teeth, and the lazy slave went to the same place. In the first case it is the place of the hypocrites; in the second it is called outer darkness. It is not mentioned that the five foolish virgins were sent anywhere, but the door was shut and they were left outside of the wedding feast. I can imagine the wailing and teeth gnashing in that case also.

Does this have to mean that they found themselves in hell for eternity? It does not. I will present all of the evidence, but first, let us take a little side trip with the next parable.

Sheep Versus Goats

The last parable of Matthew 25 is one that I am sure you know. Again, it is a long parable (25:31-46), so please read it before continuing.

You might think you understand this one, but allow me to present another view. This view is that the Lord is not talking about us as either sheep or goats. In this parable the Lord is not discussing whether **we** are allowed entry into the kingdom, but whether some among the **nations** will be. Yes, I am talking about the unsaved.

First, look at the timing of this parable. Verse 31 clearly says that the Son of Man will come and sit on His throne. It also says that He will have His angels with Him. Other places say that He will come with His saints, so I, with some others, conclude He will come with both. After all, we will meet Him in the air, right? So, if we are in the air with Him, then it has to follow that we have to be with Him when He comes down to establish His earthly kingdom.

The point is this, we must have already appeared before the judgment seat (*bema*) prior to this, because verse 32 says that He will gather all the nations to himself. If we have already been gathered together with Him in the air, then we cannot again be gathered to Him on the ground.

The second important point is the criteria that distinguish the sheep from the goats. Verses 35 and 36 say, *For I was hungry, and you gave Me something to eat; I was thirsty, and you gave Me something to drink; I was a stranger, and you invited Me in; naked, and you clothed Me; I was sick, and you visited Me; I was in prison, and you came to Me.*

Is there anything in these two verses that requires opening your heart to the Lord or calling on His name to be saved? No! This judgment is based solely on how the nations took care of God's people. To suggest anything else is to change the Lord's parable and put words into His mouth that He did not say! Here is how this parable is usually portrayed:

Since we have experienced the Lord's love in our salvation, we should want to show His love in return, and one way to do that is to love others. Therefore, the Christians are portrayed as sheep in the parable because we will love others out of our love for Christ. So, we are not actually saved by our works, since we were saved by grace to start with.

Can you see how this changes the parable by introducing new "facts?" But, you might ask, "How can unsaved people inherit the kingdom? That goes against everything I have been taught!" But do you not realize that nations are included in the last chapters of the Bible? Revelation 21:24 says, *The nations will walk by its* (the new Jerusalem's) *light, and the kings of the earth will bring their glory into it.* And Revelation 22:2b says, *And the leaves of the tree* (of life) *are for the healing of the nations.*

Who are the kings? Are the kings in Revelation 21 different from the kings in Revelation 20? Revelation 20:4 and 6 talk about those who will reign for a thousand years with Christ. Additionally, in verses 2:26-27 the overcomers are told that they will rule over the nations.

We can see then, that since there are kings and nations (let's just say "people") both during the millennium and after, then there must be something going on that most of us have not been told. If you think that we simply get saved and go to heaven, then there is no way to account for all of that. There is no continuity.

We will get to that, but the point to be made here is that if there are to be people who populate the earth, then they have to come from somewhere, and they must be qualified in some manner. This parable in Matthew 25 gives us an insight.

How are these sheep qualified? They helped, comforted, and sustained God's people during tough times, probably mainly during the tribulation, since they are alive at the Lord's return. Remember that the Lord said, *And whoever in the name of a disciple gives to one of these little ones even a cup of water to drink, truly I say to you, he shall not lose his reward* (Matthew 10:42), and, *For whoever gives you a cup of water to drink because of your name as followers of Christ, truly I say to you, he will not lose his reward* (Mark 9:41). Jesus said "whoever", and I take Him at His word, so all of these "whoevers" must be identified with the sheep in the parable. True to His word then, these who are deemed to be sheep do not lose their reward!

Here is another point. Those in the parable, both the sheep and the goats, express surprise at the Lord's declaration of their caring for Him or of their not caring for Him. They did not understand that doing these things to His own (we are His body, remember), was the same as doing to Him. But, do we not already understand that? Why would we need such an explanation? If we were the sheep in this parable, it does not make sense that we would need to have this explained to us! But, an unregenerated person would not know this. Such a concept would be totally foreign to him. The unsaved definitely would require an explanation, whether he was a sheep or a goat.

You might wonder why I included this parable if it is not about us. That is precisely the reason. Many teach that this parable **is** about us, but leave out the things that I have been showing you in the other parables, things that really **are** for us.

I hope that you found these chapters enlightening. Probably they were challenging. I know that it is not easy to immediately accept something that turns traditional teaching on its head. I assure you, however, that there are many Christians who understand these parables and other sayings by the Lord in the way that I have presented them. All I can ask is that you take this to the Lord. Study the word and allow Him to speak to you.

Mark

There are two portions of Mark's gospel that I want to cover.

How Hard for the Rich

The first is the section in chapter 10 where one came to Jesus asking what he should do to inherit eternal life (verse 10:17; see also Matthew 19). After declaring that he had kept the six things that Jesus mentioned, he balked when he heard that he had to sell his possessions and give to the poor.

Following this Jesus made three statements regarding entering the kingdom of God, verses 23-25. In verse 23 Jesus said, *How hard it will be for those who are wealthy to enter the kingdom of God!* In the next verse He gave a more general statement, *Children, how hard it is to enter the kingdom of God!* And, in verse 25 He again addressed the rich. *It is easier for a camel to go through the eye of a needle than for a rich man to enter the kingdom of God.*

Have you equated entering the kingdom of God with being saved and going to heaven? Paul wrote about inheriting the kingdom of God. He mentioned it to the church in Corinth and to the churches in Galatia. Bear in mind that Paul wrote his letters to churches, not to the unsaved. When he gave this warning, it was to those who should be following the Lord.

Here is what he wrote in his first letter to the saints in Corinth (verses 6:9-10). *Or do you not know that the unrighteous will not inherit the kingdom of God? Do not be deceived; neither fornicators, nor idolaters, not adulterers, nor effeminate, nor homosexuals, nor thieves, nor the covetous, nor drunkards, nor revilers, nor swindlers, will inherit the kingdom of God.* He said to not be deceived! We might think that we are saved, and we might actually **be** saved, but it is possible that we could miss the inheritance, God's kingdom. Prior to these two verses Paul was talking about how the brothers in Corinth should not wrong each other, defraud one another, and take each other to court. We might be brothers in the Lord, but it is **not** an automatic outcome that we inherit the kingdom!

In Galatians 5:19-21 Paul presented a similar, but even longer list of disqualifications, ending with the catch-all *and things like these.* He even said, *of which I forewarn you, just as I* **have** *forewarned you.* Paul had warned the churches previously, a warning to the Christians! What was the warning? The rest of verse 21: *that those who practice such things will* **not** *inherit the kingdom of God.* He had warned the **churches** and was warning them again that they could miss the kingdom!

Now, think about all that you have read in this book, all the warnings, all the parables. Do you still think that being saved has such a simplistic outcome as going to heaven? Be saved and go somewhere? God is concerned about His kingdom! If we want to be a part of it, we have to be qualified!

Keep on the Alert!

Mark 13 is like Matthew 24. Jesus is explained to the disciples things of the future and then closed with an admonition, a warning. Bear in mind that He was speaking to the disciples and to all of us. Here are verses 33-37:

Take heed, keep on the alert; for you do not know when the appointed time will come. It is like a man away on a journey, who upon leaving his house and putting his slaves in charge, assigning to each one his task, also commanded the doorkeeper to stay on the alert. Therefore, be on the alert – for you do not know when the master of the house is coming, whether in the evening, at midnight, or when the rooster crows, or in the morning – in case he should come suddenly and find you asleep. What I say to you I say to all, "Be on the alert!"

If we are all waiting to be called to heaven someday, then why the warning, from the Lord Himself, to stay alert? There must be consequences for not being awake and alert when He returns!

Luke 12:35-37a says it this way (and notice the similarity to the parable of the ten virgins in Matthew 25). *Be dressed in readiness, and keep your lamps lit. Be like men who are waiting for their master when he returns from the wedding feast, so that they may immediately open the door to him when he comes and knocks. Blessed are those slaves whom the master will find on the alert when he comes."* I do not know what more to say about this, except to consider again 1 John 2:28. *Now, little children, abide in Him, so that when He appears, we may have confidence and not shrink back from Him in shame at His coming.*

If we are diligent to perform our assigned tasks (back to Mark), then we can have confidence when our Lord returns. It is the same as performing your duties at work. If the boss comes around the corner, what will he see? If you are doing your job, you can confidently say "hello". But on the other hand, if you are being idle, that would **not** be a good feeling!

Luke

Early in this book I mentioned that the Lord talked at least four times about losing our soul life. Luke mentioned two of those times in 9:24 and 17:33. Here is a fifth occasion, and it opens the discussion to new dimensions.

How to Be a Disciple

If anyone comes to Me, and does not hate his own father and mother and wife and children and brothers and sisters, yes, and even his own life, he cannot be My disciple. Whoever does not carry his own cross and come after Me cannot be my disciple. That was Luke 14:26.

In those other cases Jesus talked about losing our own soul life in order to gain it, but here He expands that to include our family! Thoughts might turn to missionaries, who left everything to go to sometimes threatening environments, but we also ought to think in terms of (not) loving the soul lives of our family members. I believe that is why the Lord in the same sentence mentions the family **and** the disciple. I think not loving the family according to their soul lives is really hard, but that is the requirement.

What does that mean? What does it look like? Hating the soul life of someone does not mean to be a dictator and say "don't do this or that". If your desire is to see someone follow the Lord, then you sense a grieving when something hinders that. That something is nearly always the lust of the flesh or desire of the eyes in some form. But this should also remind us of the splinter in the other's eye and the log in ours. What a dilemma!

May the Lord enlighten our understanding to see this, give us the wisdom to know what to do, and strengthen us to do everything in love.

By Your Endurance

The next verse that I mention provides a hint of what is coming when we look at Revelation. Luke 21:19 says, *By your endurance you will gain your lives.* First, note that the last word, "lives," is the same word that we have discussed before. It is the Greek word *psuche.* Sometimes it is translated as "soul" and other times as "life."

How do we save our souls? We mistakenly believe that the blood of the Lamb does this. Strictly speaking, our Lord's shed blood cleanses us from sin, and that is a wonderful thing! It is also the cost of our redemption. Thank you, Lord, for that! But we have seen many times by now that we gain our *psuche* by what we **do**. It takes grace to "do", because our best efforts can accomplish nothing, but we have to seek the grace by coming to the throne of grace.

Recall the Roman soldier piercing our Lord's side after He died on the cross. What came out? John 19:34 says, *But one of the soldiers pierced His side with a spear, and immediately blood and water came out.*

As stated above, we all know what the blood is for, but what is the significance, even the purpose, of the water? Better than my explanation is God's Word. *Husbands, love your wives, just as Christ also loved the church and gave Himself up for her, so that He might sanctify her, having **cleansed her by the washing of water with the word**, that He might present to Himself the church in all her glory, having no spot or wrinkle or any such thing; but that she would be holy and blameless* (Ephesians 5:25-27).

Our souls have a lot of blemishes, even wrinkles! We can **not** fix ourselves, but God's Word can speak life into us. His Word washes our soul, removing the spots (our impurities) and smoothing out the wrinkles (our oldness). This purifies us and makes us new. This is our complete salvation. Notice what it says in Hebrews 5:13 to 6:1a. *For everyone who partakes only of milk is not accustomed to the word of righteousness, for he is an infant. But solid food is for the mature, who because of practice have their senses trained to* *discern good and evil. Therefore leaving the elementary teaching about the Christ, let us press on to maturity.* The forgiveness of our sins is only the beginning of our race, but it does get us to the starting line. We will **never** in this lifetime get over our need of forgiveness, but the point is that we must **run** our race! The purpose of forgiveness is to run! Hebrews 12:1 echoes the Lord's words from Luke 21:19: *.... let us also lay aside every encumbrance and the sin which so easily entangles us, and let us run with endurance the race that is set before us,...*

Strength to Escape

Speaking of encumbrances, we will continue in Luke 21. *Be on guard, so that your hearts will not be weighted down with dissipation and drunkenness and the worries of life, and that day will not come on you suddenly like a trap; for it will come upon all those who dwell on the face of all the earth. But keep on the alert at all times, praying that you may have strength to escape all these things that are about to take place, and to stand before the Son of Man* (verses 34-36).

The Lord said that we need to **pray** for strength to escape. Why would He say that? Are we not waiting for Him to suddenly return and take us away to our home in the sky? Who needs strength for that? We will get to Revelation later, but notice what the Lord said to the church in Philadelphia. *I know your deeds. Behold, I have put before you an open door which no one can shut, because* ***you have a little power,*** *and have kept My word, and have not denied My name* (Rev 3:8). The saints in that church will escape. Apparently a little is enough, because they were able to keep the Lord's word to persevere (verse 10), and that is the reason given for keeping them from the hour of testing.

What robs us of our strength? It is a weighted down heart. A race is harder to run if we are carrying a loaded backpack. Fatigue will set in fairly soon. In these verses Jesus used two extremes to show us how our hearts can be weighted down. On the one hand there is dissipation and drunkenness. Some versions say "carousing" for "dissipation". These two activities reflect lack of care and concern. On the other hand our hearts can be weighted down with worry and concern. Both hinder our running, robbing us of spiritual strength.

Jesus is warning us that the day of trial can catch us like a trap. Usually the comparison is to a thief, who comes unexpectedly, but this time He talks about getting caught in a snare. You need a keen eye to see a trap. It will be camouflaged, and if you are not paying attention, suddenly you are caught! Worldly pleasures and entertainment will surely cause us to divert our attention and make us unaware. Worrying about the cares of this life will do the same. So the Lord said to *keep on the alert at all times* and to *be on guard!*

Notice the last phrase: *and to stand before the Son of Man.* The escape that the Lord talked about refers to the rapture, I believe. That was the reason for my rhetorical questions at the beginning of this section. I think many will be surprised in a wonderful way, and others surprised in a sorrowful way. There will be more about that when we get to Revelation.

John

There is so much in the gospel according to John that I would love to share with you, but I have to keep to the subject of this book. This will be a very short chapter therefore, because I find only one direct warning, and it is in chapter 15.

Abide in the Vine

We should not talk about John 15 without first taking a look at chapter 14. Chapter 14 has been my favorite for quite a long while. Nowhere does God's Word discuss so thoroughly the means by which our triune God comes to abide in us and so makes His home in our hearts. Sadly this point is diluted or missed altogether because the enemy was able to introduce the teaching of going to a wonderful place after we die, where there will be mansions and all kinds of good stuff, all for us. This is what the gospel has become, and the real meaning of our Lord's message has become confused with stuff picked up from pagan religions.

Suffice it for now to know that chapter 14 is **entirely** about God abiding in us and our abiding in Him. Again, I refer you to a chapter in the Appendix called "About Those Mansions."

Now come to chapter 15 which takes the same discussion of abiding in a new direction. Since we have a mutual abiding with God, there should be some evidence of it. In fact, we should be one with God in accomplishing His purpose on this earth. In the first verse Jesus says very simply, *I am the true vine, and My Father is the vinedresser.* In the first sentence He tells us what He is, and He tells us the Father's role.

Then the Lord immediately goes negative! *Every branch in Me that does not bear fruit, He takes away* (verse 15:2a). It is impossible to apply this statement to anyone who has not received the Lord's precious gift of salvation. The words "in Me" bear this out. This is analogous to the parables about the faithful and unfaithful slaves. The unfaithful slave did not bear any fruit, and so suffered the consequences.

In verse 6 we see the warning repeated, but from a different angle and with the dire consequences spelled out. *If anyone does not abide in Me, he is thrown away as a branch and dries up; and they gather them, and cast them into the fire and they are burned.* "Not Christians!" you say. "Christians can't go to hell!" I agree with you, but there is more to this, and we will look at it in more depth in the chapters on the book of Revelation.

But the main point is that if we abide in the Lord, the negatives will not be an issue. Abiding was a main theme of John's. Recall that it was John who wrote: *Now, little children, abide in Him, so that when He appears, we may have confidence and not shrink away from Him in shame at His coming* (1 John 2:28). So, while the warning is definitely there in chapter 15, let us spend a couple of paragraphs on abiding!

Do not separate the vine from the branches. Do not think that the vine is the vine and the branches are the branches. The branches are in the vine, and the vine is in the branches. The vine is expressed and bears fruit through the branches, and the branches get their life from the vine. This, and only this, produces the fruit that our Father desires.

In verse 2 the issue is whether we bear fruit, but in verse 6 the requirement is changed to abiding in Christ. Verses 4 and 5 are the promises that bridge verses 2 and 6. Both 4 and 5 show that the prerequisite to bearing fruit is abiding in the Lord.

Verse 4 is very clear: *Abide in Me, and I in you. As the branch cannot bear fruit of itself unless it abides in the vine, so neither can you unless you abide in Me.* As we abide in the Lord, He abides in us, and the promise in verse 5a is this: *He who abides in Me and I in him, he bears much fruit.* Do you realize how wonderful this is?! The Lord requires fruit from us, but our responsibility is only to stay in Him!

Revelation

Introduction

The book of Revelation can seem scary to some. There is a lot of imagery and a lot of foreboding scenes. It contains big warnings to the world, but it also has warnings to the church and to individual Christians. Since the latter point is the purpose of this book, I will do my best to stick to that topic, but it will be necessary to delve off course at times in order to help clarify some things.

At the time of writing this chapter I was in a Bible study on Revelation. In this study where there were clear warnings to the inhabitants of the earth, we looked at those warnings in some detail. But there were other warnings that we did not touch. The teachers and leaders did not mention them, and our texts did not mention them. Some are very serious, but they were not discussed. Primarily those warnings are to us, we who say that we follow the Lord.

To me these unmentioned warnings were like the elephant in the room, but I did not feel the Spirit's leading to bring them up in every case. If I failed to speak when He wanted me to speak, then I ask for His forgiveness.

We covered the promises to the overcomers without mentioning that the promises were **only** to the overcomers. Bear in mind that if "A" has a certain outcome, then "not A" must have an alternative outcome, and that is what is missed in discussions about Revelation. In fact, this observation holds true, I think, in almost any fellowship about the New Testament.

I feel I should address the question of who is an overcomer. Many who teach Revelation say that an overcomer is anyone who is saved. To support this they will use the verses that indicate that that our salvation cannot be lost. I wrote in the Preface that I support the idea that once saved, we will not lose out salvation. The trouble is, the warnings to the seven churches make it appear that those who do not overcome will suffer consequences that sure make it seem that their salvation is lost!

This is what the heaven-or-hell gospel will do to you. It boxes you into a corner with no option but to say that everyone who is a Christian is an overcomer. But if that were the case, then why is the Lord making the call for overcomers? What is the point? The fact is that not everyone overcomes. I hope this book has made that very clear according to what Jesus Himself said and what His apostles wrote.

One verse in particular that makes some think that anyone who is a born-again Christians is automatically an overcomer is 1 John 5:4-5. *For whatever is born of God overcomes the world; and this is the victory that has overcome the world – our faith. Who is the one who overcomes the world, but he who believes that Jesus is the Son of God?* That seems rather definitive, does it not? It seems to leave no one out. So, no matter what kind of life I live, I am an overcomer! But then why does the Lord make the point of calling for overcomers in Revelation? First He shows the seven churches the situations and conditions that need to be addressed, then He calls for overcomers to prevail. "But everyone is an overcomer, so never mind." You know I disagree with that last quote!

What do we do with those two verses in 1 John? Am I saying that that the Bible is wrong, that 1 John 5:4-5 is incorrect? I have gone about twenty pages without mentioning context, so it's about time to bring it up again. Chapter 4 provides our context, and it flows on into chapter 5. Remember, chapters were introduced to the Bible much later; John, Paul, and the others did not write their letters in chapters. The subject of these two chapters is overcoming the world and how this is possible because: We are born of God; we are loved by God; we love God; we love the brothers and sisters; and we obey our Father. As verse 4 tells us, the victory is our faith! This overcomes the world.

What is the situation in chapters 2 and 3 of Revelation? We will see false teaching and degradation in the churches (in five of the seven), different kinds of situations, specific situations that require different kinds of overcoming. This is totally different from John's declarations in his first letter.

I will point out one other thing as a cautionary note. In the very same chapter 5 John wrote this (verse 18a): *We know that no one who is born of God sins.* What?! "We know **that** ain't true!" This follows verse 16a, which says *If anyone sees his brother committing a sin*... I'll let you do you own study on that one; I only want to point out that we have to be careful.

We need the whole Bible in order to understand the Bible. In some cases we can read something that sounds rather emphatic, but then find the opposite side of the coin somewhere else. This is **why** we need the whole Bible. We should not dare to think that we understand something based solely on what we are reading at the moment. We can pull verses from here and there without considering their context. I hope that I have not done that; I did my best to avoid it.

Now back to the subject at hand... Revelation is the "end of the story". God's story. His story with man, which started in Genesis. Genesis is not only a description of creation and Noah and Abraham and his descendants. God's purpose is revealed (and hidden) in Genesis. All of history since then leads us to the fulfillment of God's purpose. The more that we understand concerning what God has done and is doing, the better we can understand what He **will** do. Revelation does not exist in a vacuum. It is the fulfillment of God's glorious plan, and this plan has everything to do with us!

That is why I have written this book. If we finish our course, then our involvement and experience in His kingdom will be so much more glorious! Ignoring the warnings will cause loss of this wonderful experience, even some anguish. Now, let us try to tie everything together....

We will start in chapter 2, where we have letters from the Lord to four churches: Ephesus, Smyrna, Pergamum, and Thyatira.

The Tree of Life

The letter to Ephesus (verses 1–7) does not **seem** to have a specific warning, but notice that the promise to the overcoming believer is *to eat of the tree of life which is in the Paradise of God* (verse 2:7). Here is the **implied** warning: If you do not overcome, you do not eat! Right away we have the "A" and "not A" scenario. If the believer overcomes and returns to the Lord as his first love, then the tree of life is at hand. The "not A" is to apparently do everything correctly, but miss the Lord. "Not A" results in a loss.

Does this sound like not much of a big deal – not getting to eat from the tree of life? Think of it this way: If this seems like a small thing to lose, then this puts us in league with Adam, when he ignored God's tree of life. If we ignore the tree of life now, then the Lord is saying that it will be withheld from us later! If we do not care about it now, then later it will be too late to care.

Our desire for the Lord in this age has a certain (meaning "definite") impact later.

The Second Death

The second church in chapter two is Smyrna, verses 8-11. The letter to this church has the first warning that Christians do not like to talk about. The second part of verse 11 says, *He who overcomes will not be hurt by the second death.* This statement causes a lot of squirming among most who try to teach from this book. The "not A", of course, is being hurt by the second death if one does not overcome. How can that be?

Here we have a good example of the inherent problem of the heaven or hell gospel. Some point to verse 2:11 as evidence that we can lose our salvation. Others declare that we are all overcomers because of the Lord's blood, and those that are hurt by the second death obviously are not overcomers, so obviously they were never saved. It, uh, seems so obvious.

It is likely that you know about the second death, which is mentioned only in Revelation. Verse 20:14 says that *death and Hades were thrown into the lake of fire.* The next words explain that the lake of fire **is** the second death: *This is the second death, the lake of fire.* This is very clearly spoken.

In the next chapter verse 21:8 lists the characteristics of a bunch of disqualified people (sort of like us, without Christ) and says, *their part will be in the lake that burns with fire and brimstone, which is the second death."* Again, it is quite clear that the second death is that lake.

I used to think that the second death was being put into the lake of fire, but the Word definitely says that it is the lake itself. This is like realizing that eternal life is not living forever, but it is God Himself. He **is** eternal life, and He puts His life into us!

So now, seeing that the second death is the lake of fire, how is it that a Christian could be hurt by it? I know, that seems contrary to everything that you have been taught, unless you believe that you can lose your salvation. But the Lord Himself spoke those words, so we cannot pretend that they are not in the Bible.

A beautiful aspect of the Bible is that it explains itself. We have to do the seeking and knocking. In this case we can look again at 1 Corinthians 3:13-15. *Each man's work will become evident; for the day will show it because it is to be revealed with fire, and the fire itself will test the quality of each man's work. If any man's work which he has built on it remains, he will receive a reward. If any man's work is burned up, he will suffer loss; but he himself will be saved, yet so as through fire.*

Now notice that Revelation 2:11 says that *he who overcomes will not be **hurt** by the second death.* Thanks to the Lord's speaking through Paul to the church in Corinth, you can see that we **can** be hurt without being killed, without suffering eternal damnation.

For those who noticed, I realize that Paul wrote about works and the materials used in building, but verse 15 of that same third chapter talks about the **person** being saved, but as through fire. It will not be that my works are burned without the fire touching me. The Lord will purify His church, His people. If we build wrongly, then it is because of what is in us. We can take the grace now in this life to be purified (sanctified), or it will happen later. Purification is not an option!

The Sharp Two-Edged Sword

The Lord introduced Himself to the church in Pergamum as *the One who has the sharp two-edged sword* (verse 2:12). The Lord's sword is the Word. In Revelation 1:16 and 19:15 we read that a sharp sword comes out of His mouth. Hebrews 4:12 compares God's word to a two-edged sword. Clearly then, the need of this church is the purely spoken word from God. Ephesians 6:17 tells us that the sword of the Spirit is the word of God. We can see in these verses that God's word (in the aspect of a sword) has various "targets". In Revelation 19 the sword will be used against the nations. In Ephesians 6 the context tells us that it is to be used against our enemy Satan.

Here in this letter we can see that the Sword is needed. Why? The Lord identified two groups within the church that had adopted heretical teachings. The point to be made here is that it must be easier than we might think for false teaching to creep into the church, even something that in our 20/20 hindsight should have been obvious. Verse 14 talks about "the teaching of Balaam", which resulted in Israel's worship of idols and committing spiritual and physical fornication. I do not care to speculate on what form that teaching took within the church, but it should be a clear warning to us that if we are not grounded in the Word, we are susceptible to believing things that are not true.

The other teaching was that of the Nicolaitans. There are various theories about the Nicolaitans, and it is not my intent to pick one. What we need to see, though, is that the church in Ephesus was commended by the Lord for hating the deeds of the Nicolaitans. Even after scolding that church for leaving their first love, it was still an important matter to bring up. *Yet this you do have, that you hate the deeds of the Nicolaitans, which also I hate* (verse 2:6).

What was first "deeds", as described in the letter to the church in Ephesus, had progressed to a teaching, as seen in the letter to Pergamum. The Lord hates the deeds of this group, and Ephesus was one with the Lord in this. But Pergamum apparently did not take a stand, and eventually a system of error was allowed to evolve.

How do we guard ourselves from the same? Do you believe things because you have been taught them from a pulpit all your life? Can you confirm various teachings by the Word? The Word is the only remedy. We need to be able to confirm a teaching by the Word or reject it as man's teaching. Have you been challenged by this book to do that? Whether you can agree with what I have written or whether you cannot, I hope that the basis for your agreement or nonagreement is your reading the Word.

Until the End

Look at Revelation 2:18-27. The letter to the church in Thyatira starts by commending the church (verse 19): *I know your deeds, and your love and faith and service and perseverance and that your deeds of late are greater than at first.*

Then verse 20 begins: *But....* There is the tolerance of an evil situation in Thyatira, and the One *who searches the minds and hearts* gives a stern warning to those in the church who compromised with that situation: *I will give to each one of you according to your deeds.*

There were saints in that church who did not touch the evil. To those the Lord made a promise, but they had some conditions to satisfy (verses 25-26a): *Nevertheless what you have, hold fast until I come. He who overcomes, and he who keeps My deeds until **the end**....* To this church and to the church in Laodicea the promise relates to reigning with the Lord. To Thyatira John wrote (verses 26b-27), *to him I will give authority over the nations.* In resurrection Jesus received His Father's authority because He overcame. Likewise, if we expect to receive authority from Christ, then we also need to overcome.

This sounds a bit like the parables of the faithful and unfaithful servants in Matthew 25 and Luke 19. Those who are faithful will be put over various cities. In Luke 19:24 the alternative is to take away from the worthless slave that which he had been given. Maybe that does not seem so bad, but in Matthew 25:28-30 the penalty is that **plus** being thrown into the outer darkness! With the understanding of going to heaven or hell, the outer darkness, of course, has to be hell, and therefore the worthless slave could never have been a real born again Christian. This is the kind of conclusion that the simplistic gospel forces, but as I explained when covering the parables, there is no difference among the slaves except faithfulness or the lack of it. It is also important to note that there is no difference in **expectation** from the Lord!

Faithfulness, i.e., being an overcomer, is a requirement for the kingdom. Being in the outer darkness means remaining outside the kingdom. That is what is at stake here, not heaven or hell. While the faithful are reigning with Christ on this earth, those who would not be faithful will have to spend a period of time, perhaps up to a thousand years, getting the transformation that was ignored during this much shorter lifetime. We will see more about this in the next letter.

Walk in White

The Lord next addresses the church in Sardis. The Lord had told the saints in Thyatira that their latter works were better than their earlier. The opposite is the case in Sardis. Verse 3:2 says, *Wake up, and strengthen the things that remain, which were about to die.* Based on their prior works, this church had a reputation of being living, but the current reality was the opposite. But the Lord still had a few in Sardis who continued to walk with the Him. He described them this way: *But you have a few people in Sardis who have not soiled their garments* (verse 4a).

Do you believe that what we do as Christians in this life has a bearing on how glorious our experience will be in the next age? Our choices might suggest that we think it does not matter. I do not choose the Lord's side all the time, and I'm writing this book! Who am I to talk, or write? But the Lord is merciful (praise Him), and we can turn to Him (**boldly** to the throne of grace!) to receive mercy.

The Lord continues, referring to those who have not soiled their garments: *and they will walk with Me in white, for they are worthy.* Will you wear the glorious garment in the next age? Walk with the Lord in this one!

Now notice the word "worthy". It is so very true that only the Lamb is worthy to take the scroll in Chapter 5 of Revelation, but He is looking for worthy saints who will **qualify** to rule with Him in the next age. He is looking for overcomers. It is not enough to say that we all overcome in Christ. Surely we cannot be overcomers apart from Christ, but we do not automatically get that title because we can claim the Lord's name. If that were true, there would be no need for Him to dictate such warnings in His letters to the churches!

That is why the Lord provides incentives, so to speak. In verse 5 we see three. *He who **overcomes** will thus be clothed in white garments; and I will not erase his name from the book of life, and I will confess his name before My Father and before His angels.*

Even after writing all of these pages, I am not ready to expound on this verse. Read it again and let it sink in. Let the negative implications sink in: He who does not overcome will **not** wear the white garments (which signify righteousness and purity), will **not** have his name in the book of life, and the Lord will **not** confess his name before our Father.

Recall the parable in Luke 12:42-48. It starts out like this: *And the Lord said, "Who then is the faithful and sensible steward, whom his master will put in charge of his servants, to give them their rations at the proper time?* Pertaining to that guy, walking in white garments means to take care of those who are his responsibility. If he is doing this when the Lord returns, then he will continue to wear the white garments, his name will not be erased from the book of life, and our Lord will confess that servant's name to the Father. Therefore, according to the letter to the church in Smyrna, he will not be hurt by the second death.

Am I misapplying the Lord's word? Am I mixing apples and oranges? Remember what will happen to that servant if the Lord finds him abusing those that he should be caring for. *The master of that slave will come on a day when he does not expect him and at an*

*hour he does not know, **and will cut him in pieces, and assign him
a place with the unbelievers.*** Cut in pieces?! Assigned a place with
the unbelievers?! Is this not serious? What does it mean?

These are the Lord's words. They are in **your** Bible, but what
do you think about those words when you read them?

Word of Perseverance

Now we come to the church that everyone likes. The Lord liked
this church, the church of brotherly love. For many, many years I
thought that was why the Lord commended them, but "love" is not
mentioned in the letter to that church. What the Lord does say is this
(verse 3:8): *I know your deeds. Behold, I have put before you an
open door which no one can shut, because you have a little power,
and have kept My word, and have not denied My name.* It is because
of their **perseverance** that the Lord will keep them from the hour of
testing (verse 10).

The warning to this church is to not lose what they have. Verse
11 says, *I am coming quickly; hold fast what you have, so that no
one will take your crown.* Even if we are running the race as best we
can, the danger is in not finishing. As it says in Hebrews 12:1b-2a,
*And let us run with endurance the race that is set before us, fixing
our eyes on Jesus, the author and perfecter of faith.* We will never
be finished with our perfecting process on this side of the grave, so
let us keep running, dear saints, until we receive all that our Father
has ordained for us.

No Coat Tails

The seventh and last letter was written to Laodicea. The well
known warning to this church is in verse 3:16: *So because you are
lukewarm, and neither hot nor cold, I will spit you out of my mouth.*
The Lord was not finished. He told the saints there to buy three
things from Him: gold, white garments, and eye salve (verse 18).
The first two have references to letters written to the other churches.

The gold that Christ has to sell is the real riches; the church in Smyrna had this. The white garments are for the proper clothing; Sardis had some saints who walked with the Lord in white garments. The third item to buy was eye salve. Imbedded within verse 18 is the warning to not allow the shame of our nakedness to be revealed. What does this mean? Also, what did the Lord mean when He said that He would spit them out? I think the two are related, even two aspects of the same thing.

There are differing understandings on when the Lord makes His return to the earth, but most believe that He will return at the end of the great tribulation and set up His kingdom on earth. I think this is what the Bible tells us. That being the case, most who agree with that view also believe that the church in Philadelphia represents those saints whom the Lord will remove from the earth before the tribulation. I will try not to confuse you, but I have to lay some groundwork for the next point.

Again, the Lord told those in Philadelphia, *Because you have kept the word of My perseverance, I also will keep you from the hour of testing, that hour which is about to come upon the whole world* (verse 3:10). The church in Philadelphia gets this exemption because of their perseverance. The question then is, does Laodicea get a pass? Do they get to ride the coat tails of Philadelphia? It seems that the answer is a big NO, but the Lord does call on the Christian to repent and overcome the situation.

What does it mean to be spit out? I strongly believe that it means to pass through the great tribulation. Remember that this church was neither hot nor cold; tribulation will change that in a hurry.

What about being naked? That is clearly related to not having white garments to wear, which seems here to indicate not having a resurrected body. While the Philadelphia saints are spared the terrible ordeal because of their faithful endurance, the others will still be here with this body of corruption, totally exposed for their wrong attitude of being rich.

Yes, I think that both being spit out and being exposed are the same judgment, having the same result of being left here ("left behind") for the trial of the tribulation.

The saints in Laodicea did not see their real condition, and neither could they see what the Lord wanted to show them regarding Himself and God's purpose. Verse 17 shows us that they were wretched and miserable and poor and blind and naked. The water of life is free (Revelation 22:17; cf Isaiah 55:1), but these other items have a cost. That cost is our soul life, as discussed in other chapters. The more that we give to the Lord, the more of Himself He gives to us. He has some precious things for sale, and He is looking for buyers. Those buyers are the overcomers.

But all is not lost! Verse 3:19 shows us the Lord's true heart. *Those whom I love, I reprove and discipline.* Even if we find ourselves left here during that awful time, the Lord has told us that we will not be without His love. We can accept the Lord's discipline during this age of grace, so it is better to do that.

I said before that transformation is not an option. It is actually for our benefit to have that last chance to become hot for the Lord, and get the transformation that might have been neglected.

But the Lord does not wish for us to get the transformation the hard way. The rest of verse 19 says, *Therefore be zealous and repent.* It is not too late to repent. Remember, repentance is the reason for the warnings! We can do it now, and spare ourselves the hardship.

Late Warnings

There remain two very specific warnings in Revelation that present a problem to many who read it. The reason for the problem is that 1) the warnings come so very late in the sequence of events that make up the great tribulation, and 2) there is that prevalent teaching that all Christians will be taken from the earth before the start of the great tribulation.

It is going to be difficult to examine these without a deeper look at Revelation, even though such a study is not the purpose of this book. I will do my best to keep to the point.

When the sixth bowl of God's wrath is poured out (verse 16:12), we have the first late warning (verse 16:15). *("Behold, I am coming like a thief. Blessed is the one who stays awake and keeps his clothes, so that he will not walk about naked and men will not see his shame.")* Does this warning sound familiar? It should, because we have seen these same words in the letters to the churches in Sardis and Laodicea in chapter 3 of Revelation. To Sardis (verse 3:3b): *Therefore if you do not wake up, I will come like a thief, and you will not know at what hour I will come to you.* To Laodicea (verse 3:18): *I advise you to buy from Me ...... white garments so that you may clothe yourself, and that the shame of your nakedness will not be revealed.* In addition, the reference in 16:15 to keeping ones clothes refers also to the letter to Sardis, verse 3:4, *But you have a few people in Sardis who have not soiled their garments...* Remember, the unrepentant in Laodicea do **not** ride the coat tails of Philadelphia! Why else would this warning be there in chapter 16?

But there are **two** late warnings... I have to set the stage for the second late warning. Towards the end of chapter 16 there is a very brief statement about God's judgment on Babylon: *Babylon the great was remembered before God, to give her the cup of the wine of His fierce wrath* (verse 19b). Notice when this judgment occurs. This is in verse 19; the seventh and final bowl is poured out in verse 17.

After that brief declaration of Babylon's judgment the next two chapters are devoted to describing Babylon, the reason for its severe judgment, and details of its destruction. In the midst of all of this, in verse 18:4, we suddenly have this last late warning: *I heard another voice from heaven, saying, "Come out of her, my people, so that you will not participate in her sins and receive of her plagues.* Again, why would this warning be here if there was not the possibility of us still being around? This is after the seventh bowl is poured out! God is saying, "You really do not want to be around for this!"

God really does want the saints in Laodicea and all of the other churches to repent and avoid this, but human nature, even in "saved" humans, can be perplexing. Remember, I was in that boat, and I hope that I will never again be there. I am looking every day to the Lord for His keeping power. I thank Him for His mercy.

I do not think that these late warnings actually occur late in time. We have the warnings now. They are in His word already. The Lord in His mercy is telling us now what are the dire consequences of being alive at the end of this age but not being an overcomer. He is telling us now in the first late warning, as He has already told us over and over, to be awake and watchful.

This brings me to something I skipped when covering Peter's letters. I skipped it because you need the background of Revelation so that you can grasp my explanation. Here is a well known passage from 2 Peter 3: *But by His word the present heavens and earth are being reserved for fire, kept for the day of judgment and destruction of ungodly men. ...But the day of the Lord will come like a thief, in which the heavens will pass away with a roar and the elements will be destroyed with intense heat, and the earth and its works will be burned up. Since all these things are to be destroyed in this way, what sort of people ought you to be in holy conduct and godliness, looking for and hastening the coming of the day of God, because of which the elements will melt with intense heat!* (verses 7,10-12).

Most likely you have the understanding that these verses describe what will happen at the end of the thousand year reign. Doesn't this describe the destruction of this earth, so that there can be a new earth? But, notice the question that Peter asks (many translations have a question mark at the end of verse 12). *What sort of people ought you to be in holy conduct and godliness, looking for and hastening the coming of the day of God(?)* If all of this fire is for the end that age, what relevance does that have for how we live today? I will try to persuade you that this event will take place during the tribulation, and, like the late warnings in Revelation 16, Peter is saying you don't want to be here when that happens! Verse 12 associates this terrible event with the day of God, the day of the Lord in Verse 10. As far as I know, this Day belongs to the end of this age, which we ought to be *looking for and hastening*. Verse 7 also places this at the end of this age: *But by His word the present heavens and earth are being reserved for fire, kept for the day of judgment and destruction of **ungodly men**.* Look at Revelation 6:14. The sixth seal has just been broken (verse 6:12), and verse 14 says, *The sky was split apart like a scroll when it is rolled up.*

Now look at Revelation 16:8-9a. Chapter 16 describes the pouring out of the 7 bowls of wrath on the earth and the people. The fourth bowl does this: *The fourth angel poured out his bowl upon the sun, and it was given to scorch men with fire. Men were scorched with fierce heat...*

I say that this sounds like 2 Peter 3:7. *But by His word the present heavens and earth are being reserved for fire, kept for the day of judgment and destruction of ungodly men.* When is the destruction of ungodly men? It is at the end of this age!

Revelation has more to say about this. Chapter eight describes the first four trumpets. Here is verse 8:7: *The first sounded, and there came hail and fire, mixed with blood, and they were thrown to the earth; and a third of the earth was burned up, and a third of the trees were burned up, and all the green grass was burned up.* I realize that this describes "only" a third being impacted, but verses 16:8-9 are more general and will scorch the rest.

Isaiah wrote about all of this, in chapters 24 and 34. In chapter 24 he wrote of heat and shaking (among other things), and in chapter 34 he mentioned the sky being rolled up like a scroll (referenced by Hebrews 1:12). The entirety of Isaiah 24 describes God's judgment at the end of this age. You can see select verses in the Appendix, but verse 6 is one I want you to see. *Therefore, a curse devours the earth, and those who live in it are held guilty.*

Therefore, the inhabitants of the earth are burned, and few men are left. Chapter 34, verse 4a, reads, *And the host of heaven will wear away, and the sky will be rolled up like a scroll...* Traditional teaching(s) with the idea of going away to heaven, or this earth being wiped out and replaced with another earth (still heaven, somehow), want to place the verses in 2 Peter 3 between the millennium and the new earth, but Revelation places all these dreadful events squarely in the tribulation. Isaiah's descriptions, referenced by Hebrews 1 and 2 Peter 3, match Revelation's descriptions. Again, we have to pay attention to the context. In this case the context is broad, encompassing the entire revelation of God's plan in His Word.

Jesus the Christ is coming as a thief. This means, as the Lord Himself has said, that it will be without warning. Whoever is watchful, whoever is walking with Him in white, whoever is taking care of the Lord's own (that parable in Luke 12), will be ready when that moment comes. Others will be as John described in 1 John 2:28, shrinking *away from Him in shame at His coming.*

Conclusion

I appreciate that you have stayed with me until this last chapter. I do not know what it was like to have read this book with the go-to-heaven understanding that most Christians have. The purpose of this book is to sound a warning, and warnings by their nature do not sound pleasant. With that in mind, I hope that I succeeded in making this book as easy to read as was possible.

As much as the unsaved need to come to Christ, Christians also need to remain in Him. This is not a once-is-enough life. Jesus did not present the gospel in that way. He talked about being worthy, about not looking back, and about losing our soul life. He talked about being watchful and not falling asleep. Paul, in his own way, addressed these things in his letters. He didn't use the same words, but he said the same thing. He also added the concept of running a race. He was one with the Lord, and his speaking and writing reflected it.

So, while some might interpret Jesus' parables according to traditional thought, and so minimize the responsibility (our responsibility) that the Lord was illustrating, the epistles are full of "if". We see also in Revelation a different kind of speaking from the Lord in chapters 2 and 3. No more parables, no more stories. He is looking for overcomers in the churches.

One point remains that I want to make clear. I have mentioned a couple of times that I do not believe that a Christian can lose the salvation that he obtained by his profession of Jesus Christ as his Savior. I firmly believe that the Lord is clear on this, and the rest of the New Testament does not differ. If that is the case, how can all of this fit together? How can one not lose his salvation and yet suffer consequences from not heeding the New Testament warnings that have been covered in this book?

Take another look at John 1:12. *But as many as received Him, to them He gave the right to become children of God, even to those who believe in His name.* Have you received Him? Do you believe in the name of our Lord Jesus? If you have been born again, then become **full grown**. You have the **right** to become a child of God.

Some translations use "power". The Greek word is *exousia*. KJV translates this word as "right" only two times. In other places the KJV uses "power" 69 times and "authority" 29 times! Either way, are you exercising your **right**, and are you utilizing the **power** that we now have, to become a son of God?

The question is not merely whether we are saved, but do we take advantage of the salvation that now is available to us? Are we being saved not only from the death penalty of our sins, but are we being saved from our fallen nature? Are we being transformed into His image? This is exactly why Paul wrote *work out your salvation with fear and trembling* (Philippians 2:12b). If this salvation is a once-and-done deal, then why would he write such a thing?

Recall that some of the Lord's parables involved a wedding and a wedding feast. We, as the church, His bride, will be with Him with great joy and rejoicing. What if the Lord is saying that we could miss that? The Lord did His best to show us that we have to be faithful, we have to be watchful, and we have to endure. All of the verses are in this book, so please consider.

What about that place that the Lord calls the outer darkness? He clearly stated that some will find themselves there, with the hypocrites. I did not cover this fully, but now I will. Who are the hypocrites? What are they? The origin comes from the acting stage, as many know. But most consider only the aspect of talking one way and behaving another. But if you read again the places where Jesus called the Pharisees hypocrites, He was primarily calling them actors! He called them *whitewashed tombs which on the outside appear beautiful, but inside they are full of dead men's bones and all uncleanness* (Matthew 23:27). This is religion! Religion allows us to put up a good front without dealing with our fallen nature. This is absolutely contrary to the gospel.

The Jewish nation will pass through the great tribulation, and I think some Christians will also. Consider again the evil slave in Matthew 24:45-51. What does the Lord say will happen to him? *The master of that slave will come on a day when he does not expect him and at an hour which he does not know and will cut him in pieces and assign him a place with the hypocrites; in that place there will be weeping and gnashing of teeth.* He will find himself with the actors! The Lord came, and that slave was not abiding in Christ, not paying attention, and not ready. Surely that will be cause for much "weeping and gnashing of teeth."

Therefore I see two conclusions for us who have been saved, but have not allowed the Lord to lead us into full salvation: either enduring the tribulation or spending a good part (if not the whole) of the next age, the kingdom age, in an unpleasant situation. I think it primarily depends on whether we are alive at the end of this age, when the Lord gathers the faithful (Philadelphia vs Laodicea), or whether we are already passed from this life. The Lord, of course, will sort it all out, but the warnings are clearly before us.

In the end God restores all things, including, I believe, any of us who did not allow His discipline in this age. Our salvation is not lost, but because we would not be transformed into His image in this life (2 Corinthians 3:18), we will have to go through something in the next age.

The go-to-heaven gospel cannot account for these things. That says the outcome of our life on this earth is either going to heaven or going to hell. With that view, there can be only two opinions related to the five foolish virgins or to the lazy servant who hid his talent. Either they lost their salvation, or they were never saved to begin with. Nearly all Bible studies that I have seen take the latter view. I hope that I have adequately shown that there is another possible outcome.

Please try to consider these things without the influence of traditional teaching. Remember, there are no mansions in John 14:2! If you have not yet read that article in the Appendix, now is the time. It immediately follows this chapter.

I remind you of the parable in Matthew 18 where one slave did not forgive the small debt of another, even though he had received from his king forgiveness of a large debt. Here are the last two verses of that parable (18:34-35): *And his lord, moved with anger, handed him over to the torturers until he should repay all that was owed him. My heavenly Father will also do the same to you, if each of you does not forgive his brother from your heart.* The point that I am making here is that there is an end to the punishment. There is an "until". We have no idea how that will play out (and know that I am not suggesting purgatory), but it is my goal to not have firsthand knowledge of it!

I leave you with two verses. 2 Corinthians 6:1 and 1 John 2:28. I am going to run them together. *We also urge you not to receive the grace of God in vain. Now, little children, abide in Him, so that when He appears, we may have confidence.*

We have a race that we need to finish. We can do this with each other and in His grace!

Brothers and sisters, finish well.

Appendices

About Those Mansions

Two Words For "Word"

Making Pearls

Faith and Righteousness, Paul and James

Listing of Scriptures

About Those Mansions

First off I will tell you now, there are no mansions in John 14:2. Some already realize this, and some versions of the Bible do not use that unfortunate word, opting for "dwelling places," "rooms," or "abodes." But, if we do not get mansions, then what do we get? Even that question completely misses the point that Jesus was making. He was not referring even a little bit to what we get to live in for eternity. He was not saying that there are many dwelling places for us, but that there are many dwelling places for God, which **are** us!

We are God's dwelling places! You know that, of course, but for some reason the church has not applied that concept in John 14.

How can I be so sure? Let's start with the word that was translated as mansions in the KJV. The Greek word is *mone*, pronounced *mo-nae*. This word is used only one other time in the entire New Testament, and that happens to be in the same chapter! Verse 23 is where Jesus said, *If anyone loves Me, he will keep My word; and My Father will love him, and We will come to him and make Our abode with him.* So, we have one word that is translated (in KJV) as abode in verse 23, but as mansions in verse 2. Does that not seem arbitrary? Other versions use other words in verse 2, as mentioned above, but you can tell from their footnotes that the traditional understanding is that these dwelling places are for us, rather than for God.

Another point concerns the phrase *"in My father's house."* Why is that understood to be heaven? The New Testament is very clear that **we, the church,** are God's house, His spiritual house. But in this one verse, His house suddenly is transferred to heaven, with no consideration of the greater truth and greater context.

Here are just a few of the many verses about God's dwelling place.

1 Corinthians 3:17b - *For the temple of God is holy, and that is what you are.*

191

2 Corinthians 6:16 - *...For we are the temple of the living God; just as God said, "I will dwell in them and walk among them; and I will be their God, and they shall be my people.*

Ephesians 2:21-22 - *In whom the whole building, being fitted together, is growing into a holy temple in the Lord, in whom you also are being built together into a dwelling of God in the Spirit.*

1 Timothy 3:15b - *The household of God, which is the church of the living God, the pillar and support of the truth.*

So, we have a misunderstanding of Jesus' words based on the word mansions and on the non-New Testament idea of heaven being God's house. But didn't Jesus say that He was going away to prepare a place for us? Again, the idea that Jesus went away to heaven to build nice houses for us does not fit the context of the chapter, and it has nothing to do with God's divine revelation in the New Testament.

There is actually an antecedent to Jesus' speaking on this subject. In John 12:24 He said, *Truly, truly, I say to you, unless a grain of wheat falls into the earth and dies, it remains alone; but if it dies, it bears much fruit.* Jesus said that one grain, Himself, will produce many other identical grains. He was the one unique grain on the earth at the time. Likewise, when He spoke those words in John 14 He was the one unique tabernacle of God on the earth (John 1:14). Through His death and resurrection many more tabernacles of God (us!) will be produced. He would not remain forever as God's only habitation. **This** is what He would have told us! If it were not true that we would also become dwelling places of God in spirit (Ephesians 2:22), He would have told us!

Jesus actually told us where He was going and where He wants to bring us. The answer is in verse 6: *no one comes **to the Father**....* Does coming to the Father have to mean a change in location, i.e. heaven? I do not think so, of course.

That response in verse 6 came after this exchange in verses 3 to 5. *"If I go and prepare a place for you, I will come again and receive you to Myself, that where I am, there you may be also. And you know the way where I am going." Thomas said to Him, "Lord,*

we do not know where You are going, how do we know the way?"
Then Jesus said to him, "I am the way, and the truth, and the life; no
one comes to the Father but through Me."
When is it that Jesus would come again and receive us to
Himself? Maybe He already has!
Let us jump to verse 28. *You heard that **I said to you**, "I go*
away, and I will come to you." When did Jesus say that? Clearly
this refers back to verse 3. Referring to that previous statement, He
said, *Now I have told you **before** it happens, so that **when it***
***happens**, you may believe.* Helping our belief is related to this age,
when faith is required. We will cover verses 28 and 29 again, but I
mention them now to help **your** belief, to help **you** to understand
the divine revelation as it was meant to be.

How could we hope to live the Christian life if the Lord's going
and returning have not already transpired? Why should James and
Peter have to wait 2000 years for the first resurrection in order to be
received by the Lord or received to Him? The answer is that they
did have to wait a little while, until after the Lord's resurrection,
which is also mentioned in John 14.

What about the last part of verse 6.....the part about Jesus being
the only way to heaven? Oh, wait. It doesn't say that, does it? But I
have heard preachers on radio and television and others rephrase the
verse in that way. Probably you have been taught to understand it in
that way. Why do we not understand that Jesus is talking about right
now? Through Him I **have** come to the Father!

Do you need more evidence? Look at Ephesians 2:18. *For*
through Him we both (Jews and gentiles) *have our access in one*
*Spirit **to the Father**.* This is practically the same verse as John 14:6!
John 14:6 says "through Me", and Ephesians 2:18 says "through
Him" and "in one Spirit". Both verses say "to the Father"! Do you
think that Ephesians 2 is for the bye-and-bye? Let me be bold and
assume that you do not. And I say that neither is John 14 for some
later time.

Jesus said that He **is** the way, the truth, and the life. He is my
way right now. He is my truth today. He is my life. In Him I have

access right now to my Father. I have come to my Father, and He has come to me. No waiting!

Consider this. At the end of chapter 13 Jesus had just told Peter that he would deny Jesus. Then the Lord's next words were, "Do not let your heart be troubled." I ask you, what would bring comfort to Peter's heart: that he would have a nice house after he dies, or that the triune God will make His home in Peter's heart? For me the answer is easy, and I hope to persuade you of the same.

Now I will show you that the rest of chapter 14 is Jesus' **explanation** of how he planned to come to us and how this relates to our being the abodes of our Father's house.

First, Jesus showed us His relationship to the Father in verses 7 and 9-11. Verse 7 says, *If you had known Me, you would have known My Father also; from now on you know Him, and have seen Him.* Verse 9 says, *He who has seen Me has seen the Father.* In both verses 10 and 11 He declared, *I am in the Father, and the Father is in Me.*

After explaining His relationship with the Father, Jesus began to show His relationship to the Spirit in verse 16, calling Him another Helper, but also saying in verse 17, *but you know Him because He abides with you and will be in you.*

Notice the tense of Jesus' verbs in the last two paragraphs. Regarding the Father, He says, *from now on* (starting now) *you know Him* (present tense) *and have seen Him* (present perfect). Who have the disciples known? Jesus, of course! Who have they seen? Also Jesus! Regarding the Spirit, He told the eleven (Judas has left) that they already know Him, because He was already abiding with them. Again, who do they know? The answer is Jesus! Furthermore, the one who was already abiding **with** them, whom they already knew, would be **in** them!

In this Jesus told His disciples **how** He was coming to them, as promised in verse 3. He would be coming to them as the Spirit. Then later He said (verse 18), *I will not leave you as orphans; I will come to you.* Finally, He explained how it is that we are in the Father in verse 20: *In that day you will know that I am in My Father, and you in Me, and I in you.* In which day? A day far off into the future? No! In the day that He, as the Spirit and with the Father, came into us, we were able to know that **we** are in Christ and in the Father! For the disciples this was on the day of Christ's resurrection. Chapter 20 covers this. Verse 20:22 reveals Jesus breathing upon them and saying, *Receive the Holy Spirit.* The disciples were, and we are, in the Father, and verse 6 is realized!

Lastly, we come to verse 23, the verse where we see the second usage of this word for abode. *Jesus answered and said to him, "If anyone loves Me, he will keep My word; and My Father will love him, and We will come to him and make Our abode with him.* Once again, this promise is for our life in this age. The many abodes in verse 2 are the same abodes that God indwells in verse 23. This is the church!

I think this is what Jesus meant when He said, *If it were not so, I would have told you.* If He was going to be the Father's only tabernacle, or abode, then Jesus would have told us that. The first chapter of John's gospel tells us, *And the Word became flesh and dwelt* (tabernacled) *among us, and we saw His glory, glory as of the only begotten from the Father, full of grace and truth.*

While at first Jesus was the Father's only begotten, the goal was (Romans 8:29) to become the firstborn among many brothers! So now, which makes more sense: "I would have told you if you weren't getting mansions," or "I would have told you if the Father did not intend to make His abode in you?" After having just told Peter the he was going to betray his Lord (verse 13:38), which makes more sense? "That's okay, you will get a nice big house after you die," or "God's wants to make His home in your heart?" Which better fits the revelation of God's New Testament economy? Which fits the context of the rest of chapter 14?

I hope you can see now, that the entirety of chapter 14 of John's gospel has to do with our relationship in Christ to the triune God. To apply the first six verses to future events dismisses the context of the chapter. Four times in this chapter Jesus said that He would come to us. One of those times He said "We", including the Father. Do we get to pick and choose whether He meant a future event on one case and a present day event in another?

The other two times that Jesus said He is coming to us are verses 18 and 23. Verse 18: *I will not leave you as orphans; I will come to you.* Look at the context surrounding this verse. Jesus had just finished telling the disciples that the Holy Spirit would abide in them (verse 17), so does He suddenly change gears in verse 18 and talk about something way in the future? ....and then return to the present in verses 19-21?

Here is the last part of verse 23, which says the same thing as verse 21. *...My Father will love him, and We will come to him and make Our abode with him.* This results in either all four verses being about future events or verse 3 is future, verse 18 present, verse 23 present, and verse 28 future. How confusing!

Remember, Jesus said four times that He is coming to us. If I have proven that three of those times are for this present time, can you begin to see that verse 3 might also be for the present?

But here is the trap! Verse 29 says, *Now I have told you before it happens, so that **when** it happens, you may believe.* Jesus told the disciples that He was going away and coming back, so that they would believe when it happened. What good would that do if Jesus had been referring to His second coming? Jesus wants us to believe now! Therefore His coming in chapter fourteen (all of it) has to be for the present age!

The reality of this became known to the eleven after Christ's resurrection. Again, John 20:22 says, *He breathed on them and said to them, "Receive the Holy Spirit."* This was the fulfillment of John 14 in their lives, as it also is to be fulfilled in ours.

But you might point out that the second part of verse 28 says, *If you loved me, you would have rejoiced because I go to the Father, because the Father is greater than I.* Then verse 29 follows with, *Now I have told you before it happens, so that when it happens, you may believe.* "Aha! Didn't the disciples see Jesus ascend to heaven in Acts 1:9? Does that not prove that verse 3 is for the future return of Christ?" As I pointed out before, the Lord's going and returning preceded the event in Acts 1:9. Remember that when Mary Magdalene saw the Lord, He told her not to touch Him because He had not yet ascended to the Father (John 20:17). (NASB phrased it as "stop clinging," but every other translation that I checked said something like "do not…") But John 20:17 continues, the Lord saying, *But go to My brethren and say to them, "I ascend to My Father and your Father, and My God and your God."* He has just told Mary that He was going, as He said in John 14:3. When did He return? Later that same day (verse 20:19)! And we know that He had gone to the Father by this time, because He allowed the disciples to touch Him, and because He dispensed the Holy Spirit into them, completely in accord with what He said would happen in chapter 14!

Recently I was surprised by a suggestion that Jesus' breathing on the disciples was a symbolic act, and that He did not ascend to the Father until 40 days later, as described in chapter 1 of Acts. This understanding results from the traditional understanding of the first three verses of John 14 and not understanding that verse 29 designates those same verses to our believing in this age.In that bible study I explained the above reasons to show that Jesus had indeed gone to the Father after meeting Mary.

He **said** that He was ascending to the Father, and He said **receive** the Holy Spirit. These two things happened! The Son Man accomplished all that the Father had determined. I have explained above what John 14 is about. Jesus was going away and coming back. His going was to the Father, so if He went away and came back to them (which He obviously did), then by His own definition, He had to have gone to the Father after meeting with Mary. Allowing the disciples to touch Him afterwards was more confirmation.

To summarize, the risen Christ "went" on the day of His resurrection according to verses 2, 3, 4, and 28 of chapter 14. He also returned on the same day, fulfilling verses 3, 6, 18, 21, 23, and 28. Finally, He breathed the Holy Spirit into the disciples, fulfilling verses 3, 6, 16, 17, 19, 20, 23, 26, 27, and 28. What a list! This is not to say that the disciples had it all on that day. In one sense they did, but we need the Spirit's empowering teaching, reminding, and revelation every day. It is a continual process, as I hope you have gathered and are experiencing.

197

Chapter 14 is framed by verses 1-3 and verses 28-29. In verses 1-3 Jesus told us what He was going to do. Verses 28 and 29 remind us of what He said, and everything in between is the divine explanation of how, in various aspects and in heavenly detail, the wonderful triune God makes His home in our hearts! This is what God is doing in this age.

We are not finished, however. There is another glorious stage! The fulfillment of John 14 in our lives produces another fulfillment, the fulfillment of God's plan! At the end of the Bible, which is the revelation of God's full redemption of man, we see the completion of His marvelous plan; we see the new Jerusalem. This glorious city is a picture of God's most wonderful, holy, and glorious habitation with man.

The book of Revelation is filled with signs. A lot of attention is paid to negative signs, but what about the positive signs? The very first sign is of seven lampstands, and John is told in verse 1:20 that the lampstands are the churches. The last sign is the new Jerusalem, and John is told that he is looking at the Lamb's bride. Revelation 21:2 says, *And I saw the holy city, new Jerusalem, coming down out of heaven from God, made ready as a bride adorned for her husband.* And verse 21:9 says, *...I will show you the bride, the **wife** of the Lamb.* Now, if the lampstands are the churches and we have no problem with **that**, then why is it so hard for us to see the bride? Instead, we can't take our eyes off the pretty picture, and we miss seeing the most glorious sign in the Bible, the bride!

We look at the picture and we are told that we will live in our mansions in this big beautiful city. But what does the God's Word say? Verses 21:2-3a: *And I saw the holy city, new Jerusalem, coming down out of heaven from God, made ready as a bride adorned for her husband. And I heard a loud voice from the throne, saying, "Behold, the tabernacle of God is among men..."*

Did you see that? The new Jerusalem comes **down** to the earth, and the announcement is that **God's** home has arrived! **Now**, do you see it?! Not our home.....God's home!

Why do we get this backwards? You have probably heard over and over that this city is where we will live in our mansions. This largely has to do with misunderstanding the Lord's intention when He returns. He is not coming for us, to take us away somewhere. No, He is coming to take possession of this earth and establish His kingdom right here on this planet! His parables say so! He is coming **here**, and you keep hearing that we are going **there**! Since it is the case that He is coming here, it becomes **impossible** to understand John 14:3 according to that traditional way.

The new Jerusalem is not our home. It is God's home. We **are** the new Jerusalem, which was revealed to John to be the bride, the wife of the Lamb. This city is a picture of us in God and God in us. **We** are God's habitation!

Having said all of that, I have a confession. The new Jerusalem actually is our home also! This glorious city is the mutual habitation of God and man! God indwells us, and we dwell in God! How wonderful this is!

What a deal we get! We are God's tabernacle (Revelation 21:3) and He is our temple (verse 21:22). Somehow that seems unfair. God gets a tabernacle, but we get a temple! But this is His plan from the ages past.

At the end of the story, this eternal story, where is the new Jerusalem? Where are we? Where is God's house? On this earth!

God has a glorious plan to make a **living** home for Himself, and we get to be that home! To think anything else is to be robbed of this divine reality. Satan, our enemy, the subtle enemy, has done a good job of cheating the saints.

Let us know the truth and leave behind the shallow teachings, the traditions of men. The Lord wants us to know what He is doing, and the words are plainly written, but that other stuff gets in the way. From this moment, please endeavor to come to God's holy Word as not knowing anything, and see what He reveals. I come to the Word as an empty vessel, praying to be filled, **especially** when I read passages that are familiar. This is the only way to leave behind human understanding and get divine revelation.

Two Words for "Word"

I am not pretending to be a Greek scholar, but I like to study certain words as they come to my attention. In discussing chapter 7 of Matthew, I went into some detail on the Greek words behind our English word "know". It was important to the context to delve into it then. Now I want to invest a little time to explain two Greek words for "word". If you are not familiar with this topic, even a little explanation can help your Bible reading.

In the beginning was the Word, and the Word was with God, and the Word was God (John 1:1). In the beginning was the *Logos*, the expression of God, the explanation of God. But the *Logos* is also a person, One who was with God. He also is God. How mysterious and wonderful!

Logos is not abstract. It can have a legal context, as seen in Matthew 12:37, *For by your words you will be justified, and by your words you will be condemned.* Logos can be instruction: *Everyone who hears these words of Mine and acts on them, may be compared to a wise man who built his house on the rock* (Matthew 7:24). In our context *logos* is also the written Word that we hold in our hands.

The other Greek word is *rhema*. This is a wonderful word. It mainly refers to a word spoken at the moment. A simple way to contrast *logos* and *rhema* would be this: *logos* is a written word, and *rhema* is a spoken word. *Logos* is the Bible that you read; *rhema* is the Lord speaking from the pages into your heart.

It is interesting to look at the first usage of *rhema* in each of the four gospels. I will substitute the Greek word in the text.

Matthew 4:4 - *But He answered and said, "It is written, 'Man shall not live on bread alone, but on every rhema that proceeds out of the mouth of God'"*.
Mark 9:32 - *But they did not understand this rhema (statement), and they were afraid to ask Him.*
Luke 1:37-38 - *"For not any rhema [nothing] will be impossible with God." And Mary said, "Behold, the bondslave of the Lord;*

may it be done to me according to your rhema." And the angel departed from her.

John 3:34 - *For He whom God has sent speaks the rhema (plural) of God, for He gives the Spirit without measure.*

I especially enjoyed discovering Luke 1:37! Sure, we understand that nothing is impossible for God, but now we can have an entirely new appreciation for this conversation between the angel and Mary as it was written under the inspiration of the Holy Spirit. The angel referred to the *rhema* from God: It is impossible for God's *rhema* to fail. Mary's response was based on that very *rhema*: *May it be done to me according to your rhema.* (Of course we need to remember that dialog in the New Testament was not spoken in Greek, but in Aramaic, the common language of the Jews at the time. What we read today is the Holy Spirit's translation of Aramaic into the wonderful Greek language, which was specially prepared for this purpose.)

In the New Testament context, *rhema* is very much associated with the Spirit. The very best illustration that ties all of this together comes from Jesus in John 6:63. *It is the Spirit who gives life; the flesh profits nothing; the words that I have spoken to you are spirit and are life.* In the verse we have *rhema*, *zoe*, and the Spirit, even the life-giving Spirit!

I said that a little explanation might help. I hope it did! I hope that this whets your appetite to dig a little deeper into the *Logos*, and see some wonderful discoveries!

Making Pearls

Seeking forgiveness can be difficult, and granting real forgiveness can be more so. How often have you observed, or done the following? Somebody (person 1) has offended another (person 2) in some way. P1 feels the need to apologize and humbly does so. P2 says, "That's okay. No problem, forget about it." After this exchange P1 might feel like he is off the hook, but not necessarily forgiven. P2 thinks he has done his part, forgiving as instructed by the Lord.

Is this what our Lord has in mind? Out of real concern or out of obligation, we seek forgiveness and we forgive others, but what should it look like in truth? In Matthew 18:35 we read Jesus saying that we have to forgive our brother from the heart. How can we know that our forgiveness is from the heart? How can we know that the one who forgives us really means it?

We know God's forgiveness because our Lord died once on the cross for all of our sins. Not only would my death not accomplish anything for anyone, but is this not a practical way for us to extend forgiveness. So where can we look for an example of what it really means to forgive?

The title of this fellowship tells you where I am going. A mollusk, let's say an oyster, makes a pearl because it has been wounded. A grain of sand injured it or caused an irritation. Over some time the oyster covers the offending particle with its own secretions until a pearl is made.

We have an illustration of this in Revelation 21. Each of the twelve gates of the new Jerusalem is a pearl, and on each gate is the name of one of the twelve tribes of Israel. I heard a message once about how the Lord was injured by His own, and the gates of pearl illustrate how He forgave them.

I have appreciated that message for many years, but eventually I have learned that this is also what forgiveness among us should be. Every offense is an opportunity to make a pearl. How do we do this? How can we know that a pearl has been made?

Thankfully for us there is an example in the New Testament. God has not left us without a pattern. You might be familiar with Paul's admonishment to the church in Corinth because they tolerated the one who took his father's wife. We find out in 2 Corinthians that he repented, but Paul's instructions to the church were not finished. In verses 2:7-8 he wrote, *"So that on the contrary you should rather forgive and comfort him, otherwise such a one might be overwhelmed by excessive sorrow. Wherefore I urge you to reaffirm your love for him."*

I hope that three words stood out to you: forgive, comfort, and love. These make a pearl. Look back at the conversation in the first paragraph. Do you find comfort and love in that? But is this typical of what happens?

The Lord asked once (Luke 5:23) whether it is easier to say, *"Your sins have been forgiven you,"* or to say, *"Get up and walk."* Of course, the Lord has no trouble with either. But for us, is it easier to say, "I forgive you," or to show comfort and love?

Here is another parable to think about, Matthew 18:23-35. Jesus gave this illustration after the well known question from Peter, *Lord, how often shall my brother sin against me and I forgive him?* The parable is about a slave who owes a lot to a certain king, but is forgiven the debt. There was a second slave who owed the first slave a much smaller sum, and the first had the second slave thrown into prison for the small debt. We can read in verses 34-35 the king's reaction upon hearing of it. *And his lord, moved with anger, handed him over to the torturers until he should repay all that was owed him. My heavenly Father will also do the same to you, if each of you does not forgive his brother from your heart.*

This matches Matthew 6:12, you know, the part of the Lord's prayer that says, *and forgive us our debts, as we also have forgiven our debtors.* What do you think you are saying here? "Lord, I am forgiving others, so please also forgive me." The word which is translated "as" is a comparative adverb. What we are really saying is "and forgive us our debts LIKE we forgive our debtors."

Oops! Do you really want this? Do I want the Lord to forgive me like I forgive? May our forgiveness shine with comfort and love.

Faith and Righteousness,
Paul and James

In a Bible study one time we had some fellowship about the second chapter of James, verses 14-26. You might recall that James contrasts faith without works against faith that is demonstrated by works. Such discussions can delve into the differences between statements of the apostle Paul and those of James. I suggest that there really is no difference in life application.

Here is an easy test, pass/fail. The following verses (except Gal 2:21) talk about faith. What other word stands out?

Romans 4:3 - *For what does the scripture say? "Abraham believed God, and it was credited to him as righteousness."*
Romans 4:5 - *But to the one who does not work, but believes in Him who justifies the ungodly, his faith is credited as righteousness.*
Romans 4:6b - *....the man to whom God credits righteousness apart from works*
Romans 4:9b - *....faith was credited to Abraham as righteousness*
Galatians 2:21 - *I do not nullify the grace of God, for if righteousness comes through the Law, then Christ died needlessly.*
James 2:23 - *....and Abraham believed God, and it was reckoned to him as righteousness.*

James said that faith should be evidenced by deeds. He proved his case by pointing to examples from the Old Testament. James 2:23 is quoted above. Verse 2:25 speaks of Rahab the harlot, who helped the spies at Jericho. Some translations use the word righteous in describing her. Other translations say that she was justified, using the same word that is applied to Abraham in verse 2:21. *Was not Abraham our father justified by works when he offered up Isaac on the altar?*

Coming back to Paul, here are two verses that you might know well, both from Romans: *As it is written, "there is none righteous, not even one"* (3:10) *....even so through the obedience of the One many will be made righteous* (5:19b)

I think we hold two concepts regarding righteousness, and they seem to be contradictory. One is that righteousness is equivalent to proper conduct or behavior. The other is that we are automatically made righteous in Christ. On one hand we know that we are not and never can be righteous in ourselves, but on the other hand we might think we should live up to a certain standard. That standard might be the Mosaic law, it might be self imposed, or maybe it might even be WWJD (what would Jesus do?). So it does seem that there are two aspects of righteousness: inward and outward.

Some translations use the word "constituted" in Romans 5:19. Here is the entire verse: *For as through the one man's disobedience the many were made* (constituted) *sinners, even so through the obedience of the One the many will be made* (constituted) *righteous.* We need an inward change, and we all know it. Our constitution is messed up. We need to be reconstituted!

The other aspect of righteousness is outward expression. It is this that is reflected in the six verses listed above. It involves an action. If a person is unrighteous, you know it by what he does. Likewise righteousness has an expression.

But the interesting thing is that the actions described in the above verses do not "look" like righteousness, at least maybe not according to our concept. Abraham left Ur in answer to God's calling. He took Isaac up on the mountain in obedience to God. Rahab took in the spies.

What did Paul say? In Romans 6:13 he said that we should present the members of our body as instruments of righteousness. That certainly suggests an outward expression. Then in verse 16b we have this: *you are slaves of the one whom you obey, either of sin resulting in death, or of obedience **resulting** in righteousness.* This also shows an outward expression in committing sin or obedience to God. The latter has a wonderful result, righteousness!

In 2 Corinthians 9:7-8 Paul wrote of the cheerful giver and of having an abundance for every good deed. Verses 9-10 sum up by quoting from Psalm 112:9. *As it is written He scattered abroad, He gave to the poor, His righteousness endures forever. Now he who supplies seed to the sower and bread for food will supply and* *multiply **your** seed for **sowing** and increase the harvest of **your** **righteousness**.* Verse 10 is not from the psalm; it is Paul's explanation that giving to the poor is God's equivalence to righteousness.

Now let's return to James 2. I mentioned that James proved his case by highlighting Abraham and Rahab. By their obedience, they were considered righteous before God. The case he was proving was that faith is justified when we feed and clothe the poor and honor all men, so in this context we have to conclude that this is what righteousness looks like!

Seven times in the New Testament we have the phrase "love your neighbor as yourself". James included that in this section. Paul wrote those words to the church in Rome and to the churches in Galatia. Both refer to this as fulfilling the law, and well they should, because Jesus said it first, as we know.

Remember what I quoted from Galatians 6 in the Preface. *God is not mocked, for whatever a man sows, this he will also reap.* The next verse (verse 8) says *for the one who sows to his own flesh will from the flesh reap corruption, but the one who sows to the Spirit will from the Spirit reap eternal life.* That seems logical, but do you know the verses that make a "sandwich" around verses 7 and 8? We looked at those briefly in the Galatians chapter. Verse 6 says *the one who is taught the word is to share all good things with the one who teaches him.* Verses 9 and 10 continue the theme. *Let us not lose heart in doing good, for in due time we will reap if we do not grow weary. So then, while we have opportunity, let us do good to all people, and especially to those who are of the household of the faith.* What do we reap? Eternal Life! As we obey the Lord, we gain more of Him.

Does this change your idea of what righteousness is? It is two words: obedience and love, and these are summed up in faith.

Scriptures
(OT follows NT)

Matthew

4:4
But He answered and said, "It is written, 'Man shall not live on bread alone, but on every word that proceeds out of the mouth of God.'" (pg 201)

4:23
Jesus was going throughout all Galilee, teaching in their synagogues and proclaiming the gospel of the kingdom, and healing every kind of disease and every kind of sickness among the people. (pg 115)

5:22
But I say to you that everyone who is angry with his brother shall be guilty before the court; and whoever says to his brother, "You good-for-nothing," shall be guilty before the supreme court; and whoever says, "You fool," shall be guilty enough to go into the fiery hell. (pg 114)

5:48
Therefore you are to be perfect, as your heavenly Father is perfect. (pg 82)

6:12
And forgive us our debts, as we also have forgiven our debtors. (pg 111,204)

6:14-15
For if you forgive others for their transgressions, your heavenly Father will also forgive you. But if you do not forgive others, then your Father will not forgive your transgressions. (pg 143-144)

6:20
But store up for yourselves treasures in heaven, where neither moth nor rust destroys, and where thieves do not break in and steal. (pg 12)

7:1-2
Do not judge so that you will not be judged. For in the way you judge, you will be judged; and by your standard of measure, it will be measured to you. (pg 113)

7:7
Ask, and it shall be given to you; seek, and you will find; knock, and it will be opened to you (pg 120)

7:12
In everything, therefore, treat people the same way you want them to treat you, for this is the Law and the Prophets. (pg 61)

7:13-14
Enter through the narrow gate; for the gate is wide and the way is broad that leads to destruction, and there are many who enter through it. For the gate is small and the way is narrow that leads to life, and there are few who find it. (pg 114-115,117,138)

7:15-20
Beware of the false prophets, who come to you in sheep's clothing, but inwardly are ravenous wolves. You will know them by their fruits. Grapes are not gathered from thorn bushes nor figs from thistles, are they? So every good tree bears good fruit, but the bad tree bears bad fruit. A good tree cannot produce bad fruit, nor can a bad tree produce good fruit. Every tree that does not bear good fruit is cut down and thrown into the fire. So then, you will know them by their fruits. (pg 117,121)

7:21-23
Not everyone who says to Me, 'Lord, Lord,' will enter the kingdom of heaven, but he who does the will of My Father who is in heaven will enter. Many will say to Me on that day, 'Lord, Lord, did we not prophesy in Your name, and in Your name cast out demons, and in Your name perform many miracles?' And then I will declare to them, 'I never knew you; depart from me, you who practice lawlessness.' (pg 125-126,127-128)

7:24
Therefore everyone who hears these words of Mine and acts on them, may be compared to a wise man who built his house on the rock. (pg 115,201)

7:26
Everyone who hears these words of Mine and does not act on them, will be like a foolish man who built his house on the sand. (pg 115)

9:35a
Jesus was going through all the cities and villages, teaching in their synagogues and proclaiming the gospel of the kingdom,.. (pg 115)

10:19-20
But when they hand you over, do not worry about how or what you are to say; for it will be given you in that hour what you are to say. For it is not you who speak, but it is the Spirit of your Father who speaks in you. (pg 132)

10:22
You will be hated by all because of My name, but it is the one who has endured to the end who will be saved. (pg 13,129,131)

10:28
Do not fear those who kill the body but are unable to kill the soul. (pg 132)

10:32-33
Therefore everyone who confesses Me before men, I will also confess him before My Father who is in heaven. But whoever denies Me before men, I will also deny him before My father who is in heaven. (pg 12-13,131)

10:37
He who loves father or mother more than Me is not worth of Me; and he who loves son or daughter more than Me is not worthy of Me. (pg 133)

10:38-39
And he who does not take his cross and follow after Me is not worthy of Me. He who has found his life will lose it, and he who has lost his life for My sake will find it. (*psuche*) (pg 77,133)

10:40-42
He who receives you receives Me, and he who receives Me receives Him who sent Me. He who receives a prophet in the name of a prophet shall receive a prophet's reward; and he who receives a righteous man in the name of a righteous man shall receive a righteous man's reward. And whoever in the name of a disciple gives to one of these little ones even a cup of cold water to drink, truly I say to you, he shall not lose his reward. (pg 135-136,158)

12:37
For by your words you will be justified, and by your words you will be condemned. (pg 201)

13:11-12
Jesus answered them, "To you it has been granted to know the mysteries of the kingdom of heaven, but to them it has not been granted. For whoever has, to him more shall be given, and he will have an abundance; but whoever does not have, even what he has shall be taken away from him." (pg 137)

13:33
He spoke another parable to them, "The kingdom of heaven is like leaven, which a woman took and hid in three pecks of flour until it was all leavened." (pg 139)

16:6,12
And Jesus said to them, "Watch out and beware of the leaven of the Pharisees and Sadducees." ...Then they understood that He did not say to beware of the leaven of bread, but of the teaching of the Pharisees and Sadducees. (pg 139)

16:24-26
Then Jesus said to His disciples, "If anyone wishes to come after Me, he must deny himself, and take up his cross and follow Me. For whoever wishes to save his life will lose it; but whoever loses his life for My sake will find it. For what will it profit a man if he gains the whole world and forfeits his soul? Or what will a man give in exchange for his soul?" (pg 10,77,85)

18:8-9
"If your hand or your foot causes you to stumble, cut it off and throw it from you; it is better for you to enter life crippled or lame, than to have two hands or two feet and be cast into the eternal fire. If your eye causes you to stumble, pluck it out and throw it from you. It is better for you to enter life with one eye, than to have two eyes and be cast into the fiery hell." (pg 141)

18:23-35
[The unforgiving slave] ..."My heavenly Father will also do the same to you, if each of you does not forgive his brother from your heart." (pg 112,143,144,148,187-188,203,204)

22:9,11-14
"Go therefore to the main highways, and as many as you find there, invite to the wedding feast" ... But when the king came in to look over the dinner guests, he saw a man there who was not dressed in

wedding clothes, and he said to him, 'Friend, how did you come in here without wedding clothes?' And the man was speechless. Then the king said to the servants, 'Bind him hand and foot, and throw him into the outer darkness; in that place there will be weeping and gnashing of teeth. For many are called, but few are chosen." (pg 145)

23:27
Woe to you, scribes and Pharisees, hypocrites! For you are like whitewashed tombs which on the outside appear beautiful, but inside they are full of dead men's bones and all uncleanness. (pg 186)

24:13
But the one who endures to the end, he will be saved. (pg 129)

24:45-51
Who then is the faithful and sensible slave whom his master put in charge of his household to give them their food at the proper time? Blessed is that slave whom his master finds so doing when he comes. Truly I say to you that he will put him in charge of all his possessions. But if that evil slaves says in his heart, 'My master is not coming for a long time," and begins to beat his fellow slaves and eat and drink with the drunkards; the master of that slave will come on a day when he does not expect him and at an hour which he does not know, and will cut him in pieces and assign him a place with the hypocrites; in that place there will be weeping and gnashing of teeth. (pg 147,177-178,186)

25:1-13
[The ten virgins] ..."Be on the alert then, for you do not know the day nor the hour." (pg 149-154,155,160-161,187)

25:14-30
[Talents given to the slaves] ..."Throw out the worthless slave into the outer darkness; in that place there will be weeping and gnashing of teeth." (pg 154-156,175-176)

25:31-46
[Sheep and goats] But when the Son of Man comes in His glory, and all the angels with Him, then He will on His glorious throne. All the nations will be gathered before Him; and He will separate them from one another, as the shepherd separates the sheep from the goats; and He will put the sheep on His right, and the goats on His left. Then the King will say to those on His right, 'Come, you who are blessed of My Father, inherit the kingdom prepared for you from the foundation of the world...... (pg 138,156-158)

28:19-20
Go therefore and make disciples of all the nations, baptizing them in the name of the Father and the Son and the Holy Spirit, teaching them to observe all that I commanded you. (pg iv,115)

Mark

1:14
Now after John had been taken into custody, Jesus came into Galilee, preaching the gospel of God. (pg 115)

4:24
And He was saying to them, "Take care what you listen to. By your standard of measure it will be measured to you; and more will be given to you besides." (pg 113)

8:15-17
And He was giving orders to them, saying, "Watch out! Beware of the leaven of the Pharisees and the leaven of Herod." They began to discuss with one another the fact that they had no bread. And Jesus,

aware of this, said to them, "Why do you discuss the fact that you have no bread? Do you not yet see or understand? Do you have a hardened heart?" (pg 139)

8:34-38
And He summoned the crowd with His disciples, and said to them, "If anyone wishes to come after Me, he must deny himself, and take up his cross and follow Me. For whoever wishes to save his life will lose it, but whoever loses his life for My sake and the gospel's will save it. For what does it profit a man to gain the whole world, and forfeit his soul? For what will a man give in exchange for his soul? For whoever is ashamed of Me and My words in the adulterous and sinful generation, the Son of Man will also be ashamed of him when He comes in the glory of His Father with the holy angels." (pg 10,77,85)

9:32
But they did not understand this statement, and they were afraid to ask Him. (pg 201)

9:38-41
John said to Him, "Teacher, we saw someone casting out demons in Your name, and we tried to prevent him because he was not following us." But Jesus said, "Do not hinder him, for there is no one who will perform a miracle in My name, and be able soon afterward to speak evil of Me. For he who is not against us is for us. For whoever gives you a cup of water to drink because of your name as followers of Christ, truly I say to you, he will not lose his reward. (pg 158)

9:42-48
"Whoever causes one of these little ones who believe to stumble, it would be better for him if, with a heavy millstone hung around his neck, he had been cast into the sea. "If your hand causes you to stumble, cut it off; it is better for you to enter life crippled, than, having your two hands, to go into hell, into the unquenchable fire,

where their worm does not die, and the worm is not quenched. "If your foot causes you to stumble, cut it off; it is better for you to enter life lame, than, having your two feet, to be cast into hell, where their worm does not die, and the worm is not quenched. "If your eye causes you to stumble, throw it out; it is better for you to enter the kingdom of God with one eye, than, having two eyes, to be cast into hell, where their worm does not die, and the worm is not quenched. (pg 141)

10:17
As He was setting out on a journey, a man ran up to Him and knelt before Him, and asked Him, "Good Teacher, what shall I do to inherit eternal life?" (pg 159)

10:23,24b-25,27
And Jesus, looking around, said to His disciples, "How hard it will be for those who are wealthy to enter the kingdom of God!" ... "Children, how hard it is to enter the kingdom of God! It is easier for a camel to go through the eye of a needle than for a rich man to enter the kingdom of God." Looking at them, Jesus said, "With people it is impossible, but not with God; for all things are possible with God." (pg 159)

11:25
Whenever you stand praying, forgive, if you have anything against anyone, so that your Father who is in heaven will also forgive you your transgressions. (pg 111)

13:13
"You will be hated by all because of My name, but the one who endures to the end, he will be saved. (pg 129)

13:33-37
Take heed, keep on the alert; for you do not know when the appointed time will come. It is like a man away on a journey, who upon leaving his house and putting his slaves in charge, assigning to

each one his task, also commanded the doorkeeper to stay on the alert. Therefore, be on the alert – for you do not know when the master of the house is coming, whether in the evening, at midnight, or when the rooster crows, or in the morning – in case he should come suddenly and find you asleep. What I say to you I say to all, 'Be on the alert!' (pg 160-161)

Luke

1:37-38
"For nothing will be impossible with God." And Mary said, "Behold, the bondslave of the Lord; may it be done to me according to your word" And the angel departed from her. (pg 201-202)

4:18
The Spirit of the Lord is upon Me, because He anointed Me to preach the gospel to the poor. (pg 115)

5:23
Which is easier, to say, 'Your sins have been forgiven you,' or to say, 'Get up and walk'? (pg 204)

6:31
Treat others the same way you want them to treat you. (pg 61)

6:36-37
Be merciful, just as your Father is merciful. Do not judge, and you will not be judged; and do not condemn, and you will not be condemned; pardon, and you will be pardoned. (pg 113)

9:23-26
And He was saying to them all, "If anyone wishes to come after Me, he must deny himself, and take up his cross daily and follow Me. For whoever wishes to save his life will lose it, but whoever loses his life for My sake, he is the one who will save it. For what is a man

profited if he gains the whole world, and loses or forfeits himself? For whoever is ashamed of Me and My words, the Son of Man will be ashamed of him when He comes in His glory, and the glory of the Father and of the holy angels. (pg 10,77)

11:4a
And forgive us our sins, for we ourselves also forgive everyone who is indebted to us. (pg 111)

12:8-9
And I say to you, everyone who confesses Me before men, the Son of Man will confess him also before the angels of God; but he who denies Me before men will be denied before the angels of God. (pg 131)

12:35-37a
Be dressed in readiness, and keep your lamps lit. Be like men who are waiting for their master when he returns from the wedding feast, so that they may immediately open the door to him he comes and knocks. Blessed are those slaves whom the master will find on the alert when he comes." (pg 154,130-161)

12:41-47
Peter said, "Lord, are You addressing this parable to us, or to everyone else as well?" And the Lord said, "Who then is the faithful and sensible steward, whom his master will put in charge of his servants, to give them their rations at the proper time? Blessed is that slave whom his master finds so doing when he comes..." (pg 148,177,184)

13:23-28
And someone said to Him, "Lord, are there just a few who are being saved?" And He said to them, "Strive to enter through the narrow door; for many, I tell you, will seek to enter and will not be able. Once the head of the house gets up and shuts the door, and you begin to stand outside and knock on the door, saying, 'Lord open up

to us!' then He will answer and say to you, 'I do not know where you are from.' Then you will begin to say, 'We ate and drank in Your presence, and You taught in our streets'; and He will say, 'I tell you, I do not know where you are from; depart from Me, all you evildoers.' In that place there will be weeping and gnashing of teeth when you see Abraham and Isaac and Jacob and all the prophets in the kingdom of God, but yourselves being thrown out. (pg 123-124,125)

14:26-27,33
If anyone comes to Me, and does not hate his own father and mother and wife and children and brothers and sisters, yes, and even his own life, he cannot be My disciple. Whoever does not carry his own cross and come after Me cannot be my disciple. (pg 163)

17:33
Whoever seeks to keep his life will lose it, and whoever loses his life will preserve it. (pg 10,77)

18:24
And Jesus looked at him and said, "How hard it is for those who are wealthy to enter the kingdom of God!" (pg 57)

19:12-27
[Parable of 10 slaves and 10 minas]…"And he said to him, 'Well done, good slave, because you have been faithful in a very little thing, you are to be in authority over ten cities.' …… I tell you that everyone who has, more shall be given, but from the one who does not have, even what he does have shall be taken away……"
(pg 12,175-176)

20:1
On one of the days while He was teaching the people in the temple and preaching the gospel,... (pg 115)

21:19
By your endurance you will gain your lives. (pg 164-165)

21:34-36
Be on guard, so that your hearts will not be weighted down with dissipation and drunkenness and the worries of life, and that day will not come on you suddenly like a trap; for it will come upon all those who dwell on the face of all the earth. But keep on the alert at all times, praying that you may have strength to escape all these things that are about to take place, and to stand before the Son of Man. (pg 165,166)

24:27
Then beginning with Moses and with all the prophets, He explained to them the things concerning Himself in all the Scriptures. (pg 71)

John

1:1
In the beginning was the Word, and the Word was with God, and the Word was God. (pg 201)

1:2
But as many as received Him, to them He gave the right to become children of God, even to those who believe in His name (pg 185)

1:4
In Him was life, and the life was the Light of men. (pg 6)

3:34
For He whom God has sent speaks the words of God, for He gives the Spirit without measure. (pg 184)

5:27
And He [the Father] gave Him authority to execute judgment, because He is the Son of Man. (pg 113)

5:39-40
You search the Scriptures because you think that in them you have eternal life; it is these that testify about Me; and you are unwilling to come to Me so that you may have life. (pg 6)

6:63
It is the Spirit who gives life; the flesh profits nothing; the words that I have spoken to you are spirit and are life. (pg 202)

12:23-25
And Jesus answered them, saying, "The hour has come for the Son of Man to be glorified. Truly, truly, I say to you, unless a grain of wheat falls into the earth and dies, it remains alone; but if it dies, it bears much fruit. He who loves his life loses it, and he who hates his life in this world will keep it to life eternal." (pg 10,77,192)

13:38
Jesus answered, "Will you lay down your life for Me? Truly, truly, I say to you, a rooster will not crow until you deny Me three times. (pg 195)

14:1-29 Yes, the whole chapter (pg 99,116,167,191-199)

15:1-2
I am the true vine, and My Father is the vinedresser. Every branch in Me that does not bear fruit, He takes away; and every branch that bears fruit, He prunes it so that it may bear more fruit. (pg 167-168)

15:4-5a
Abide in Me, and I in you. As the branch cannot bear fruit of itself unless it abides in the vine, so neither can you unless you abide in

Me. I am the vine, you are the branches; he who abides in Me and I in him, he bears much fruit. (pg 168)

15:6
If anyone does not abide in Me, he is thrown away as a branch and dries up; and they gather them, and cast them into the fire and they are burned. (pg 168)

17:3
This is eternal life, that they may know You, the only true God, and Jesus Christ whom You have sent. (pg 35,116)

19:34
But one of the soldiers pierced His side with a spear, and immediately blood and water came out. (pg 164)

20:17
Jesus said to her, "Stop clinging to Me, for I have not yet ascended to the Father; but go to My brethren and say to them, 'I ascend to My Father and your Father, and My God and your God.'" (pg 197)

20:22
And when He had said this, He breathed on them and said to them, "Receive the Holy Spirit." (pg 195,196)

Acts

1:9
And after He had said these things, He was lifted up while they were looking on, and a cloud received Him out of their sight. (pg 196)

3:21
Whom heaven must receive until the period of restoration of all
things about which God spoke by the mouth of His holy prophets
from ancient time (pg 23)

4:12
And there is salvation in no one else; for there is no other name
under heaven that has been given among men by which we must be
saved. (pg 115)

Romans

3:10
As it is written, "There is none righteous, not even one"
(pg 205)

3:23
For all have sinned and fall short of the glory of God. (pg 86,95)

4:3
For what does the Scripture say? "Abraham believed God, and it
was credited to him as righteousness. (pg 205)

4:5
But to the one who does not work, but believes in Him who justifies
the ungodly, his faith is credited as righteousness. (pg 205)

4:6b
...the man to whom God credits righteousness apart from works.
(pg 205)

4:9b
..."Faith was credited to Abraham as righteousness." (pg 205)

5:10

For if while we were enemies we were reconciled to God through the death of His Son, much more, having been reconciled, we shall be saved by His life. (pg 5,69)

5:15

But the free gift is not like the transgression. For if by the transgression of the one the many died, much more did the grace of God and the gift by the grace of the one Man, Jesus Christ, abound to the many. (pg 105)

5:19

For as through the one man's disobedience the many were made sinners, even so through the obedience of the One the many will be made righteous. (pg 26,205)

5:20

The Law came in so that the transgression would increase; but where sin increased, grace abounded all the more (pg 105)

6:1

What shall we say then? Are we to continue in sin so that grace may increase? (pg 105)

6:13b

...but present yourselves to God as those alive from the dead, and your members as instruments of righteousness to God. (pg 206)

6:15

What then? Shall we sin because we are not under law but under grace? May it never be! (pg 119)

6:16b

You are slaves of the one whom you obey, either of sin resulting in death, or of obedience resulting in righteousness. (pg 206)

6:22
But now having been freed from sin and enslaved to God, you derive your benefit, resulting in sanctification, and the outcome, eternal life (pg 119)

6:23
For the wages of sin is death, but the free gift of God is eternal life in Christ Jesus our Lord. (pg 83,119)

7:24-25
Wretched man that I am! Who will set me free from the body of this death? Thanks be to God through Jesus Christ our Lord! So then, on the one hand I myself with my mind am serving the law of God, but on the other, with my flesh the law of sin (pg 62)

8:1-2
Therefore there is now no condemnation for those who are in Christ Jesus. For the law of the Spirit of life in Christ Jesus has set you free from the law of sin and of death. (pg 62)

8:3,4
For what the Law could not do, weak as it was through the flesh, God did: sending His own Son in the likeness of sinful flesh and as an offering for sin, He condemned sin in the flesh, so that the requirement of the Law might be fulfilled in us, who do not walk according to the flesh but according to the Spirit. (pg 62,118)

8:16
The Spirit Himself testifies with our spirit that we are children of God. (pg 149)

8:28
And we know that God causes all things to work together for good to those who love God, to those who are called according to His purpose. (pg 82,152)

8:29-30
For those whom He foreknew, He also predestined to become conformed to the image of His Son, so that He would be the firstborn among many brethren; and these whom He predestinated, He also called; and these whom He called, He also justified; and these whom He justified, He also glorified. (pg 85,152,195)

11:20-23
Quite right, they were broken off for their unbelief, but you stand by your faith. Do not be conceited, but fear; for if God did not spare the natural branches, He will not spare you, either. Behold then the kindness and severity of God; to those who fell, severity, but to you, God's kindness, if you continue in His kindness; otherwise you also will be cut off. (pg 7)

12:3
For through the grace given to me I say to everyone among you not to think more highly of himself than he ought to think; but to think so as to have sound judgment, as God has allotted to each a measure of faith. (pg 105,106)

12:6
Since we have gifts that differ according to the grace given to us, each of us is to exercise them accordingly: if prophecy, according to the proportion of his faith, (pg 105,108)

12:12a
And do not be conformed to this world, but be transformed by the renewing of your mind... (pg 6)

14:10-12
But you, why do you judge your brother? Or you again, why do you regard your brother with contempt? For we will all stand before the judgment seat of God. For it is written, "As I live, says the Lord,

every knee shall bow to Me, and every tongue shall give praise to God." So then each one of us will give an account of himself to God (pg 153)

15:15-16a
But I have written very boldly to you on some points so as to remind you again, because of the grace that was given me from God to be a minister of Christ Jesus to the Gentiles (pg 105-106)

15:30
Now I urge you, brethren, by our Lord Jesus Christ and by the love of the Spirit, to strive together with me in your prayers to God for me. (pg 130)

1 Corinthians

2:9
But just as it is written, "Things which the eye has not seen and ear has not heard, and which have not entered the heart of man, all that God has prepared for those who love Him." (pg 29)

2:10a
For to us God revealed them through the Spirit (pg 30)

2:12
Now we have received, not the spirit of the world, but the Spirit who is from God, so that we may know the things freely given to us by God. (pg 30)

3:9a,10,12-15
For we are God's fellow workers... According to the grace of God which was given to me, like a wise master builder I laid a foundation, and another is building on it. But each man must be careful how he builds on it. Now if any man builds on the foundation with gold, silver, precious stones, wood, hay, straw,

each man's work will become evident; for the day will show it because it is to *be* revealed with fire, and the fire itself will test the quality of each man's work. If any man's work which he has built on it remains, he will receive a reward. If any man's work is burned up, he will suffer loss; but he himself will be saved, yet so as through fire. (pg 17-19,25,75,92-93,106,128,142,173)

3:16-17
Do you not know that you are a temple of God and that the Spirit of God dwells in you? If any man destroys the temple of God, God will destroy him, for the temple of God is holy, and that is what you are. (pg 22,191)

5:5
I have decided to deliver such a one to Satan for the destruction of his flesh, so that his spirit may be saved in the day of the Lord Jesus. (pg 87)

6:9-10
Or do you not know that the unrighteous will not inherit the kingdom of God? Do not be deceived; neither fornicators, nor idolaters, not adulterers, nor effeminate, nor homosexuals, nor thieves, nor the covetous, nor drunkards, nor revilers, nor swindlers, will inherit the kingdom of God. (pg 159)

6:19
Or do you not know that your body is a temple of the Holy Spirit who is in you, whom you have from God, and that you are not your own? (pg 22)

7:1
Therefore, having these promises, beloved, let us cleanse ourselves from all defilement of flesh and spirit, perfecting holiness in the fear of God. (pg 29)

9:24
Do you not know that those who run in a race all run, but only one receives the prize? Run in such a way that you may win. (pg 6,130)

9:26-27
Therefore I run in such a way, as not without aim; I box in such a way, as not beating the air, but I discipline my body and make it my slave, so that, after I have preached to others, I myself will not be disqualified. (pg 6,64,124)

10:1,5-6,12
For I do not want you to be unaware, brethren, that our fathers were all under the cloud and all passed through the sea; ... Nevertheless, with most of them God was not well-pleased; for they were laid low in the wilderness. Now these things happened as examples for us, so that we would not crave evil things as they also craved. ... Therefore let him who thinks he stands take heed that he does not fall. (pg 101-102)

10:13
No temptation has overtaken you but such as is common to man; and God is faithful, who will not allow you to be tempted beyond what you are able, but with the temptation will provide the way of escape also; so that you will be able to endure it. (pg 102)

12:3b
And no one can say, "Jesus is Lord," except by the Holy Spirit. (pg 125)

12:21
And the eye cannot say to the hand, "I have no need of you"; or again the head to the feet, "I have no need of you." (pg 131)

13:12

For now we see in a mirror dimly, but then face to face; now I know in part, but then I will know fully just as I also have been fully known. (pg 126,127)

15:10

But by the grace of God I am what I am, and His grace toward me did not prove vain; but I labored even more than all of them, yet not I, but the grace of God with me (pg 68,107)

2 Corinthians

2:7-8

...so that on the contrary you should rather forgive and comfort him, otherwise such a one might be overwhelmed by excessive sorrow. Wherefore I urge you to reaffirm your love for him. (pg 204)

3:18

But we all with unveiled face, beholding as in a mirror the glory of the Lord, are being transformed into the same image from glory to glory, just as from the Lord, the Spirit. (pg 96)

4:7a

But we have this treasure in earthen vessels... (pg 150)

5:9-10

Therefore we also have as our ambition, whether at home or absent, to be pleasing to Him. For we must all appear before the judgment seat of Christ, so that each one may be recompensed for his deeds in the body, according to what he has done, whether good or bad. (pg 25,76,128,153)

5:20
Therefore, we are ambassadors for Christ, as though God were making an appeal through us; we beg you on behalf of Christ, be reconciled to God. (pg 26)

5:21
He made Him who did not know sin to be sin on our behalf, so that we might become the righteousness of God in Him. (pg 26)

6:1-2
And working together with Him, we also urge you not to receive the grace of God in vain. – for He says, "At the acceptable time I listened to you, and on the day of salvation I helped you." Behold, now is "the acceptable time," behold, now is "the day of salvation." (pg 26)

6:16
Or what agreement has the temple of God with idols? For we are the temple of the living God; just as God said, "I will dwell in them and walk among them; and I will be their God, and they shall be my people. (pg 28,192)

6:17-18
"Therefore come out from their midst and be separated, says the Lord, and do not touch what is unclean; and I will welcome you. And I will be a father to you, and you shall be sons and daughters to Me," says the Lord Almighty. (pg 28,99)

7:1
Therefore having these promises, beloved, let us cleanse ourselves from all defilement of flesh and spirit, perfecting holiness in the fear of God. (pg 27-28,31)

7:3b
You are in our hearts to die together and to live together. (pg 130)

9:7-8
Each one must do just as he has purposed in his heart, not grudgingly or under compulsion, for God loves a cheerful giver. And God is able to make all grace abound to you, so that always having all sufficiency in everything, you may have an abundance for every good deed. (pg 206)

9:9-10
As it is written, "He scattered abroad, He gave to the poor, His righteousness endure forever." Now He who supplies seed to the sower and bread for food will supply and multiply your seed for sowing and increase the harvest of your righteousness. (pg 206-207)

12:9
And He has said to me, "My grace is sufficient for you, for power is perfected in weakness." Most gladly, therefore, I will rather boast about my weaknesses, so that the power of Christ may dwell in me. (pg 67,107)

Galatians

1:11-12
For I would have you know, brethren, that the gospel which was preached by me is not according to man, for I neither received it from man, nor was I taught it, but I received it through a revelation of Jesus Christ. (pg 3)

2:21
I do not nullify the grace of God, for if righteousness comes through the Law, then Christ died needlessly. (pg 205)

3:21b
For if a law had been given which was able to impart life, then righteousness would indeed have been based on law. (pg 97)

4:9a
But now that you have come to know God, or rather to be known by God. (pg 126,127)

4:19
My children, with whom I am again in labor until Christ is formed in you. (pg 33)

5:4
You have been severed from Christ, you who are seeking to be justified by law; you have fallen from grace. (pg 68)

5:7
You were running well; who hindered you from obeying the truth? (pg 6)

5:16-17a,18
But I say, walk by the Spirit and you will not carry out the desire of the flesh. For the flesh sets its desire against the Spirit, and the Spirit against the flesh; ... But if you are led by the Spirit, you are not under the Law. (pg 36,174)

5:19-21
Now the deeds of the flesh are evident, which are: immorality, impurity, sensuality, idolatry, sorcery, enmities, strife, jealousy, outbursts of anger, disputes, dissensions, factions, envying, drunkenness, carousing, and things like these, of which I forewarn you, just as I have forewarned you, that those who practice such things will not inherit the kingdom of God. (pg 36,160)

5:22-23a
But the fruit of the Sprit is love, joy, peace, patience, kindness, goodness, faithfulness, gentleness, self-control. (pg 121)

6:1-2
Brethren, even if anyone is caught in any trespass, you who are spiritual, restore such a one in a spirit of gentleness; each one looking to yourself, so that you too will not be tempted. Bear one another's burdens, and thereby fulfill the law of Christ. (pg 34)

6:6
The one who is taught the word is to share all good things with the one who teaches him. For the one who sows to his own flesh will from the flesh reap corruption, but the one who sows to the Spirit will from the Spirit reap eternal life. (pg 34,207)

6:7-8
Do not be deceived, God is not mocked; for whatever a man sows, this he will also reap. For the one who sows to his own flesh will from the flesh reap corruption, but the one who sows to the Spirit will from the Spirit reap eternal life. (pg v,25,34,87,207)

6:9-10
Let us not lose heart in doing good, for in due time we will reap if we do not grow weary. So then, while we have opportunity, let us do good to all people, and especially to those who are of the household of the faith. (pg 34-35,207)

6:15
For neither is circumcision anything, nor uncircumcision, but a new creation. (pg 23)

Ephesians

2:5b
...(God) made us alive together with Christ... (pg 130)

2:18
For through Him we both have our access in one Spirit to the Father. (pg 193)

2:21-22
In whom the whole building, being fitted together, is growing into a holy temple in the Lord, in whom you also are being built together into a dwelling of God in the Spirit. (pg 130,192)

3:3
That by revelation there was made known to me the mystery, as I wrote before in brief. (pg 3)

3:17
So that Christ may dwell in your hearts through faith. (pg 150)

4:11-12,15-16
And He gave some as apostles, and some as prophets, and some as evangelists, and some as pastors and teachers, for the equipping of the saints for the work of service, to the building up of the body of Christ;... but speaking the truth in love, we are to grow up in all aspects into Him who is the head, even Christ, ... from whom the whole body, being fitted and held together by what every joint supplies, according to the proper working of each individual part, causes the growth of the body for the building up of itself in love. (pg 20,130)

4:28-29
He who steals must steal no longer; but rather he must labor, performing with his own hands what is good, so that he will have something to share with one who has need. Let no unwholesome word proceed from your mouth, but only such a word as is good for edification according to the need of the moment, so that it will give grace to those who hear. (pg 21)

4:30-32
Do not grieve the Holy Spirit of God, by whom you were sealed for the day of redemption. Let all bitterness and wrath and anger and clamor and slander be put away from you, along with all malice. Be kind to one another, tender-hearted, forgiving each other, just as God in Christ also has forgiven you. (pg 113-114)

5:1-2a,3-5
Therefore be imitators of God, as beloved children; And walk in love, ... But immorality or any impurity or greed, must not even be named among you, as is proper among saints; and there must be no filthiness and silly talk, or course jesting, which are not fitting, but rather giving of thanks. For this you know with certainty, that no immoral or impure person or covetous man, who is an idolater, has an inheritance in the kingdom of Christ and God. (pg 38)

5:6-7
Let no one deceive you with empty words, for because of these things the wrath of God comes upon the sons of disobedience. Therefore do not be partakers with them; (pg 39,41)

5:8-10
For you were formerly darkness, but now you are Light in the Lord; walk as children of Light (for the fruit of the Light consists in all goodness and righteousness and truth), trying to learn what is pleasing to the Lord. . (pg 122)

5:13-15,17-18
But all things become visible when they are exposed by the light, for everything that becomes visible is light. For this reason it says, "Awake, sleeper, and arise from the dead, and Christ will shine on you." Therefore be careful how you walk, not as unwise men but as wise, ... So then do not be foolish, but understand what the will of the Lord is. And do not get drunk with wine, for that is dissipation, but be filled with the Spirit. (pg 40,153)

5:26-27
Husbands, love your wives, just as Christ also loved the church and gave Himself up for her, so that He might sanctify her, having cleansed her by the washing of water with the word, that He might present to Himself the church in all her glory, having no spot or wrinkle or any such thing; but that she would be holy and blameless. (pg 93-94,96,164)

6:17
And take The helmet of salvation, and the sword of the Spirit, which is the word of God. (pg 174)

Philippians

1:6
For I am confident of this very thing, that He who began a good work in you will perfect it until the day of Christ Jesus. (pg 11,85,93)

1:9-11
And this I pray, that your love may abound still more and more in real knowledge and all discernment, so that you may approve the things that are excellent, in order to be sincere and blameless until the day of Christ; having been filled with the fruit of righteousness which comes through Jesus Christ, to the glory and praise of God. (pg 122)

1:18-20
What then? Only that in every way, whether in pretense or in truth, Christ is proclaimed; and in this I rejoice. Yes, and I will rejoice, for I know that this will turn out for my deliverance through your prayers and the provision of the Spirit of Jesus Christ, according to my earnest expectation and hope, that I will not be put to shame in

anything, but that with all boldness, Christ will even now, as always, be exalted in my body, whether by life or by death. (pg 132)

1:27b
...that you are standing firm in one spirit, with one mind striving together... (pg 130)

2:12b
...work out your salvation with fear and trembling. (pg 186)

2:16
Holding fast the word of life, so that in the day of Christ I will have reason to glory because I did not run in vain nor toil in vain. (pg 6)

3:7-9
But whatever things were gain to me, those things I have counted as loss for the sake of Christ. More than that, I count all things to be loss in view of the surpassing value of knowing Christ Jesus my Lord, for whom I have suffered the loss of all things, and count them but rubbish so that I may gain Christ, and may be found in Him, not having a righteousness of my own derived from the Law, but that which is through faith in Christ, the righteousness which comes from God on the basis of faith. (pg 44,134)

3:10-11
That I may know Him and the power of His resurrection and the fellowship of His sufferings, being conformed to His death; in order that I may attain to the resurrection from the dead. (pg 44,134)

3:12
Not that I have already obtained it or have already become perfect, but I press on so that I may lay hold of that for which also I was laid hold of by Christ Jesus. (pg 43,66-67)

3:17-19
Brethren, join in following my example, and observe those who walk according to the pattern you have in us. For many walk, of whom I often told you, and now tell you even weeping, that they are the enemies of the cross of Christ, whose end is destruction, whose god is their appetite, and whose glory is in their shame, who set their minds on earthly things. (pg 47,134-135)

4:1
Therefore, my beloved brethren whom I long to see, my joy and crown, in this way stand firm in the Lord, my beloved. (pg 64)

4:15-18
You yourselves also know, Philippians, that at the first preaching of the gospel, after I left Macedonia, no church shared with me in the matter of giving and receiving but you alone; for even in Thessalonica you sent a gift more than once for my needs. Not that I seek the gift itself, but I seek for the profit which increases to your account. But I have received everything in full and have an abundance; I am amply supplied, having received from Epaphroditus what you have sent, a fragrant aroma, an acceptable sacrifice, well-pleasing to God. (pg 120)

Colossians

1:22-23a
Yet He has now reconciled you in His fleshly body through death, in order to present you before Him holy and blameless and beyond reproach - if indeed you continue in the faith firmly established and steadfast, and not moved away from the hope of the gospel that you have heard. (pg 8,49)

2:2a
That their hearts may be encouraged, having been knit together in love... (pg 131)

2:13b

...He made you alive together with Him... (pg 131)

2:16-17

Therefore no one is to act as your judge in regard to food or drink or in respect to a festival or a new moon or a Sabbath day – things which are a mere shadow of what is to come; but the substance belongs to Christ (pg 45,46)

2:19b

...the entire body, being supplied and held together... (pg 131)

2:20-23

If you have died with Christ to the elementary principals of the world, why, as if you were living in the world, do you submit yourself to decrees, such as, "do not handle, do not taste, do not touch!" (which all refer to things destined to perish with use) – in accordance with the commandments and teaching of men? These are matters which have, to be sure, the appearance of wisdom in self-made religion and self-abasement and severe treatment of the body, but are of no value against fleshly indulgence. (pg 45)

1 Thessalonians

2:19-20

For who is our hope or joy or crown of exultation? Is it not even you, in the presence of our Lord Jesus at His coming? For you are our glory and joy. (pg 64)

3:12-13

And may the Lord cause you to increase and abound in love for one another, and for all people, just as we also do for you; so that He may establish your hearts without blame in holiness before our God and Father at the coming of our Lord Jesus with all His saints. (pg 51)

5:23-24
Now may the God of peace Himself sanctify you entirely; and may your spirit and soul and body be preserved complete, without blame at the coming of our Lord Jesus Christ. Faithful is He who calls you, and He also will bring it to pass. (pg 52,150)

2 Thessalonians

1:5
This is a plain indication of God's righteous judgment so that you will be considered worthy of the kingdom of God, for which indeed you are suffering. (pg 55)

2:11
For this reason God will send upon them a deluding influence so that they will believe what is false. (pg 41)

2:13b-14
...because God has chosen you from the beginning for salvation through sanctification by the Spirit and faith in the truth. It was for this He called you through our gospel, that you may gain the glory of our Lord Jesus Christ. (pg 55,59-60)

1 Timothy

3:15b
The household of God, which is the church of the living God, the pillar and support of the truth. (pg 192)

6:18-19
Instruct them to do good, to be rich in good works, to be generous and ready to share, storing up for themselves the treasure of a good foundation for the future, so that they may take hold of that which is life indeed. (pg 57)

2 Timothy

1:9
Who has saved us and called us with a holy calling, not according to our works, but according to His own purpose and grace which was granted us in Christ Jesus from all eternity. (pg 68)

2:4-5
No soldier in active service entangles himself in the affairs of everyday life, so that he may please the one who enlisted him as a soldier. Also if anyone competes as an athlete, he does not win the prize unless he competes according to the rules. (pg 60-61)

2:10
For this reason I endure all things for the sake of those who are chosen, so that they also may obtain the salvation which is in Christ Jesus and with it eternal glory. (pg 10,59-60)

2:11-14
It is a trustworthy statement: For if we died with Him, we will also live with Him; if we endure, we will also reign with Him; if we deny Him, He also will deny us; if we are faithless, He remains faithful, for He cannot deny Himself. Remind them of these things, and solemnly charge them in the presence of God not to wrangle about words, which is useless and leads to the ruin of the hearers. (pg 10,12,13,60,62-63)

4:7-8
I have fought the good fight, I have finished the course, I have kept the faith; in the future there is laid up for me the crown of righteousness, which the Lord, the righteous Judge, will award to me on that day; and not only to me, but also to all who have loved His appearing. (pg 6,63,65,66)

Titus

2:11-14

For the grace of God has appeared, bringing salvation to all men, instructing us to deny ungodliness and worldly desires and to live sensibly, righteously and godly in the present age, looking for the blessed hope and the appearing of the glory of our great God and Savior, Christ Jesus, who gave Himself for us to redeem us from every lawless deed, and to purify for Himself a people for His own possession, zealous for good deeds. (pg 66-69)

Hebrews

1:14

Are they not all ministering spirits, sent out to render service for the sake of those who will inherit salvation? (pg 71)

2:1-3a

For this reason we must pay much closer attention to what we have heard, so that we do not drift away from it. For if the word spoken through angels proved unalterable, and every transgression and disobedience received a just penalty, how shall we escape if we neglect so great a salvation? (pg 71-72)

3:6

But Christ was faithful as a Son over His house - whose house we are, if we hold fast our confidence and the boast of our hope firm to the end. (pg 72,129)

3:7-10

Therefore, just as the Holy Spirit says, "Today if you hear His voice, do not harden your hearts as when they provoked Me, as in the day of trial in the wilderness, where your fathers tried Me by testing Me, and saw My works for forty years. "Therefore I was angry with this generation, and said, 'They always go astray in their heart, and they did not know My ways'" (pg 72,102)

3:11-12
"As I swore in My wrath, "They shall not enter into My rest." Take care, brethren, that there not be in any one of you an evil, unbelieving heart that falls away from the living God. (pg 72-73)

3:14-15
For we have become partakers of Christ, if we hold fast the beginning of our assurance firm until the end, while it is said, "Today if you hear His voice, do not harden your hearts, as when they provoked Me." (pg 9, 73)

3:19-4:1
So we see that they were not able to enter because of unbelief. Therefore, let us fear if, while a promise remains of entering His rest, any one of you may seem to have come short of it. (pg 73)

4:2-3a
For indeed we have had good news preached to us, just as they also; but the word they heard did not profit them, because it was not united by faith in those who heard. For we who have believed enter that rest. (pg 74)

4:7b
just as has been said before, "Today if you hear His voice, do not harden your hearts. (pg 74)

4:9,11-12
So there remains a Sabbath rest for the people of God. .... Therefore let us be diligent to enter that rest, so that no one will fall, through following the same example of disobedience. For the word of God is living and active and sharper that any two-edged sword, and

piercing as far as the division of soul and spirit, of both joints and marrow, and able to judge the thoughts and intentions of the heart. (pg 52,74)

4:16
Therefore let us draw near with confidence to the throne of grace, so that we may receive mercy and find grace to help in time of need. (pg 74)

5:13-6:1a
For everyone who partakes only of milk is not accustomed to the word of righteousness, for he is an infant. But solid food is for the mature, who because of practice have their senses trained to discern good and evil. Therefore leaving the elementary teaching about the Christ, let us press on to maturity. (pg 164-165)

6:7-9
For ground that drinks the rain which often falls on it and brings forth vegetation useful to those for whose sake it is also tilled, receives a blessing from God; But if it (the ground) yields thorns and thistles, it is worthless and close to being cursed, and it ends up being burned. But, beloved, we are convinced of better things concerning you, and things that accompany salvation though we are speaking this way. (pg 75)

6:10
For God is not unjust so as to forget your work and the love which you have shown toward His name, in having ministered and in still ministering to the saints. (pg 75)

6:11-12
And we desire that each one of you show the same diligence so as to realize the full assurance of hope until the end, so that you will not be sluggish, but imitators of those who through faith and patience inherit the promises. (pg 76)

10:25a
Not forsaking our own assembling together... (pg 131)

10:35-36
Therefore, do not throw away your confidence, which has a great reward. For you have need of endurance, so that when you have done the will of God, you may receive what was promised. (pg 76)

10:37
For yet in a very little while, He who is coming will come, and will not delay. (pg 76)

10:38-39
But my righteous one shall live by faith, and if he shrinks back, My soul has no pleasure in him. But we are not of those who shrink back to destruction, but of those who have faith to the preserving of the soul. (pg 77)

11:1-2
Now faith is the assurance of things hoped for, the conviction of things not seen. For by it the men of old gained approval. (pg 64)

11:35
Women received back their dead by resurrection; and others were tortured, not accepting their release, so that they might obtain a better resurrection; (pg 44)

12:1-2
Therefore, since we have so great a cloud of witnesses surrounding us, let us also lay aside every encumbrance and the sin which so easily entangles us, and let us run with endurance the race that is set before us, fixing our eyes on Jesus, the author and perfecter of faith, who for the joy set before Him endured the cross, despising the shame, and has sat down at the right hand of the throne of God. (pg 64,77,130,165,178)

12:9,10b
Furthermore, we had earthly fathers to discipline us, and we respected them; shall we not much rather be subject to the Father of spirits, and live? ...but He disciplines us for our good, so that we may share His holiness. (pg 77)

12:11
All discipline for the moment seems not to be joyful, but sorrowful; yet to those who have been trained by it, afterwards it yields the peaceful fruit of righteousness. (pg 78,122)

12:12-13
Therefore strengthen the hands that are weak and the knees that are feeble, and make straight paths for your feet, so that the limb which is lame may not be put out of joint, but rather be healed. (pg 78)

12:14
Pursue peace with all men, and the sanctification without which no one will see the Lord. (pg 78)

12:25
See to it that you do not refuse Him who is speaking. For if those did not escape when they refused him who warned them on earth, much less will we escape who turn away from Him who warns from heaven. (pg 79)

13:16
And do not neglect doing good and sharing, for with such sacrifices God is pleased. (pg 35)

James

1:12
Blessed is a man who perseveres under trial, for once he has been approved, he will receive the crown of life which the Lord has promised to those who love Him. (pg 65,82-83)

1:15
Then when lust has conceived, it gives birth to sin; and when sin is accomplished, it brings forth death. (pg 83)

1:21
Therefore, putting aside all filthiness and all that remains of wickedness, in humility receive the word implanted, which is able to save your souls. (pg 84)

2:14-26
What use is it, my brethren, if someone says he has faith but he has no works? Can that faith save him? ... Abraham ... Rahab ... For just as the body without the spirit is dead, so also faith without works is dead. (pg 205)

5:9
Do not complain, brethren, against one another, so that you yourselves may not be judged; behold, the Judge is standing right at the door. (pg 85)

5:19-20
My brethren, if any among you strays from the truth and one turns him back, let him know that he who turns a sinner from the error of his way will save his soul from death and will cover a multitude of sins. (pg 86)

1 Peter

1:3-4a

Blessed be the God and Father of our Lord Jesus Christ, who according to His great mercy has caused us to be born again to a living hope through the resurrection of Jesus Christ from the dead, to obtain an inheritance... (pg 89)

1:7-8

So that the proof of your faith, being more precious that gold which is perishable, even though tested by fire, may be found to result in praise and glory and honor at the revelation of Jesus Christ, And though you have not seen Him, you love Him, and though you do not see Him now, but believe in Him, you greatly rejoice with joy inexpressible and full of glory. (pg 90)

1:9

...obtaining as the outcome of your faith the salvation of your souls. (pg 60,89-91)

2:24

And He Himself bore our sins in His body on the cross, so that we might die to sin and live to righteousness; for by His wounds you were healed. (pg 149)

4:8-10a

Above all, keep fervent in your love for one another, because love covers a multitude of sins. Be hospitable to one another without complaint. As each one has received a special gift, employ it in serving one another as good stewards of the manifold grace of God. (pg 51-52)

5:4

And when the Chief Shepherd appears, you will receive the unfading crown of glory. (pg 65)

2 Peter

1:5-7

Now for this very reason also, applying all diligence, in your faith supply moral excellence, and in your moral excellence, knowledge, and in your knowledge, self-control, and in your self-control, perseverance, and in your perseverance, godliness, and in your godliness, brotherly kindness, and in your brotherly kindness, love. (pg 92)

1:10-11

Therefore, brethren, be all the more diligent to make certain about His calling and choosing you; for as long as you practice these things, you will never stumble; for in this way the entrance into the eternal kingdom of our Lord and Savior Jesus Christ will be abundantly supplied to you. (pg 91-92)

2:5

And did not spare the ancient world, but preserved Noah, a preacher of righteousness, with seven others, when He brought a flood upon the world of the ungodly; (pg iii)

3:7

But by His word the present heavens and earth are being reserved for fire, kept for the day of judgment and destruction of ungodly men. (pg 182,183)

3:10-12

But the day of the Lord will come like a thief, in which the heavens will pass away with a roar and the elements will be destroyed with intense heat, and the earth and its works will be burned up. Since all these things are to be destroyed in this way, what sort of people ought you to be in holy conduct and godliness, looking for and hastening the coming of the day of God, because of which the elements will melt with intense heat! (pg 182-184)

3:14-15
Therefore, beloved, since you look for these things, be diligent to be found by Him in peace, spotless and blameless, and regard the patience of our Lord as salvation; just as also our beloved brother Paul, according to the wisdom given him, wrote to you. (pg 89,93,98)

3:16a
As also in all his letters, speaking in them of these things, in which are some things hard to understand. (pg 89)

1 John

1:8
If we say that we have no sin, we are deceiving ourselves and the truth is not in us. (pg 95)

1:9
If we confess our sins, He is faithful and righteous to forgive us our sins and to cleanse us from all unrighteousness. (pg 86,95-96,97)

2:1
My little children, I am writing these things to you so that you may not sin. And if anyone sins, we have an Advocate with the Father, Jesus Christ the righteous. (pg 98)

2:3
By this we know that we have come to know Him, if we keep His commandments. (pg 98)

2:4
The one who says, "I have come to know Him," and does not keep His commandments, is a liar, and the truth is not in him. (pg 99)

2:17
The world is passing away, and also its lusts; but the one who does the will of God lives forever. (pg 97,98)

2:25
This is the promise which He Himself made to us: eternal life. (pg 35)

2:28
Now, little children, abide in Him, so that when He appears, we may have confidence and not shrink away from Him in shame at His coming. (pg iii,90-91,97,152,161,168,188)

5:4-5
For whatever is born of God overcomes the world; and this is the victory that has overcome the world – our faith. Who is the one who overcomes the world, but he who believes that Jesus is the Son of God? (pg 170)

5:16a
If anyone sees his brother committing a sin,... (pg 171)

5:18a
We know that no one who is born of God sins. (pg 171)

Jude

1:3
Beloved, while I was making every effort to write you about our common salvation, I felt the necessity to write to you appealing that you contend earnestly for the faith which was once for all handed down to the saints. (pg 101)

1:5
Now I desire to remind you, though you know all things once for
all, that the Lord, after saving a people out of the land of Egypt,
subsequently destroyed those who did not believe. (pg 101)

1:20-25
But you, beloved, building yourselves up on your most holy faith,
praying in the Holy Spirit, keep yourselves in the love of God,
waiting anxiously for the mercy of our Lord Jesus Christ to eternal
life. And have mercy on some, who are doubting; save others,
snatching them out of the fire; and on some have mercy with fear,
hating even the garment polluted by the flesh. Now to Him who is
able to keep you from stumbling, and to make you stand in the
presence of His glory blameless with great joy, to the only God our
Savior, through Jesus Christ our Lord, be glory, majesty, dominion
and authority, before all time and now and forever. Amen.
(pg 102)

Revelation

1:16
And out of His mouth came a sharp two-edged sword. (pg 174)

1:20
As for the mystery of the seven stars which you saw in My right
hand, and the seven golden lampstands: the seven stars are the
angels of the seven churches, and the seven lampstands are the
seven churches. (pg 197)

2:6
Yet this you do have, that you hate the deeds of the Nicolaitans,
which I also hate. (pg 174)

2:7b
To him who overcomes, I will grant to eat of the tree of life which is in the Paradise of God. (pg 172)

2:10b
Be faithful until death, and I will give you the crown of life. (pg 65)

2:11b
He who overcomes will not be hurt by the second death. (pg 142,172-173)

2:12
And to the angel of the church in Pergamum write: The One who has the sharp two-edged sword says this: (pg 174)

2:19,20b
I know your deeds, and your love and faith and service and perseverance, and that your deeds of late are greater than at first. ...I am He who searches the minds and hearts; and I will give to each one of you according to your deeds. (pg 175)

2:23
...and all the churches will know that I am He who searches the minds and hearts; and I will give to each one of you according to your deeds. (pg 175)

2:25-26
Nevertheless what you have, hold fast until I come. He who overcomes, and he who keeps My deeds until the end, to him I will give authority over the nations. (pg 129,157,175)

2:27
And he shall rule them with a rod of iron, as the vessels of the potter are broken to pieces, as I also have received authority from My Father. (pg 175)

3:2
Wake up, and strengthen the things that remain, which were about to die; for I have not found your deeds completed in the sight of My God. (pg 176)

3:3b
Therefore if you do not wake up, I will come like a thief, and you will not know at what hour I will come to you. (pg 181)

3:4-5
But you have a few people in Sardis who have not soiled their garments; and they will walk with Me in white, for they are worthy. He who overcomes will thus be clothed in white garments; and I will not erase his name from the book of life, and I will confess his name before My Father and before His angels.
(pg 13,145,176-177)

3:8
I know your deeds. Behold, I have put before you an open door which no one can shut, because you have a little power, and have kept My word, and have not denied My name. (pg 165,178)

3:10
Because you have kept the word of My perseverance, I also will keep you from the hour of testing, that hour which is about to come upon the whole world, to test those who dwell on the earth.
(pg 165,179)

3:11
I am coming quickly; hold fast what you have, so that no one will take your crown. (pg 178)

3:16
So because you are lukewarm, and neither hot nor cold, I will spit you out of my mouth. (pg 178)

3:17b-18
You do not know that you are wretched and miserable and poor and blind and naked, I advise you to buy from Me gold refined by fire so that you may become rich, and white garments so that you may clothe yourself, and that the shame of your nakedness will not be revealed; and eye salve to anoint your eyes so that you may see. (pg 145,151,178-179,181)

3:19
Those whom I love, I reprove and discipline; therefore be zealous and repent. (pg 180)

6:14
The sky was split apart like a scroll when it is rolled up, and every mountain and island were moved out of their places. (pg 183)

8:7
The first sounded, and there came hail and fire, mixed with blood, and they were thrown to the earth; and a third of the earth was burned up, and a third of the trees were burned up, and all the green grass was burned up. (pg 183)

9:20a
The rest of mankind, who were not killed by these plagues, did not repent of the works of their hands. (pg iii)

9:21
and they did not repent of their murders nor of their sorceries nor of their immorality nor of their thefts. (pg iii)

16:8-9
The fourth angel poured out his bowl upon the sun, and it was given to it to scorch men with fire. Men were scorched with fierce heat; and they blasphemed the name of God who has the power over these plagues, and they did not repent so as to give Him glory. (pg iii,183)

16:15
("Behold, I am coming like a thief. Blessed is the one who stays awake and keeps his clothes, so that he will not walk about naked and men will not see his shame.") (pg 181)

16:19b
Babylon the great was remembered before God, to give her the cup of the wine of His fierce wrath. (pg 181)

18:4
I heard another voice from heaven, saying, "Come out of her, my people, so that you will not participate in her sins and receive of her plagues. (pg 40,181)

19:15
From His mouth comes a sharp sword,... (pg 174)

20:3
And he threw him into the abyss, and shut it and sealed it over him, so that he would not deceive the nations any longer, until the thousand years were completed; after these things he must be released for a short time. (pg 25)

20:5
The rest of the dead did not come to life until the thousand years were completed. This is the first resurrection. (pg 25)

20:4,6
Then I saw thrones, and they sat on them, and judgment was given to them, ... and they came to life and reigned with Christ for a thousand years. ...they will be priests of God and of Christ and will reign with Him for a thousand years. (pg 157)

20:14
Then death and Hades were thrown into the lake of fire. This is the second death, the lake of fire. (pg 172)

20:11a,12a
Then I saw a great white throne and Him who sat upon it...And I saw the dead, the great and the small, standing before the throne, (pg 25)

21:2-3a
And I saw the holy city, new Jerusalem, coming down out of heaven from God, made ready as a bride adorned for her husband. And I heard a loud voice from the throne, saying, "Behold, the tabernacle of God is among men... (pg 94,198,199)

21:8
But for the cowardly and unbelieving and abominable and murderers and immoral persons and sorcerers and idolaters and all liars, their part will be in the lake that burns with fire and brimstone, which is the second death. (pg 173)

21:9
Then one of the seven angels who had the seven bowls full of the seven last plagues came and spoke with me, saying, "Come here, I will show you the bride, the wife of the Lamb." (pg 198)

21:22
I saw no temple in it, for the Lord God the Almighty and the Lamb are its temple. (pg 199)

21:24,26
The nations will walk by its light, and the kings of the earth will bring their glory into it. ... and they will bring the glory and the honor of the nations into it. (pg 39,157)

22:2b
And the leaves of the tree are for the healing of the nations. (pg 157)

22:17
And let the one who is thirsty come; let the one who wishes take the water of life without cost. (pg 180)

22:21
The grace of our Lord Jesus Christ be with you all. Amen. (pg 53)

Genesis

2:17
But from the tree of the knowledge of good and evil you shall not eat, for in the day that you eat from it you will surely die. (pg iii)

3:24
He stationed the cherubim and the flaming sword which turned every direction to guard the way to the tree of life. (pg 5-6)

Psalms

112:9
He has given freely to the poor, His righteousness endures forever; His horn will be exalted in honor. (pg 206-207)

116:13
I shall lift up the cup of salvation and call upon the name of the Lord. (pg 96)

Proverbs

20:27
The spirit of man is the lamp of the Lord, searching all the innermost parts of his being. (pg 149,150)

Isaiah

1:18
"Come now, and let us reason together," Says the LORD, "Though your sins are as scarlet, They will be as white as snow; Though they are red like crimson, They will be like wool." (pg 95)

24:1
Behold, the LORD lays the earth waste, devastates it, distorts its surface and scatters its inhabitants. (pg 183???)

24:5
The earth is also polluted by its inhabitants, for they transgressed laws, violated statutes, broke the everlasting covenant. (pg 183???)

24:6
Therefore, a curse devours the earth, and those who live in it are held guilty. Therefore, the inhabitants of the earth are burned, and few men are left. (pg 183-184)

24:19
The earth is broken asunder, the earth is split through, the earth is shaken violently. (pg 183???)

34:4a
And all the host of heaven will wear away, and the sky will be rolled up like a scroll (pg 184)

49:8a
Thus says the LORD, "In a favorable time I have answered you, And in a day of salvation I have helped you." (pg 27)

55:1
Ho! Every one who thirsts, come to the waters; and you who have no money come, buy and eat. Come, buy wine and milk without money and without cost. (pg 180)

Jeremiah

17:9
The heart is more deceitful than all else and is desperately sick; who can understand it? (pg 96)

Ezekiel

31:33
But this is the covenant which I will make with the house of Israel after those days," declares the LORD, "I will put My law within them and on their heart I will write it; and I will be their God, and they shall be My people. (pg 118)

36:26
Moreover, I will give you a new heart and put a new spirit within you; and I will remove the heart of stone from your flesh and give you a heart of flesh. (pg 95)

Made in United States
North Haven, CT
02 May 2022

18778630R00153